For Michelle and Mary
Stories from Texas
and wishes for happiness.

Dancing Naked

&

Mary Rogers

Aug 24, 2009

dancing naked

MARY ROGERS

TCU Press / Fort Worth, Texas

Library of Congress Cataloging-in-Publication Data

Rogers, Mary (Mary Russell)
Dancing naked / by Mary Rogers.
p. cm.
Collection of articles that appeared in the *Fort Worth Star-Telegram,*
from 1991-2006.
ISBN 978-0-87565-374-7 paper
ISBN 978-0-87565-383-9 cloth
1. Biography--Miscellanea. 2. Texas--Miscellanea. 3. Interpersonal
relations—Texas. I. Title.

CT262.R64 2008
976.4'53150630922--dc22
2007049503

TCU Press
P. O. Box 298300
Fort Worth, Texas 76129
817.257.7822
http://www.prs.tcu.edu
To order books: 800.826.8911

Design by Barbara Mathews Whitehead

CONTENTS

For Charles, *my love,*
Ben, *our light,* and Morgan.

INTRODUCTION

W HEN I was nineteen, I was a college student, a cub
reporter at a small West Texas newspaper and, I
believed, a serious searcher for the Truth with a capital T. It was then that I read a book that changed my life. I have a
number of books on my personal list of favorites, but none has
altered my thinking so much as *Man's Search for Meaning* by
Viktor E. Frankl. I've read it again and again over the years, and I
always feel a new surge of optimism when I close the cover.

Frankl was a survivor of Auschwitz and other World War II
concentration camps, but he penned a surprisingly gentle story
about every man's freedom to transcend suffering and discover
the meaning of his own unique life. This thin volume is not an
accounting of the horrors of those Nazi death camps; he left it to
others to record those atrocities. It is instead a story of choice and
survival and a suggestion that at every moment life is asking
something of each of us—and at every moment we are answering.

The answer makes us who we are. The questions offer us an
opportunity for redemption or growth—or a chance to become
someone else entirely. One day we may be heroic, another day
cowardly, but in a time of quiet peace or in moments of personal
turmoil, the questions come. When I first read this little book, I
had no idea that Frankl was an internationally recognized psychi-
atrist or that this work had already become a classic. All I knew
was that his story touched me in an important way.

Forget what you've read about food, shelter, sex, or even
recognition being the prime motivators of life. It is, says Frankl,
the need to understand the significance of our own lives that is the

most important motivation of all. At nineteen, I certainly didn't know how I should invest my life, but I did know that whatever you spend your time on is what you're dying to do. I had written my first short story when I was nine years old, and I suppose I always knew I'd write, but at nineteen I suddenly knew that I wanted to tell the stories of individuals caught in frantic circumstances and those who seem to live "ordinary" lives—people who somehow manage to triumph. Maybe by studying their stories others could do as well, I thought.

I took some detours along the way, but after all these years I've been lucky to tell the stories of dozens of remarkable people who exercised what Frankl calls "the last of the human freedoms"—the ability to choose one's attitude in a given set of circumstances. Some of those stories and others about interesting characters are part of this collection. Some of my subjects were introspective; others were not. These stories are no more than small snapshots at a given moment in time. Since these pieces were written, the lives of all these people have changed. Some have had new successes. Some have known failure and discontent. Children have been born, divorces have been finalized, a few have died. Those who have survived are all older living in new skins in a new day.

Many of them bravely showed me their hearts. I call that "dancing naked." It is the most generous of gestures. I'll never forget the woman rancher who was forced by drought to sell the flocks of sheep and goats and herds of cattle she had devoted a lifetime to improving. For her, that barren, rocky land near Sonora, Texas, is the center of the earth, and she grieved that she had no heirs. I was touched by the devotion of a ninety-one-year-old man who still reads aloud with his mentally handicapped son each night and worries that when he is gone there will be no one left to love his sixty-year-old boy.

I still cry when I think of the father who sat and talked with me while his son lay dying of cancer in another room. He told me he'd done all he could to save his precious child. He'd taken him to every specialist, wept bitterly, loved deeply, and if the boy should slip into the next world while we talked, he would have no regrets that he hadn't been there to hold his hand at the moment of his passing. He had done his best, he said. He gave his suffering dignity, embraced it as a part of his life's unique story. No one else could have loved exactly as he had. No one else could have suffered in the same way. No one could take his place in that suffering and, in the end, he owned it as no one else could.

The choices people make are the stories of their lives.

The stories and essays in this collection were written over the last eighteen years for the *Fort Worth Star-Telegram*. Most were written for a reason: to acknowledge an award, a holiday, an accomplishment, some marker along life's highway. The collection itself is a reflection of print journalism at a crossroads, too. Today, newspaper readership all across the nation is declining, space for long stories is shrinking, and the entire industry is struggling to understand how to remain important to readers while delivering the profit margins investors demand. I believe we will always need individual stories about generosity, endurance and struggle.

When I was nine I had no idea where my stories would be printed. I had only a slightly better idea at nineteen. Now I feel lucky—no blessed—to have done what I wanted to do.

Mary Rogers
Fort Worth, Texas
July 2007

PART ONE
Love Stories

৵৹ ৵৹ ৵৹
৵৹ ৵৹
৵৹

The Love Endures ✌ *February 14, 1993*

Rolly Schur cherishes the memory of the man she loved.
Courtesy, the Fort Worth Star-Telegram.

OF COURSE, she knew something was wrong.

Everyone knew something was wrong. The rabbi kept losing his place. Even when the pages were marked, even when he used his finger as a guide, the rabbi was losing his place.

Rabbi Robert Schur had been the temple leader for more than thirty years, organizing many interfaith community projects as well as civil rights marches. He'd helped in the formation of the Child Study Center and the Fort Worth Community Council, but something was wrong. Everyday tasks whirled out of control. He was sometimes frantic, sometimes lost in confusion. Life became a tangle of emotions.

In the midst of the bewilderment, on Valentine's Day 1985, the rabbi sent his wife Rolly a card. The words penned in his graceful handwriting reach out to her now across a chasm of loneliness and despair.

"I love you beyond the boundaries of verbal expression," he wrote. "I cherish your love and all we have shared. . . . Your Bob, February 14, 1985."

Two months earlier the articulate, respected leader of Temple Beth-El had been diagnosed with Alzheimer's disease, a degenerative condition that attacks the brain and ravages the memory.

There would be no more valentines.

Now, after a lifetime together—after raising children, building congregations, and carving out a place in the community; after fish fries, birthday parties, and graduation exercises; after a thousand Sabbath dinners and as many prayers—only Rolly owns the memories of their life together. She measures her breath as she remembers the afternoon in December 1984, when they learned the name of the sickness that would steal their happiness. They had lived with the symptoms for five years, and it was a terrifying pronouncement. "I went out in the waiting room and wept. And Bob came out and put his arms around me and comforted me," she says.

Less than two weeks later, the rabbi told the congregation he had the disease. From that moment on, he preached seldom but continued to write the eloquent prayers that had been a hallmark of his service.

"Today . . ." he wrote in 1984, "the sun was slow to rise; the green of grass seemed darker than its customary hue. The birds were almost silent when I rose to dress. No wind stirred the leaves. Something stirred in me . . . I thought of Grandpa's cuckoo clock . . . and once again I saw him set the weights. It was the weight that made the pendulum swing. It was the weight that made the cuckoo sing!

"There is no song in life, without the burden's pull! And so, today, we thank you God . . . that we can pull the weight . . . and earn the right to hear the song in praise of Thee."

By the early fall of 1986, he could not continue his temple duties. He agreed to a videotaped interview with longtime friend Ellen Mack. It was, she says, the end of his cogency. He sat before the camera and said his condition was a good thing to discuss. He smiled and sometimes laughed and talked openly about Alzheimer's disease and how it scrambled his memory. No, he didn't know what day or month or year it was. No, he didn't know who was in the White House. But he did know he was losing his grip on things. Near the end of the interview, he admitted he did not know what they'd been talking about.

"I have to deal with reality," he said with a shrug. "What bothers me most of all is what it's doing to those close to me." And then, just at the end of the tape, he spoke directly to Rolly, his wife, his childhood sweetheart. The camera zoomed in for a close shot. "I wish, not for myself, but for you—my wife, my love, my partner—I wish it weren't necessary," he said of the disease. "But ... I know that we will deal with it together, because I know what you are. And somehow or other our togetherness will make it better than it would have been."

He choked and covered his eyes with a trembling hand. His friend reached to touch him and motioned for the camera to stop.

As the year progressed, so did the rabbi's anguish. "Lots of confusion in my mind—also much anxiety," he wrote at the end of 1986. "Nothing is crystal-clear except that I have great anxiety."

Rolly worked to keep things on level ground, but her husband began a frenzied regimen of pacing. He sometimes walked away from the house and became lost. She slept with one eye open. Her nerves were frayed. She nursed a rash. Finally, after several years, his acute anxiety and sometimes combative behavior became more than she could physically handle.

In 1988, the family moved the rabbi to a permanent-care facility in Dallas. It was the first time Rolly had rested in months, but for her it was also the beginning of a five-year passage into despair. "It was like a divorce I didn't want," she says. "He was here, but we weren't together."

Rolly points to a cluttered desk stacked high with files and papers and says her life is like that—a jumble of neglected projects. "I went down for five years. It's taken five years for me to want to get my house in order." She is unemotional, matter-of-fact, clear eyed. She is seventy and coming home again, clearing the desk, making a life for herself. She volunteers at the Child Study Center, goes to Sabbath services, visits museums, and shops with friends.

Once a week she makes the 100-mile round-trip to see her husband in a Dallas care facility. He is seventy-one. She gets there in time to feed him lunch and stays to straighten his closet and drawers.

On a recent visit, her husband of forty-seven years sits hunched forward in a wheelchair when she arrives. She strokes his hair and kisses him. Bending close, she tells him that she loves him, then turns away to get his luncheon plate. A shadow of embarrassment seems to cross his face. He leans forward and puts his head in his hands. It is a tiny glimmer of recognition, a slim understanding of what his life has become, but it is gone in a second and he sinks back into the dim world of Alzheimer's.

She holds his hands as she feeds him, and once she wipes his nose. His hands tremble and jerk. A tear slides slowly down his cheek, a light flickers in his eyes, but it is gone in a second and his eyes are wide and vacant again. Just before she leaves for the day, she kisses him again. "I love you, Bob Schur. Are you in there? Do you hear me? I love you, Bob," she says.

He straightens just a bit and then, as she walks behind his chair, he reaches forward. His arms open wide and then close as he embraces air—but it is over in a second, and he retreats quickly into himself again.

Those little flashes are what one Alzheimer's expert calls "little miracles." Some say those moments of recognition are precious gifts to be treasured, but Rolly and others who care for Alzheimer's patients aren't so sure. As the disease takes its terrible toll, family members don't know where to put their hope.

Rolly's life seems suspended, she says. She is forever waiting, but for what? "I don't expect he'll ever be better," she says and so she must sort through her feelings and the recollections of her time with Bob. She alone is the keeper of their life's story. She is the only one who recalls their childhood days in Cincinnati, Ohio. Only she remembers that first trip together to Coney Island when they were barely in their teens. "Going out, I sat here," she says indicating a place on an imaginary train seat. "He sat there, and the coats were in between. Coming back, I sat here. He sat there." She marked places side by side on the remembered seat. "The coats were over there," she says.

Only Rolly remembers Bob's decision to become a rabbi. She was away at the University of Wisconsin, and their relationship had cooled. He was considering skipping college to go into the dress manufacturing business with his father, but Rolly wanted to marry a college man. He couldn't let her go and so he wrote her a letter. "I got his letter and I was so excited, I rushed to tell a friend all about it," she says.

She remembers the war years and their decision to marry in 1945. She recalls their wedding day, the long white wedding dress, the young man waiting for her, the flowers, the cake, the reception. "I was a nursery school teacher, and I thought I could keep working," she says. She shrugs. Life is full of unexpected turns. Two children came, a girl and a boy. There were several moves, several congregations. Finally, in the 1950s, they settled in Fort Worth.

The memories are good. Her eyes sparkle. She laughs. Her hands dance before her. There are other happy stories and then she remembers a Sabbath dinner. The rain beats a melancholy rhythm against the windows as she tells the story.

They were alone together. The candles flickered and her husband, the man she has known since she was a girl, said, "I don't know who you are. I don't know who I am. I don't know what we're doing."

She was startled. She told him he was Rabbi Robert Schur. She said she was Rolly, his wife. She explained that they were eating Sabbath dinner.

"I regret that I didn't say, 'I love you,'" she says. "I wish I had said 'I love you, Bob Schur.'"

Love, Actually ✆ March 19, 2006

David and Stacie McDavid cuddle on the porch of their country retreat. Courtesy, the Fort Worth Star-Telegram. © *Jill Johnson.*

FROM THE windows of the farmhouse they restored near Weatherford, Stacie and David McDavid can see a half-dozen broodmares with new foals in the pasture across the road. The baby horses gambol about, kicking their heels in the air, feeling the power of life and the approaching spring, but on this day, a chill north wind dances over the standing seam roof of the McDavids' weekend retreat. The house, with two front rooms dating from the 1850s, was their gift to each other on their twentieth anniversary three years ago.

Inside, the fires are burning, and David pulls a chair close to the hearth. He is smiling—the good ol' boy in jeans and ostrich-skin boots, the eternal salesman—but there is tiredness around his blue eyes. It is the look of a traveler who has just returned from a perilous journey and carries with him the burden—and the joy— of an important discovery.

He glances often at Stacie and peppers his language with the word "we." "We went to a specialist in Dallas …" he says. "We got the news and it was very sobering … We began to look into treatments . . . We decided to go to Houston . . ." He seldom uses the word "I," and it is clear that this is a partnership of the spirit.

She is the one who drew close to him in the darkness and listened for his steady breathing. She is the one who cradled him in her arms when she thought he slept. Sometimes he only lay still, awake in her embrace, wrapped in a shining moment of grace. She is the one who swallowed her fear and laid her hands on him, willing his recovery. She is the one who could not—would not—let go.

She is his traveling companion.

Now David is certain that last year's tonsil cancer is both a thing of the past and a blessing; an important and affirming chapter in their own private story.

Stacie, forty-nine, and David, sixty-four, are among North Texas' most public couples, with ties to the cutting-horse circuit and the world of professional sports. They are also known for the television commercials they made with Wide Track, a Great Dane who barked on cue, advertising the David McDavid car dealerships, which he sold in 1998 but that still carry his name.

Champions of the National Cowgirl Museum and Hall of Fame and the Fort Worth Museum of Science and History, they are also arts benefactors. In fact, the plaques have not yet been installed at Maddox-Muse Center, but a room there has been named the McDavid Studio, in recognition of their gift to Performing Arts Fort Worth.

Stacie says this commemoration is more about tomorrow than today. "It's more for the grandchildren and future generations than for us," she says, and David nods agreement.

They are gregarious people, active on Fort Worth's benefit party circuit and accustomed to media attention. In 1996, he was part of the group that bought the Dallas Mavericks. In 2000, that team sold for a reported $280 million, doubling the McDavids' investment. They made news again in 2003 when their bid to buy the Atlanta-based Hawks, a National Basketball Association team, and the National Hockey League's Thrashers, went south. They filed a suit accusing Time Warner of breach of contract and fraud, among other things. According to David, legendary attorney Johnnie Cochran wanted to take the case, but the family decided on an Atlanta firm instead. The suit is still pending.

For all their public presence, Stacie and David have kept their private life out of the spotlight, while making it appear that their story is a completely open book.

When they met in 1980, David had been married and divorced twice. The first marriage was to his high school sweetheart, Tenie Braniff, a woman he still regards with great admiration and affection. Their two sons, David Jr., now forty-four, and Jimmy, now forty-two, eventually joined him in the car business, but back then the teens lived in Tennessee and visited in the summer.

David says it took only about a year to hop in and out of the next marriage. After that, most people thought there would be no more ties to bind him—but one man wasn't buying that. A Dallas jeweler, who was also a rabbi and matchmaker, knew both David and Stacie Dieb. He thought the two would hit it off, but they refused to meet.

By then David had a string of car dealerships, plenty of jingle in his jeans, a jet plane, gold chains around his neck, a taste for diamonds—and a reputation as a high-flying ladies' man. David says that was an image he was eager to shed.

He had grown tired of the glittering nightlife, the constant inner noise of the social game. He was already looking inward and attending a nondenominational church with his sister. "I was trying to get my life straight," he says. It was a tall order.

"He'd surrounded himself with the wrong people," says his youngest son, Jimmy.

Stacie was a savvy college grad who had attended Texas Woman's University on a track-and-field scholarship. She'd been so skilled at throwing the javelin, some thought she had Olympic potential. She was living with her younger brother, Steve Dieb, and they were operating a string of fitness clubs that had more than twenty locations. This brother/sister team had been unusually close since their mother died of leukemia when Stacie was ten and Steve eight. Their father, a teacher, always encouraged their independence.

The jeweler, certain that this was a match made in heaven, continued to nag the two to meet. One day David called Stacie. "Let's just meet for lunch," David said. "It won't take but an hour."

"Let's meet for drinks," Stacie snapped. "That will only take ten minutes."

Neither was prepared for the meeting. "It wasn't love at first sight, but it was close," says Stacie. "We clicked. We enjoyed being together."

The ten-minute meeting stretched into two hours, followed by other dates—but then *Cosmopolitan* magazine editor Helen Gurley Brown got in the way.

Brown invited David and his brother, Bill McDavid, to be the featured gents in the magazine's bachelor issue. Who could turn down such heady stuff? But that decision almost killed the budding romance between Stacie and David. "It tested our relationship," she says. "The fan mail came in knapsacks every day for a year! It was unbelievable. There are some desperate single women out there—a lot of them prisoners."

She flashes David a smile, then turns serious. "This was a pivotal moment," she says. "David had to decide to stick our relationship out. It was clear that we loved each other's company, but he had to decide if we could go on."

"You don't marry to live with someone. You marry because you can't live without them," David says, and before long he was down on one knee on the Great Wall of China, asking Stacie to be his wife.

The McDavids were married in 1983. He was forty-one; she was twenty-seven.

"Stacie brought balance into my life," says David. "The business was growing, doing great. Before long we had seventeen stores …"

They didn't see the storm coming; no one did, but the red-hot economy was cooling fast. "The wheels started coming off about 1987," David remembers. Soon no one was buying cars, and real estate went into a death spin.

"I had a piece of property I'd paid $12 a square foot for and the best offer I could get was $3 a square foot," he says. The car business was just as bad. By 1989, the year their daughter Sterling was born, David was trying to raise some cash, but it was tough.

The value of their Aspen retreat plummeted. Property that had sold for a million and more suddenly drew anemic bids of "$300,000 or so," says David. The worst part was that even at those bargain-basement prices there were no takers.

"I remember going up to our place in Aspen with Stacie. We had a glass of wine and sat down in these easy chairs looking out on this beautiful country. We held hands and tried to figure a way out. I was willing to sell everything. . . . I hoped I could hold on to one store and I thought Stacie and I could run it with this one salesman. . . ."

But there were no buyers. He sold his helicopter and tried to sell the jet. "If I could have found a buyer, I would have sold the house we lived in.... We weren't looking for the cheese. We just wanted out of the trap," David says.

He dug in, got rid of what he could and vowed he'd never be in that position again. Then the economy began to turn around and his legendary luck kicked in. The things he owned suddenly had value again. Real estate prices rose and people started buying cars. David took a deep breath and jumped into the business of changing his business.

David made sure the dealership had the most modern computer technology, tracking systems and state-of-the-art accounting programs available. By the time it was accomplished, he had made up his mind to get out of the business. He sold to the Asbury Automotive Group in 1998. He and his sons walked away completely in 2003 when their five-year management contract ended.

David had spent his entire life in the car business. His father had owned a Weatherford dealership. David was fourteen when the family business expanded to Houston. He had a hard time leaving his hometown.

"Son, if you want to hunt bears, you've got to go where the bears live," his father said, while giving him a lesson about earning money. When he was twenty, David bought the Weatherford dealership from his father. "Dad carried the note, but I was in business," David recalls. Soon, he jumped at the chance to open another location in Irving. He never looked back.

But once it was over, he says, he had few regrets. They had lots of money and plenty of interests, but the McDavids had no idea what was coming next.

David's sore throat began in September of 2004, but it was more a niggling aggravation than a real pain. Still, it wouldn't go away, and Stacie, a member of the M.D. Anderson Cancer Center board, was worried. David refused to see a doctor. "I cowboyed up," he says. "It was a stupid thing to do."

One night he asked a neighbor, Dr. George Kostohryz, to have a look. When tests came back negative the doctor sent David for more tests. "You still have the sore throat. We can't find the reason, but there's something wrong," he said. Because of that friend's dogged persistence, David's cancer was detected early. They were at the farm when they got the news.

"We didn't know how we were going to tell Sterling," says Stacie. "But you know, for her generation, cancer is curable and treatable."

"I knew God would take care of him and that people would pray for him as they have," says Sterling, now seventeen.

David was more concerned for Stacie than for himself. "I got my life right with God a long time ago," he says. "But I worried about my family." Stacie and David took an apartment in Houston last summer while he went through rounds of radiation and chemotherapy treatment at M.D. Anderson.

On his last day of treatment in the fall, the family gathered for a ceremony that is also a celebration of life. It's a ceremony that takes place every day at the cancer center, but for David, ringing a small brass school bell mounted on the wall was emotional.

He pulled the foot-long chain and the tears started. The bell's chime reverberated through the halls, a signal that one more person had made it through the arduous course of treatments. He pulled the chain again and the bell rang out, a reminder that one more patient had stayed the course. David pulled the chain one last time and everyone who heard it knew that one more man was on his way.

For David, it is a new way. "I am changed," he says.

The fire crackles and the wind sings in the eaves of the house. "I'm more tolerant, more understanding of those who have health problems. I'm more forgiving than I was before the cancer…."

Across the road the foals prance and the mares lift their noses to smell the approaching spring. David considers his life's journey silently. "I wouldn't take the cancer away even if I could," he says, looking at Stacie. "It was my teacher."

Life is Beautiful ❧ *July 18, 1999*

Holly and Jeff Smith should have had a lifetime ahead of them, but it wasn't in the cards. Courtesy, the Fort Worth Star-Telegram. © *Jill Johnson.*

SHE PERCHES on the edge of the hospital bed, her sandaled feet dangling above the polished floor. Her toenails are painted a bright red, and there's a small cross tattooed on the inside of her right ankle. She has come from work at an insurance company wearing denim trousers and a T-shirt. A silver charm bracelet jangles on her wrist. She is animated and smiling a Colgate smile as she turns the pages of the scrapbook.

Her husband of three years sits beside her. His brown hair is mussed from the pillows and he breathes with the help of oxygen pumped from a bottle beside the bed. His cheeks are flushed with fever and he coughs often, a thick, choking sound that punctuates their days.

The scrapbook is her favorite color, red, and on the rough sheets she has glued a hundred reminders of their life together. Holly Reynolds Smith, twenty-two, hasn't left out a thing: not the good times, not the bad times. This scrapbook might chronicle a thousand marriages. It is the story of Everyman's small pleasures and stinging regrets. It is also a unique record of the ebb and flow of Holly and Jeff Smith's time together, a volume filled with a poignant hope for a future they may never know.

Jeff has cystic fibrosis, a genetic disease that attacks the respiratory and digestive systems. The disorder has invaded his pancreas, leaving him an insulin-dependent diabetic, and filled his lungs with a gooey mucus. He won't be twenty-five until September, but he has already lost a full inch in height since high school, and after recent days in the hospital he has gained weight but still tips the scales at only 111 pounds.

In a last-ditch effort to save his life, doctors have recommended a lung transplant. He has been on the list since February—and may not find the right donor match in time. Jeff believes he can survive only a little more than a year without a transplant, but even new lungs won't guarantee a new life. So many things can go wrong. Rejection. Infection. Hemorrhage.

Jeff knows the dangers, but he doesn't dwell on them. Every day, he thanks God for giving him one more day. Every day, Holly prays for more time with Jeff.

She is, she says, supremely happy, but she is also very candid about life with her husband. It's a life she chose willingly, one she'd choose again, but it's tough, very tough—harder than she ever imagined. Keenly aware of their own mortality, they have grown old before their time—but it wasn't always so.

On the first page of the scrapbook there's a snapshot of Holly and Jeff. He's wearing cut-off jeans and a ball cap. She's got on shorts and hiking boots. His arm is around her shoulders. In the upper left-hand corner of the page there's a ticket stub from a Neil Young concert at Dallas' Coca-Cola Starplex—September 19, 1993—the day they met. It was the eve of her seventeenth birthday. Jeff was tan, attractive, what she called a "hotty" who owned a ten-year-old Mustang convertible and knew how to savor every moment. She was effervescent, optimistic, and smiling. Introduced by mutual friends, they were drawn to each other immediately, but Holly was involved with someone else. In no time, Jeff made that duo a trio, and for almost a year the three went everywhere together: the mall, concerts, ball games.

Soon Holly and Jeff began palling around alone like longtime friends. When Jeff looked at Holly and their friend together, it was not jealousy he felt but a sense of wonder and maybe envy that his friend could be so lucky. Holly was so easy to be with, so much fun.

They knew their relationship was changing, but still they had no real date. Once when she took a trip to Indiana, he told her to think of him at twilight. "You look south and I'll look north. Look up and I'll be there, " he said. It is the sort of secret code used by lovers worldwide, a romantic reminder that each is always in the other's thoughts. Even today, Jeff and Holly whisper those words—often when she leaves the hospital. "Look up and I'll be there."

On July 4, 1994, they joined crowds of people gathered on Fort Worth's river levee to watch the annual fireworks display. Holly and Jeff sat on the grass, watching the rockets explode in starbursts. It was their first date, and they knew that from that night on, everything would be different.

Jeff was amazingly healthy for someone who had struggled his entire life with CF, so their summer passed in a happy blur of volleyball, shows, and dinners at Wild Bill's Bar-B-Q, where Jeff held a job. The two had grown up in the Mid-Cities area of North Texas, a cluster of communities sandwiched between Fort Worth and Dallas. They moved easily back and forth across the invisible city lines that divide North Richland Hills from Keller or Hurst or Haltom City. All summer, they happily prowled that district and thought nothing of driving to Fort Worth or Dallas or even Oklahoma for a concert. They basked in the glow of romance.

Jeff sold his Mustang and put all the money down on a white Ford Splash pickup. When he'd pick Holly up for a date, he'd leave a single red rose or a daisy in the passenger seat for her to find. He wrote poetry filled with romantic images and for the first time began to take an interest in his treatment. Until then, he'd often missed his clinic appointments and had been cavalier about his health unless the disease demanded attention.

One day Jeff decided to trust Holly with his biggest confidence. He resolved to tell her face to face that he had cystic fibrosis. His friends knew, of course, but Jeff had never actually told anyone he had the fatal disease. He practiced the words he would use. That night they drove to a grassy field. A summer sky bloomed above them. They sat on the tailgate of the pickup. He was trembling when he turned to face her. "I've got something to tell you," he said. "I have cystic fibrosis."

"I know," she said. "It doesn't matter. Not to me."

Jeff was more than relieved; he was giddy with happiness. For him the greatest obstacle had been conquered. For the first time, he entertained the idea of a "normal" life with a partner, a soul mate who understood without explanation, who loved without reservation.

Then in October of 1994, the disease struck with a vengeance, sending Jeff for a long hospital stay and an even longer period of recovery. Holly was shaken and as he grew sicker, she pulled away. She wouldn't go to see him, wouldn't return his phone calls. "I knew about CF, but I guess I just didn't realize until then how serious it is—how it can be fatal at such a young age," she says now, sitting beside him on the hospital bed.

Stung by her rebuff, Jeff was frustrated and angry. "I thought we'd worked through all that," he says now. "I tried to understand, but I just saw her trying to bail out of this relationship. I was mad—mad at the disease, mad at myself, mad at Holly. It took awhile for us to get it back together."

They worked through the problems and by March 1995 they were talking of marriage. They bought a diamond ring together and then drove to the levee just north of Fort Worth's central business district. They walked across the dry grass together until they found the spot they shared on that first date. Jeff was shaking. Holly was smiling. He dropped quickly to one knee.

"Will you marry me?"

"What do you think?" Her bell-like laugh drifted out across the river.

They would be each other's to have and to hold, for better or for worse, in sickness and in health, for the rest of their lives.

She was eighteen—and afraid to tell her folks.

They decided a yearlong engagement would give everyone time to get used to the idea.

The scrapbook contains a snapshot of their wedding day—June 8, 1996. In the photo, Jeff and Holly hurry down the church steps to a white limo waiting at the curb. A stiff breeze snags Holly's borrowed veil and scatters the red and white balloons that well wishers released instead of throwing rice. A receipt for one night at the Omni Mandalay hotel in Las Colinas, Room 2402, is glued next to the photo.

Their marriage license is on the next page. Over it are pasted ticket stubs from SeaWorld, Natural Bridge Caverns, and the Hard Rock Cafe in San Antonio. There's also a paper liner from a Pringles Potato Chip can, a reminder of their incredible luck. On the return trip from San Antonio, they stopped to buy gas, a can of Pringles—and a lottery ticket. The ticket was a winner that brought them $100.

Life was remarkably good for the Smiths. They had a little apartment on the third level of a large Haltom City complex. They had a little dog, a pug-Chihuahua mix called Gerty. Holly and Jeff both had jobs at a North Richland Hills insurance company. Then one morning in March 1997, Jeff woke coughing up blood. They rushed to the hospital.

In June, they celebrated their first wedding anniversary and in July, Jeff's left lung collapsed. The climb to the third-floor apartment was too much. They moved to the second level, but that was just the beginning of their downward adjustment. Over the next year, Jeff was in and out of the hospital often. They tried to make the best of what they had. They cuddled on the blue denim couch—and sometimes fought.

"I didn't want to talk to her because I was afraid it would upset her. She didn't want to talk to me because she was afraid it would upset me," Jeff says with a shrug of his thin shoulders.

The cards in the scrapbook tell the story. "I will love you forever, Holl."

"I'm sorry. I know I hurt you. I love you, Baby."

"I know you're not happy. The ball is in your court. Whatever is broken we need to fix. I'm sorry. . . ."

"I didn't like the way we argued today. . . . I feel like every second we have is starting to count. I think sometimes I am in God's time clock and He's waiting to punch me out to go home. . . . I love you."

"I'm sorry. Hang in there. We'll get through this."

"I know it's been hard the last few days. I want you to know that I am here for you always."

On their second anniversary, Jeff gave her another card. Inside he wrote, "Two people. Two hugs. Two kisses, Two years turn into a lifetime." He gave her a silver charm: XX over OO, shorthand for two hugs and two kisses. She put the charm on her bracelet and fastened the card into the scrapbook, next to the one she gave him.

"The past two years have been the best for me. I know we have some ups and downs, but through it all we stick together. I think that is what makes us us. I love you. Your partner, Holl," she wrote.

Jeff sits on the hospital bed now and looks at the words. "We grew up," he says.

Even as they settled into a more confident understanding, their life together was about to become even more difficult. Last year, after months in the hospital followed by a regimen of home medication, IVs, and bed rest, Jeff had used up all his sick leave at the Mid-Cities insurance company where he and Holly both worked. The Smiths were forced to live only on Holly's salary. It was harder than either could have imagined.

They sold the Ford, but finances were not Jeff's only concern.

He worried about Holly working all day, rushing to the hospital to see him, and then going home to a dark apartment to walk Gerty alone. Holly was swimming with fatigue by the time she reached her door. Loneliness became her companion. She would leave a light on in the kitchen and most often fall asleep with the television running. Hungry for companionship, she began to drop by her parents' house. If she joined co-workers for dinner or a drink, she felt guilty and hurried home.

Then Jeff lost his job.

They both knew it was coming, knew it was the best thing— at least then he could collect disability. He'd used up all of his sick days and it had been two months since he had gotten a paycheck. Now they have only Holly's income and Jeff's small Social Security check.

In January of this year, they gave up their apartment and moved into her parents' North Richland Hills home. The couple share the upstairs bedroom Holly had when she was a student at Keller High School. It is better, they know, but oh so difficult to give up that independence, but it means that when Jeff is hospitalized, Holly comes home to other people. That's a relief for him— and for her, but hospital stays are tough, she says. It means she eats lunch at her desk so she can leave early and see Jeff. If he's up to a stroll, she pulls the oxygen bottle and they walk the hospital corridors together. They talk about her work, about their dogs: Audrey, a dachshund puppy, and Gerty, their old friend who knows when to kiss away the inevitable tears.

At the hospital Holly gets into bed with Jeff, and they watch television. Sometimes they play Uno. He makes her leave before dark.

"Look up and I'll be there," he whispers as she goes.

The scrapbook records dozens of hospital stays. There are cards from Holly and cards from the dogs.

"Come home soon. Mommy doesn't cuddle as well as you do, Gerty."

"We miss you. Gerty and Audrey."

The good times are there, too: Christmas snapshots and birthday celebrations and photos of other friends, some of whom have CF. Some now gone.

Holly and Jeff pose in front of the Italian Inn, "home of the singing waiters." They smile on a white-sand beach while an azure sea laps around their bare feet. There are stubs from shows and concerts. In September of last year, Jeff won a writing contest sponsored by a pharmaceutical company and a trip to the Big Apple. His winning entry was called "Rules of Life." It is a list of ways to cope with cystic fibrosis. Jeff's health was failing badly, but their families encouraged them to go to New York, Jeff's dream city. Enjoy every minute, they'd said.

Jeff gave Holly a card that she glued into the scrapbook. "Baby, If I've learned one thing this past year, it's to make the most of each and every day.... We are going to have the time of our lives in New York.... All I am begins with you."

The trip was exhilarating, exciting—and very difficult. Jeff was sick every day, struggling for breath, pushing himself to see a Broadway show, working to take the carriage ride through Central Park, determined to have one never-to-be-forgotten dinner at the Rainbow Room.

"It was romantic and magical," he says of that dinner. He looks at Holly beside him on the hospital bed. "You wore that new gray dress."

"You wore that gray suit with a blue shirt," she says and smiles a sunshine smile.

Jeff grew weaker, thinner, sicker by the day. They came home on a Monday. By Friday he was in the hospital again. His doctor said it was time to talk about a lung transplant. The Smiths had always told their doctor that if Jeff's condition ever warranted it, they wanted to talk about the possibility of a transplant, but when Jeff actually heard the news, he was numb.

He seemed suspended between life and eternity, twisting from sunlight to shadow as he dialed Holly's work number. She was excited and optimistic. Holly saw this announcement as Jeff's second chance at life—and she was determined to keep his spirits high. After he'd been on the transplant list for three months, Holly threw a party. It was time to celebrate, she said.

She planned a picnic at Chisholm Park in Hurst. She wore a purple ribbon to symbolize their fight against cystic fibrosis and a blue ribbon as a reminder of the importance of organ donation. It was May 23, 1999.

The first week of June, the Smiths celebrated their third wedding anniversary and the next week, Jeff was hospitalized. He is home now, but there is no rhythm to their days. The chronic nature of this illness prevents it. Jeff bounces from the bedroom he shares with Holly to the hospital and back again in an unpredictable cycle.

The future is only a beautiful dream, and neither Holly nor Jeff will say where they may be even a year from now. Hoping for the best, Holly has left several blank sheets in the scrapbook, waiting to be filled with mementos from the days to come—but these are not the last pages in the book.

Closer to the back, Holly has fastened other keepsakes of their life together. These obituaries report the loss of friends—Anna Marie Infante, fifteen; Amy Pack, twenty-one; Chrystina Mari Melanson, eighteen; William E. Bill Ross, thirty-eight; Frank Houston Manan—reminders that life can be short, that friendship and family and hope matter—and that love counts as much as life itself.

The Keys to Life ✌ *May 13, 2001*

At this time in their life, Dace Sultanov clung to the idea that her husband, 1999 Cliburn Gold Medalist Alexei Sultanov, would play again. Courtesy, the Fort Worth Star-Telegram, Ron Ennis.

HE LIES heavily against the pillows, eyes squeezed shut. The hair above his left temple is growing back. The surgeons didn't remove the thick, dark braid and it rests against his shoulder.

His right hand moves restlessly across an imagined keyboard. Perhaps he plays Liszt's "Mephisto Waltz" or maybe it's a Mozart sonata or something from Chopin or Beethoven. It could be one of his own compositions, some jazz or even his own arrangement of *La Traviata*. His left hand is a tight fist.

The silent music rises through the ether, reminding heaven that he is here, a prisoner longing to escape.

Some might say that Alexei Sultanov is a magician who bewitches his audiences and sends them soaring into the uncharted territory of celestial rapture—or diving into the muddy watercolor realm of melancholy. Some critics say he is a rebel whose musical interpretations are too unorthodox, too crass, and too immature to be considered great.

In fact, Alexei is a fearless performer, a concert pianist who stirs emotion wherever he goes. He has a large and enthusiastic following of international devotees who adore him, but his career might have been different if he hadn't won the Van Cliburn International Piano Competition in 1989.

He was nineteen that year, a puzzling mix of shy schoolboy and bold performer. He wore a white turtleneck under a dark suit too warm for Texas in May. His socks were white. His thick, dark hair was a shaggy, shoulder-length mane that almost covered his dark eyes. There was the faintest shadow of a boyish mustache across his upper lip that made him appear all the more youthful, but his command of the keyboard made the audience hold its breath. His fingers flashed over the keys. The sweat dripped into his eyes and ran down his smooth cheeks. His hair grew damp. The music thundered and whispered and groaned. He shut his eyes as if enraptured by the sound.

A piano string snapped, but Alexei played on. He leaned close to the piano and caressed the keyboard as if it were a lover, and the piano sighed. When the music ended, he bowed low to the audience, then took a backward step and pointed to the piano as if to share the spotlight with a fellow performer—and maybe, from that moment on, Alexei was meant to win the gold.

Now, at thirty-one, Alexei is a veteran of the international concert circuit who has played hundreds of concerts in the world's music capitals, including New York, London, Tokyo, Amsterdam, Vienna, and Seoul. He is also a man struggling to reclaim his life and his art after a massive stroke two months ago left him teetering between life and death.

He has known since childhood that his destiny would be forever tied to the piano—and the stage, but on February 26, his life took an unexpected and abrupt turn. A subdural hematoma—a tumor-like blood clot outside a blood vessel—almost took his life. Doctors aren't sure why it formed, but they are certain that it is not the first time. Only five years ago, Alexei suffered a small stroke that didn't disrupt his performance schedule but showed up on a CAT scan. The February bleed was different. It was potentially deadly.

Surgeons at Osteopathic Medical Center of Texas in Fort Worth rushed to remove a blood clot on his brain but, that night another hemorrhage plunged him into an even more desperate situation. Again doctors scrambled to snatch him back from the edge of death.

Outside the operating room, Alexei's wife, Dace Sultanov, thirty-two, waited and paced. She may have prayed and cried, but she never doubted that he would live.

"He is half my body," she says. "How can you separate half the body from itself? Alexei is all that matters now. We can fight. We can love. It does not matter. We must be together."

She will not—cannot—believe that Alexei's destiny could be changed. For her, Alexei is the music.

Now he is a patient at Baylor Institute for Rehabilitation in Dallas, struggling to relearn the basics of how to walk, how to dress, how to brush his teeth, and how to read. He wants his fans to know about his condition.

"Tell them everything," he says in a hoarse whisper that is barely audible. "All the good. All the bad. I cannot play hide-and-seek."

His doctor, Mary Carlile, the medical director for traumatic brain injury at Baylor, is "cautiously optimistic" about his recovery. She points out that his left side is "very weak and his vision impaired." In fact, she believes that he may have lost all sight in his left eye. In spite of the trauma, Alexei still speaks and understands both Russian and English. He listens to music and occasionally plays on a battery-operated keyboard, using only his right hand. "He's hard-wired for that and plays beautifully with only one hand," says Carlile.

There is a rhythm to the days now. Dace comes early every morning with bits of chocolate for the nurses and flowers from the garden and more e-mails from fans for Alexei. The walls are papered with e-mails and get-well cards from fans around the world. As soon as breakfast is cleared away, he begins the rounds of therapy sessions. There is speech therapy, physical therapy, occupational therapy, and hydrotherapy in the pool.

Every day, a message arrives from Moscow. It is expected now, a familiar part of the routine. Alexei's mother, Natalia Sultanov, fills the paper with large hand-lettered print. Each page contains only a few letters of the Russian alphabet. She writes a few words beside each character. More come each day. These are taped to the wall with the e-mails.

"A is for Alexei. Endlessly lovable son, we are praying for your recovery.

B is for brother, Sergei. Dear and loving son, may God give you health and happiness.

D is for Dace, the angel savior, for Alexei," she writes.

She does not say that Dace is the bedrock beneath the shifting sand of their lives. She does not need to.

Dace Sultanov is all shocking blond hair and gray-blue eyes the color of a Baltic lake. Her pale skin is smooth and her quick laugh is deep and throaty, the sound of a woman who has left girl-hood behind. She is a true believer, that rare spirit who trusts beyond understanding. She insists that Alexei will play again—not just for himself or for her, but for an audience.

Alexei's father, Faizul Sultanov, hurried from Russia weeks ago to be with his son. The Russian government forbids two family members to leave the country together, Dace explains. Faizul will go home in a few weeks and Alexei's mother will come.

In the meantime, Faizul sleeps on a cot in the corner of the crowded hospital room to be near Alexei around the clock. Every day, he hauls Alexei from the bed and helps his son move about the room. First, the right foot, then the left. Some mornings, they sing together—sometimes the scales, sometimes Russian chil-dren's songs.

He knows all about encouraging his son. He and his wife fanned the spark of musical genius they saw early in Alexei. When Alexei was only six, he began lessons in Tashkent with Tamara Popovitch, a taskmaster and now one of Alexei's most trusted advisers. Not long ago when she was in New York, she learned of

Alexei's illness. She flew to his side. "There is only one Alexei," she says through an interpreter, but Alexei seems not to hear.

When Alexei was a child, she arranged for him to have lessons at the Moscow Conservatory several times a year. Accompanied by one of his parents, young Alexei traveled by train from Uzbekistan for those lessons. It was a staggering expense and huge sacrifice, but it paid off, and in his teen years, Alexei was accepted at the Moscow Conservatory.

Faizul is a musician, too, a cellist. He understands the life of an artist, the delicate measures of life's song.

He nods. Yes. Yes. Alexei will play again.

He and Dace mean to encourage the man in the bed—but there is something else here, something mysterious and powerful. It can't be called by any single word, but it vibrates through the room like the low hum of a tuning fork. It is Dace's steadfast belief that Alexei will not simply survive—but that he will triumph.

Dace was not there the night Alexei won the Cliburn gold. She did not see him leap from his seat and hold his fists above his head in a jubilant victory salute. She didn't watch as he bounded onto the stage and hefted a silver loving cup into the air. She didn't hear him later joke that it should be filled with wine.

Dace was still in Russia when Alexei began the dizzy 200-concert tour that began after the Cliburn and stretched over the next two years. There were music camps and performances, talk shows, and dinner parties. Amiable and curious, Alexei lacked the social confidence to "work a room," but patrons were drawn to him and some whispered that he was that unique treasure—a youthful, attractive artist who was both passionate and marketable.

Even the famous wanted to be close to him. One night after appearing on the David Letterman Show, Alexei was invited to play privately for the legendary Vladimir Horowitz. It was a memorable highlight of the young Russian's life. They met in Horowitz's New York apartment. They spoke Russian and played the piano together. Alexei told him the story of meeting Dace at a Horowitz concert at Moscow's Bolshoi Theatre. Dace was only a girl of about fifteen, a cello student at the Moscow Conservatory herself, the afternoon she met Alexei. It was a fateful—and romantic —meeting.

She smiles now at that memory. Horowitz, the celebrated pianist, was playing at the Bolshoi and a crowd of some fifteen music students wanted to see the great man perform. There were no more tickets for the sold-out performance, and so the little band of students climbed to the roof of an adjoining building and jumped one by one to the sloping roof of the theater.

"It was a rainy day. I was fortunate and unfortunate at the same time," Dace says. "My foot slipped and somebody grabbed me—somebody whom I liked before, somebody whom I knew, but he didn't know me."

Alexei takes up the story. "I grabbed the girl. I looked at the girl. It was not bad—so I saved her."

The students climbed through the theater's attic space and found themselves above the stage at the Bolshoi, looking down through the magnificent chandelier. "It was so beautiful. You can see through the crystals Horowitz's hands moving," Dace says as she plays imaginary piano keys. Her eyes are shut and she sways slightly. She blinks, then smiles. "This is the first time Alexei and I are talking. The first time we are meeting. It is amazing."

From that moment on, the two seemed destined to be together —for better or for worse, but that would come later.

If Alexei's life was busy in the first years after the Cliburn win, it may have also been lonely, says Denise Mullins, who was then working for the Cliburn, managing Alexei's engagements. But she also admits that this is a newfound sympathy. Their relationship was strained to the breaking point when Alexei refused to leave Moscow and play at the important Linz Festival in 1990.

"This was a big-deal festival," Mullins says. "A European manager was going to be there. Conductors were coming to hear him. The whole thing was going to be on television. He didn't want to leave Moscow, because he wanted me to bring his girlfriend, Dace, to the U.S. for a visit and her visa hadn't arrived in Moscow yet. He wasn't going to leave without her. I was very angered by this and so were the people at the Linz. We didn't know at that time, they planned to get married. We just thought it was a visit. Anyway, he wouldn't leave without her and he missed a very important engagement because he so wanted her to be part of his life.

"In retrospect, I have to respect his decision. His priorities were different than mine. Actually, they were good for each other. Dace was certainly good for him. He got so much better when she came. She was a very grounding influence."

Soon after, Dace arrived in Fort Worth on a tourist visa and stayed—like Alexei—at the home of Susan and Jon Wilcox, the host family that had provided housing for Alexei during the Cliburn competition. In 1989, the Wilcoxes thought they were making a three-week commitment to house a competitor. That arrangement had stretched into a two-year run while Alexei completed the Cliburn-managed concert tour. Before it was over, the Wilcoxes thought of Alexei as their son.

It was to their house he came back when the concerts were over. Susan calls Alexei "one of the most generous" people she has ever met, a sentiment echoed by everyone who knows him. "He'd give you the shirt off his back. If you admire something he has, he just gives it to you," says Dr. Edward Kramer, a close friend and the physician whom the Sultanovs turned to first when the stroke hit in February.

"When Alexei won at the Cliburn, he didn't speak any English. He had never had more than a dollar in his pocket at one time. He didn't know how to do the simplest things like make change. He couldn't travel by himself and suddenly he had all these concert dates. We just decided we couldn't stop helping then," says Susan.

In 1991, on the day before the visa expired, Alexei and Dace were married by a justice of the peace at the Tarrant County Courthouse after a judge caught between sessions waived the waiting period. Naturally, they went home to the Wilcox house and settled in, but after several months they dipped into Alexei's savings gleaned from concerts and bought their own modest home on the city's southwest side. They share the place with several cats and an iguana.

Red roses bloom in the garden there and now Dace brings bouquets to Alexei as a reminder of the world beyond this cramped hospital cocoon. She kisses his forehead and whispers words of love to him—reminding him of what it's like to fly, promising him that she can still see his wings.

The Private Lives of a Public Couple ✌
May 16, 1993

ON THE outside, they looked very different.

He seemed to have it all: prominence, power, money. She was a mechanic's daughter, raised in rural isolation, bringing up a son alone.

But they say they were alike on the inside: troubled, lonely, searching.

From that crucible of understanding, they have forged a commitment to each other and to myriad worthy causes and emerged as one of Texas' most public couples, but State Senator Mike Moncrief and his wife Rosie guard their private lives so well that only a small circle of friends know their story.

Just before receiving the latest award for their long commitment to improving the lives of mentally retarded Texans, they talked about their first date, their individual histories, and their life together. The Moncriefs sat close to each other on a comfortable sofa in their home in West Fort Worth.

They seemed relaxed and happy, but as they examined their history, they became pensive and protective and struggled to explain their lives.

"We are very much aware of the fact that in another place and time our relationship might not have had the magic that it has now—but we also know that all those other experiences made us what we are today and may be why our marriage is so successful," says Rosie, forty-five.

She had already married and divorced twice when she came to Fort Worth with her young son Troy in the late 1970s to work at the then-new Century II Club. She didn't want to move, but she had already turned down a couple of other offers from the management at Club Corp of America. "I was afraid I was eliminating my options," she says.

Mike was only in his thirties, but he'd already served a stint in the Texas Legislature and landed the job as a Tarrant County judge. Outsiders might have thought he had it made, that he could write his own ticket, but he knew that his personal life was coming apart at the seams and his thirteen-year marriage to his college sweetheart was failing.

He insists now that he loved Rosie the instant he saw her. They arranged a dinner date and very soon he told her he was married. "It was not something I wanted to hear," she says.

"I remember the most intriguing thing about Mike was that there was such a kindness in his eyes. I felt that underneath all the stuff was a really kind and gentle person," she says, then pauses and looks at him. "I don't think Mike knew that person was in there."

He reaches for her hand. No, he hadn't known, not then, but now he sends flowers each month to commemorate the anniversary of that first date. It was a life affirming, life changing moment.

They were married on New Year's Eve 1980.

Rosie's Story

Now an outspoken advocate for people who are mentally ill, mentally handicapped, disabled, and underserved by health care systems, Rosie says that once she was painfully shy. She grew up the youngest of five children in Steep Hollow, Texas, a small farming community outside Bryan. The family rented a two-bedroom house on five acres. They had cows, chickens, and a garden and for a time, her mother sold butter, eggs, and produce to make ends meet.

Neighbors were distant, and a small Baptist church was the hub of their social life. It was, she says, a solitary childhood in a house filled with so much tension that she remembers few incidents from those early years. She has no family snapshots to jog those memories. Money was too scarce for that indulgence. Her father, a mechanic, was brooding and immensely unhappy.

"We cut a wide path around that man," she says. "He never touched me, but he was horrible to my brothers. He was horrible to my mother."

The tiny house could hardly hold the family. Two brothers shared a bedroom. Two slept on a screened breezeway. Rosie slept with her mother while her father spent the nights on a rollaway bed. Discontent haunted every room.

"They weren't afraid of him really," she said of her four brothers' attitude toward their father. "There was just no respect."

When Rosie was twelve, her father killed himself.

Her mother, who died in 1984, never remarried—never really looked at another man. "I think life with him was so difficult, she didn't ever want another man in her life," she says.

With her father gone, the stress of day-to-day existence changed, but for Rosie, the crushing loneliness continued. "I was always alone … surrounded by people, but always alone," she muses. When only fourteen, she secured a Social Security card and took a job as a gift wrapper and layaway clerk in a Bryan department store. By the time she was seventeen, her mother owned a dress shop and Rosie went to work for her.

"Mom was a strict disciplinarian," she says. "She was a good woman, a Christian woman . . . but she was a victim of her environment. She was a person who didn't show affection. I don't now, nor did I ever, hold that against her, because that's what she learned, but it was hard. You could always get criticism, but not much praise."

Rosie wanted something more and so at eighteen she married. She was a mother at nineteen and divorced by twenty-two.

"I was mentally, financially, and emotionally on my own with Troy," she says of those years with her baby son. There was no time or money for advanced schooling, but she says that looking back, she never doubted she could make it alone. She had no choice. In only five years, she was managing twenty-three apartment complexes and a doctors' building in Houston. Things were looking up—and then the company sold.

The new management transferred her to Arlington. She was unhappy with the work and began to look for something new, but she was a woman alone. She sometimes took two jobs to pay the bills, and it seemed as if she worked all the time. Then she landed a position with Club Corp of America selling memberships in a classy club in Mississippi. Eventually that company sent her to Fort Worth.

She says she did not want a new relationship then. A second brief marriage had ended in divorce and she was left feeling empty and more lonely than ever, but she was determined to change her life's story. "I knew there had to be a better life than what I had," she says.

For Rosie, life began with Mike.

Mike's Story

Mike Moncrief, forty-nine, is the most public member of a moneyed Texas family that is the stuff of legend. Now a Democratic state senator, he was once one of the youngest members of the legislature and then Tarrant County's outspoken and often controversial judge, heading the Commissioners Court. Early in his public life, he championed causes that addressed drug and alcohol abuse and issues surrounding mental health and retardation amid whispers that such matters touched his own family.

He is at once reflective and guarded about the subject. "I won't deny that our family—like many, if not most—has had some of those problems. We've had our share of tragedy, but those tragedies have somehow made us stronger, closer," he says.

Born Michael Joseph Trapp, Mike was adopted by R.B. "Dick" Moncrief when Dick married the boy's mother, Dee. Dee's marriage to Mike's biological father, Jack Trapp, had ended in divorce when Mike was very young.

Trapp's mother was the sister of W.A. "Monty" Moncrief Sr., the patriarch of the influential Fort Worth oil family—and Trapp was Dick Moncrief's first cousin.

Dick Moncrief was the son of oil tycoon "Monty" Moncrief Sr. and the only brother of W.A. "Tex" Moncrief Jr. For reasons left unexplained, Dick fell out of favor with his powerful father and was distanced from his brother.

Three more children were born to Dick and Dee Moncrief: Richard Barton Moncrief Jr., Elizabeth Scott "Scotty" Moncrief, and Lee Wiley Moncrief.

"Our family, that being my father and his side of the family, has always been on the outside," says Mike. "This is hard for me to express. There was an imbalance. An imbalance of love, I think, and of everything that goes along with it. Tex was clearly the favorite son and consequently that led to a split that was never repaired. My dad went his own way."

As Mike, then twenty-six, made his first bid for public office in 1970, Dick, then only forty-eight, died of a massive stroke at his Crestwood home. It was the end of only one painful story. Through the years Dick had been plagued with failing health. "He had kidney failure and then consequently he had strokes. The strokes led to partial paralysis on one side, then partial paralysis on the other side, then total paralysis," says Mike. "He was home at the end and he had a trach that had to be cut. He was having suction every hour. It was just … it was one of the toughest things I've ever seen."

The family was still numb from a tragedy only three years earlier. Scotty was a girl of only seventeen when she died in a fiery car crash. Her death sent the family into a tailspin of grief.

Blinking back tears, Mike describes the 1967 accident. As he speaks, Rosie moves closer, lightly stroking his neck. Mike was a student at Tarleton State University then, he says. He flipped on the television and saw the footage of a Corvette on fire.

"I see it now like it was yesterday … the wheel slowly spinning. It was burning and it was going around and around real slowly." He traces wide circles in the air. "I saw the three thin white-walls and my stomach became just a hard knot. The phone started ringing, and I knew it was Scotty." The accident was a turning point that sent the family sometimes to the brink of despair, he says.

"Scotty was the good one. She was angelic. But she was gone," he says. He draws a ragged breath. Lee, the youngest, tried to fill the void. She moved to Scotty's room. She drove Scotty's car.

"It just never worked," he says. "Lee had problems from that day on. My sister is now, unfortunately, suffering a degree of retardation because of brain damage. She was injured in an incident. She is totally dependent. She lives at home with a full-time nurse. Lee has had a rough life."

Lee's picture is displayed on a piano in a corner of the Moncrief house along with a collection of family photographs. He visits her often and grieves over her misfortunes, but he confides that he has other regrets even closer to his heart.

He wants a better relationship with his son from his previous marriage, Mitch, who is now twenty-four. Mike says he never knew how to be a father until he married Rosie and adopted her son, Troy, who is now twenty-six.

"It hurts," he says of his relationship with Mitch. "I wish things were different, but I was not the greatest father and that is my burden to bear. We exchange gifts on holidays, but we seldom see each other. It's not what I want, and frankly, I don't think it's what he wants."

Mike becomes reflective. Sunlight flecks the lavender-tinted walls. There are tulips in a crystal vase on the coffee table. A white cockatoo climbs its perch, parroting "Hi" to no one in particular.

The senator recalls those early struggles: demands that interfered with family life; campaigning for Republican presidential hopeful Barry Goldwater; his own successful bid for president of the Tarleton State student body; that first Austin job as the assistant to the assistant calendar clerk, which fueled his political ambition.

As a senator, Moncrief is a leading advocate for mental health and mental retardation services. He and Rosie were honored last month with the Association for Retarded Citizens/Texas' first Leadership Award. Although still clearly dedicated to public service, he says he has learned that family time is the seedbed of happiness and energy. Sharing life is what makes it worth living, he says.

Now he always involves his wife in his political life, always seeks her counsel. He tells constituents that she is part of a two-person team.

"I want to be part of Rosie's life and I want her to be part of mine," he says. And so they constantly work to keep an element of wonder and romance in their relationship. He was enormously pleased when she surprised him with a rafting trip through the Grand Canyon. He thought he was going to a golf tournament.

She was equally delighted when, in the heat of a campaign, he rented a room at the Fort Worth Club and ordered flowers and lunch. She thought they were going to the dining room for a fast meal.

But as her role in the community broadens, they are challenged to find new ways to be together. Trapped by legislative committee work in Austin, Mike could not go to Washington, D.C., in January for the presidential inauguration. Rosie attended with former U.S. House Speaker Jim Wright and his wife Betty. As the bands played and the crowd cheered, Rosie called Mike on a cellular phone. "I wanted him to be part of that historic moment," she says, but he was locked in a meeting and only his staff could hear the excitement.

She is glad she went, but she says she won't go again without Mike. "I put my family first," she explains. "I'm very aware that anything could happen. There are no guarantees in life. Something could happen to one of us today or tomorrow. I want the most out of our relationship every day."

PART TWO
Fathers and Sons

Loving Freddie ❧ *August 29, 2004*

At almost 60, Freddie Cobb believes there is always tomorrow, but his 91-year-old father Howard knows better. Courtesy, the Fort Worth Star-Telegram. © *Joyce Marshall.*

HIGHLAND PARK—The two men huddle together in the amber circle of lamplight, bending their heads toward the page as they have on a thousand other nights. Howard Cobb adjusts his glasses and reads a single sentence aloud, then his son reads the same sentence. Freddie's voice jerks over the printed words.

Howard hopes his son understands the story—but he can't be sure.

It doesn't matter.

Freddie is almost sixty now, and these two men have grown old together in this old house. They seem to live in their own private orbits, brushing against each other in the familiar routines that morning and evening bring, but at ninety-one, Howard Cobb knows he no longer has the luxury of time.

He made up his mind long ago that he'd "do right" by his son, give him every advantage possible; love him completely and without reservation. It's a choice he has never regretted, but now he wonders if he always did the right thing.

Love, he'll tell you, can be tricky.

He has made arrangements for his son: an allowance, a guardian, a place to live—but will it be enough?

Who, he wonders, will love Freddie when he is gone?

Freddie Cobb wears his Whataburger uniform as he lopes awkwardly past the multimillion-dollar homes on Highland Park's Lexington Avenue, never noticing the immaculate lawns or the profusion of flowers that bloom in carefully tended beds. He doesn't wonder what's behind those gilded or gleaming doors, can't appreciate that Highland Park, a small city completely surrounded by Dallas, is one of the Lone Star State's most exclusive enclaves. Freddie and his dad live here in a white frame house built in 1913. The magnolia tree in the front yard was planted that same year, and now its waxy leaves stretch past the second-story roof. Most mornings, Freddie hoists an American flag up the pole beside the porch, and in the evenings he hauls it down. He carries a key to the wide front door in one of his pockets.

Since Freddie's mother went to a nursing home three years ago, he and his father have been batching it. She calls each day to be sure they're eating right. Howard does the cooking: frozen corn dogs nuked in the microwave and a can of beans, or fried chicken from a carry-out place. He eats in the kitchen; Freddie in front of the big-screen TV in the living room. Without a housekeeper, the rooms are a jumble of laundry and mail. Dozens of Freddie's Special Olympics trophies collect dust on the mantel. No one washes the windows.

Friends wonder why Howard doesn't sell this place and move them both into something more manageable—someplace where a meal is served and someone runs the vacuum.

Sometimes Howard wonders, too. He brought his family to this home in the late 1940s, and now the property value has skyrocketed. In this neighborhood where houses sell for more than a million dollars and are then torn down to make room for new construction, he knows his place would command top dollar, but for Howard, the decision to sell is a tangle of emotion and practicality.

What would happen to Freddie? he wonders.

After all, Freddie's home extends beyond the walls of this creaking house to the borders of this little city within a city. Freddie has a routine here, friends—and a measure of safety, says

Howard. Everywhere Freddie goes in Highland Park, people recognize him, accept him—protect him.

If the two of them move, how can Freddie drop by the fire hall, or go to the pool—or walk unharmed through the streets?

And yet, Howard knows that when he is gone, Freddie can't stay in this house. He has made arrangements for Freddie to live with a guardian, a gentle family friend who loves Freddie, but Howard sometimes worries that circumstances may confound that plan. The guardian, after all, is a woman in her seventies, a time when life can take unwelcome and unexpected turns.

Howard flicks the thought away with a wave of his hand, but his gray eyes are clouded with concern. Howard Cobb knows that when he is gone, Freddie's life will change dramatically—and there is nothing he can do to stop it.

Freddie is at home in this burg of some 9,000, happily hurrying down the shady walkways to the Highland Park Swimming Pool all by himself—and on this day all he can think about is the girls he'll see there.

"Maggie. Ellen. That other one," he says, his lips working to make the names intelligible. "I'm on lifeguard patrol," he announces proudly as he rushes forward, his billed Whataburger hat set carelessly on his gray head, a smile plastered on his lined face.

Freddie is always smiling, the skin creasing in pleasant starbursts around his narrow blue-gray eyes and his lips pulled back over straight teeth the color of old ivory. He is a big man at almost six feet and more than 200 pounds, but his shoulders droop a little now, and there's a bit of a paunch beneath his shirt. Sometimes a small tremor shakes his right hand.

But to those who know him, Freddie is a man forgotten by time, a forever-child who reminds them that enthusiasm is its own reward and that the future is a gleaming prize to be cherished. It is this single characteristic, this unfettered optimism and absolute trust that tomorrow holds infinite possibility for joy, that most impresses Howard Cobb about his son. He smiles and shakes his head, proud and amazed at Freddie's invincible trust in the future.

"Maybe next year," Freddie declares when someone says he can't go to their school or to their house or to help with a chore. "Maybe tomorrow," he'll chirp and then busy himself with some bit of make-believe.

Freddie's pretend world is as full of adventure as that of any six-year-old's. As pool lifeguards watch, he pretends to tame a circus lion. He plays at taking someone's temperature, carefully shaking down the mercury in an imaginary thermometer, pumping up an invisible blood-pressure cuff and letting it go with a shushing sound. He puts out a make-believe fire with an invisible fire extinguisher or shoots off imaginary fireworks. When a plane roars overhead, Freddie pretends to be the man on the tarmac guiding the big jet to a gate only he sees.

"Freddie, do you get mad?" a friend recently asked.

Freddie closed his eyes and shook his head, making the Whataburger hat wobble back and forth. No. Never.

The anger gene may have skipped him, but other human frailties did not.

Most days he could use a nap, but his schedule is too full for that—and Freddie doesn't want to miss a thing. Three nights every week, he and his father go to Bachman Recreation Center, where Freddie plays basketball or does group exercises or takes a nature hike—and his father logs a few volunteer hours answering the phone.

Most nights Freddie stops at Highland Park's fire hall, where he hangs out with the firefighters. Each Fourth of July, he rides on the firetruck in the Highland Park parade and afterward attends the firefighters' company picnic.

Once, when Howard fell into a deep sleep in front of the television, Freddie thought his father was dead and rushed to the Fire Hall for help. When Howard woke, he was surrounded by Highland Park police officers and firefighters.

But Freddie works, too: a part-time job at Whataburger where he buses tables, mops floors, and carries a condiment tray to diners, and another at the Community Development Center, where he boxes cosmetics or does other kinds of workshop labor. Howard drives his son to all these places, not exactly rocketing through Dallas' busy streets in his 1995 Mercury Grand Marquis but holding a steady course, taking a careful forty-five minutes to drive the four miles from his house to the Whataburger on Greenville Avenue.

On an August afternoon, Freddie circles around the Highland Park pool, carefully folding towels the swimmers have discarded in rumpled heaps, telling children not to run on the slippery deck. Freddie says he's on lifeguard duty, but he wears his Whataburger uniform instead of swim trunks. No one cares. Everyone at the pool knows him. Freddie has been coming to this pool since it was built in 1953. He was eight then. Now he swims with the children, sometimes the grandchildren, of people he met there when he was a child.

Most of the burger joint customers give him the cold shoulder, leery of his odd manner and his tendency to stand too close, but here in the heart of this wealthy enclave, Freddie is accepted as a member of the family. Anne Reece grew up in Highland Park. Now in her forties, she is glad her nine-year-old daughter, Caroline, knows Freddie, too.

"Everyone who grew up at the Highland Park pool knows Freddie," she says while watching her daughter swim. "We love him. Everyone always asks about him, too. If we bump into someone we haven't seen for a while, it's one of the first things we say to each other. 'Hey, how's Freddie?'"

Anne laughs about Freddie's peculiar problem with personal distance. "He'll break your sphere in a minute, reach out and touch you," she says. "His movements are jerky, and it could be frightening, I guess, but even when we were kids we were never afraid of him. Freddie taught us that's it's OK to be different. Touching doesn't hurt.

"I'm glad Caroline knows him. This quiet nonverbal exposure teaches her about people's differences, too. She knows everyone isn't born the same. Not everyone needs the same personal space."

Occasionally, if the weather turns bad or the hour grows late, Howard will appear at the top of the stairs that lead from the street to the pool and call to his son.

"Fred. Time to come home," he shouts. And those at the pool who've known Freddie their whole lives hear those words echo across the decades to their own childhood—and for one brief moment the world stops.

Howard Cobb quit asking why long ago. "The doctor used forceps, and I think maybe that caused some damage," he offers, but the why of the matter has long ago lost its sting.

"It was a normal pregnancy," says Freddie's mother, Phyllis, as she settles into a comfy chair in her room. Howard reaches out and covers one of her hands with his.

"Oh, we knew right away that something was wrong," she says. "We had another boy and, well, Freddie was not progressing the same way." But now, in her eighties, she can't remember the details of those worrisome days.

Doctors said it would be best to "send him away," put him in a state school, focus on their son David, who was a couple of years older, move on with their lives. The Cobbs couldn't do that. Freddie belonged with them. Maybe the doctors were wrong. Maybe if given enough attention, he could learn more than anyone guessed.

The heaviest burden of teaching—and coping—fell to Phyllis, who was with her children around the clock. Howard had his job as a geophysicist, and a life away from Freddie. But at night, Howard read to his son and had him read to him. He drilled Freddie on simple math problems. He still does. Freddie can add 9 plus 9 or subtract 8 from 16—but he doesn't know how old he is.

The Cobbs became pioneers helping organize the forerunner of the Arc of Dallas, an organization that advocates for people with mental disabilities. They pushed to change laws and social attitudes that kept their son and others like him from reaching their fullest potential.

Howard calls it "the agency work," but he can't recall the details of those days now. He worked to organize Special Olympics in Texas, too, and helped found a group home in northwest Dallas. It was one of the first in the state, but in the end he didn't send Freddie there. Instead, he kept his son home with him—home in Highland Park. He doesn't regret the time he devoted to Freddie in those early years, but he wonders if his older son, David, suffered because of it.

"I tried to do the right thing," he says. But he'll tell you there's a trick to recognizing the right thing when it comes along.

David was a student at Southern Methodist University when he died in the 1960s. "He was killed by gunshot," Howard explains, his voice flat. He clears his throat and casts his eyes toward the steep stairs at the end of the living room. "I don't know if he was playing with the gun, or if...."

Phyllis heard the shot, rushed up the stairs . . .

"David was troubled," Howard admits. He sighs and turns his head away.

Suddenly, in one awful moment, Freddie became his only child, and the memory is heavy in the morning air.

Howard dreams the days away now, the cicadas' shrill song a lullaby outside his window. "I don't know why I sleep so much, but I sleep all the time," he says and chuckles. He wakes in time to pick Freddie up from work and then sends him off to the pool. Before bedtime, Freddie will stop at the fire hall and hang out with the firefighters until almost dark.

For almost sixty years, Howard and Freddie have been bound together by need and duty, admiration and love, but now Howard knows the future dangles on the thinnest thread of chance. Standing in the gravel drive, he looks up at the tall magnolia tree in his front yard. His gray eyes skim over the roof and take in the porch.

"Sometimes I'd like to sell this place," he says, his voice brimming with melancholy, "but how would Fred get to the fire hall?"

A Father's Long Goodbye ❧ September 28, 2002

From left: Hayley, Mike, Jay, and Holley Hendrickson. Mike Hendrickson thought he could save his son's fate, but even with the support of his wife Holley and his daughter Hayley, he couldn't win. Courtesy, the Fort Worth Star-Telegram.

BEDFORD—Who knows how long the enemy slept in his house? It hid in the darkness and kept so still that he had no idea it was there. Then, just when he thought he'd turned it out, it crept back in and waited to strike again.

He knew from the beginning that it would be a hard fight, but he was sure he could win. He would carry his family on his shoulders, stay the course—will his son to get well again.

He never said it was Jay's battle alone, Jay's treatment, Jay's chemotherapy. He always said it was "ours" or that "we" went to the emergency room; through the stem cell replacement program; to the clinical trials at Memorial Sloan-Kettering Cancer Center in New York. "We" had surgery to remove a stretch of bone and more to pluck tumors from the lungs. "We" were hungry or sick. "We" were hopeful or happy—or out of sorts. "We" were free of disease. "We" had active cancer cells again.

"We" missed starting seventh grade.

"We" included the whole family—but it stood, most of all, for him.

If one out of five of those stricken with the deadly bone cancer called metastatic osteogenic sarcoma survive, then his son would be that one, he said—but in the end, Mike Hendrickson could not stop the enemy. It lived in his bedroom, and even while he and his wife and daughter watched, it stole his son's last breath.

Each year, hundreds of children die of cancer in the United States. They leave behind grieving family members and heartsick friends, but Jay left something more. His two-and-a-half-year struggle to survive produced a remarkable chronicle of everyday details of his fight, written by his father. Only three days after Jay's bone cancer was diagnosed on March 20, 2000, Mike began a series of postings on a protected website as a way to keep friends informed of Jay's progress.

Of the hundreds of postings on the site, only a dozen or so are written by Mike's wife, Holley, who seldom had access to a computer. Mike always did, so the postings became his responsibility—and, later, his catharsis. It is a record of a father's devotion to his family, a long goodbye to a son he loved and loves still, a reminder of the frailty of life and the strength of hope.

When the end came, Mike and Holley put their arms around each other and around their daughter, Hayley, and cried. Then Mike dressed his boy in a basketball uniform and put a stuffed dog at his side. The long struggle was finished. They had been like fugitives on the run, looking over their shoulders for more than two years and at last, they were apprehended. It was over.

They waited for someone to take away this shell that had housed Jay's brave spirit, this little body swollen from medication and scarred from more than half a dozen surgeries.

On Saturday, September 14, young Jay Hendrickson left home for the last time. The funeral home sent not a hearse, but a white Suburban. The attendant didn't cover the boy's head as he was carried out and the bright sunlight fell across Jay's dark hair and pale face. Neighbors who saw the Suburban roll slowly down the Bedford street came to stand on the family's porch and cry with them.

Jay was twelve. He was Holley and Mike Hendrickson's only son, Hayley's only sibling.

Long before that day arrived, the family had decided Jay would be cremated and that they would hold a memorial service for him the second Saturday after his passing. There were times in the past two years that they were certain this day was not Jay's destiny, others when they were sure they could not escape it.

The Hendricksons' terrifying journey began, innocently enough, at a basketball game. Jay, a skinny fourth-grader with freckles and braces, was playing for the Spring Garden Elementary School Rockets when he took a hard knock on his left thigh.

Hours later, his leg still hurt. His mother, now fifty, who had survived breast cancer twice, once in 1998 and again in 1999, felt a knot and called to Mike. "Oh, it's only a muscle knot," he said. But days passed and Jay continued to complain.

A series of x-rays revealed trouble with Jay's left femur—and a dozen tumors in his lungs. Jay began treatment at Fort Worth's Cook Children's Medical Center. In addition to chemotherapy, he was part of a cutting-edge treatment program called stem cell replacement. White blood cells are harvested from the patient's own blood, frozen and then, after an aggressive chemotherapy program, put back into circulation.

Mike was more than hopeful.

"This treatment protocol will only last five to six months rather than the more conventional yearlong protocol," he wrote in his first posting on March 23, 2000. He was a confident man then. He dealt with facts. Jay had cancer. There were new treatments. It was a bump in the road. They'd be back on track soon.

Mike, now forty-eight, is a partner in an insurance agency. He is a man accustomed to making decisions, solving problems. He could stand strong.

Before the end of March, the Hendricksons had memorized the medical center's corridors. They knew more about the enemy, too. The cancer had started in Jay's femur. The bone had become porous "somewhat like a nylon stocking," Mike wrote in a posting. That portion of the weakened bone had to come out. Jay would receive a bone graft. It meant that contact sports and anything else that might stress the bone would be stopped permanently. It was hard news for this budding athlete—and for his parents. Holley cried, but Mike was optimistic.

"I've been busy reminding Jay that hiking, fishing, hunting, archery, and golf are but a few of the activities he'll be able to continue," Mike wrote. But by that time, Mike didn't sound so completely independent. "Please, oh, please keep in touch with us, that contact has been vital to Holley and Jay. Hayley and I like it, too," he wrote.

By April, Jay began to lose his hair. Mike offered to shave his head, which he later did along with some of Jay's school friends, but underneath the levity coiled a knot of uncertainty. "I hope and pray that chemo has vanquished the nodules from his lungs. This is possible, though not likely. Somehow the thought of two lung surgeries on Jay is pretty hard for me to contemplate," he wrote in a posting as if he were confiding in one longtime friend instead of the large group that logged onto the website.

The Hendricksons tried to maintain a "normal" routine, but it was impossible. "Good days" were treasured: the dove hunting trip to West Texas, a visit to an Oregon beach where Jay lay down in the sand and moved his arms and legs to make "angels" as if the sand were snow, one more chance to play outfield in a baseball game, a day at Six Flags Over Texas. One June evening in 2000, they attended a Rangers game and Jay was allowed on the field with a *Star-Telegram* photographer. "Well, if I can't play sports, maybe I can become a sports photographer," he told his dad.

Later that month, Jay had more surgery. Mike noted that he and Holley were both "teary." He wrote that "Jay faced the day like a brave general marching into battle, although he did ask 'Will I ever run free again?' which broke our hearts."

Mike was relieved when doctors left the operating room smiling. "Holley and I feel blessed and touched by a higher presence," he wrote. If the Hendricksons' lives had been on hold, the life around them ebbed and flowed in universal rhythms. Sandy, the Hendricksons' yellow Labrador, had puppies, and Mike took photos or videos of the wriggling litter to the hospital each evening. Test results showed no cancer.

Mike's spirits soared. "I believe that we are in God's hands and that the many prayers offered by our friends and families are being heard," he wrote. "We're blessed and wish to acknowledge that we are."

By the end of September 2000, Jay had his last stem cell infusion, and the family thought the end was in sight. He turned eleven on October 6, 2000, and Mike wrote that Jay was hospitalized. This birthday posting also introduced a new concern that was to be repeated over and over during the coming months. "One of the patients in this unit faces a tough surgery with a somewhat uncertain outcome later this morning," Mike wrote. "Could you please remember this unnamed patient in your private thoughts and prayers please?"

In the months to come, Mike would name the patients and ask for prayers. In October 2000, twelve-year-old Megan Newstrom, who lived only a short distance from the Hendricksons, died. When he got the news, Mike grieved openly.

Then Jay took a turn for the better and the Hendricksons were hopeful again. Jay was disease-free from October 2000 to May 2001. Holley and Jay hosted their annual Christmas party, and Jay even put his crutches aside and hit the dance floor—but another of his hospital friends was fighting for her life. Mike couldn't forget her. On December 18, he wrote, "If you have a quiet moment, please remember Gabby Napadano, a fellow patient in Rochester, New York."

Gabby did not survive.

The Hendricksons felt lucky that Jay was "able to put all the suffering and misery from the last year behind him." Mike wrote, "I'm committed and optimistic that we'll all be together for many years to come."

Of course, he couldn't see into the future.

～

At the end of May 2001, Mike wrote: "We're pretty crushed that the ground gained since last October has now all been given back . . . I look into the eyes of my family and see a bit of fear. We're a bit tender but resolved to fight on, filled with hope that there will be an effective treatment."

By June 2001, Jay was in a rush to live every minute. A different friend spent the night each night. He even made it to summer camp, but on Father's Day, Jay had a fever and Mike took him to the hospital for another round of tests.

Mike found it harder to push away his doubts—even more difficult to control his fear. "Emotionally, I've struggled a bit the last few days and have been bitter about the physical and emotional toll that osteosarcoma has exacted on Jay. We still have him and I still believe we will keep him, but the toll has been tremendous and more dues have yet to be paid," he wrote.

In August, Jay was ready to begin sixth grade. Hayley, almost sixteen, was eager to get a driver's license. Then, on August 15, Jay asked to go back to the hospital. Feverish and in great pain he said, "Daddy, I can't do this." Mike ached. "I'm holding up OK, but wish there were more hours to work and spend at home," he mused.

A few days later he wrote, "Jay and I were released from the hospital … I was so happy I sang and shouted most of the way there." The school year started, and while Jay had a home tutor much of the time, he did attend many classes and even took part in the sixth-grade play.

Mike and Holley were elated when Jay was accepted into a new clinical trial at New York's famous Memorial Sloan-Kettering Cancer Center in October 2001. The program consisted of a series of vaccinations administered over a year. Surely this was the ticket.

Less than two weeks later, the Hendricksons received the bad news that Jay had another tumor in his left lung. "Pray for us. We'll need it," Mike implored in a posting.

Sometimes Mike and Jay went to New York for the treatments. Sometimes it was Holley and Jay. Sometimes Hayley went along, and the whole family treated the trip as an adventure. They stayed at the Ronald McDonald House and made friends there. "The work of saving our son with the help of so many seems to be at hand," he wrote in November.

The Hendricksons were hopeful as the new year approached. They had celebrated Mike's parents' fiftieth wedding anniversary and enjoyed Christmas, but even then a new tumor was growing and Jay faced another surgery.

On December 30, Mike and Jay talked about the struggle to survive. Mike was so moved by Jay's "unflagging resolve to fight on," he had to fight back the tears. "We concluded our father-and-son talk with a handshake," he wrote. "I explained to Jay that when two men really admire one another … they shook hands…. Please pray for our strength and healing," he wrote. The year 2002 held great promise, but before the leaves would fall, the Hendricksons would need all the strength they could muster.

In late May, Jay and Holley walked together in the Survivors Lap in the American Cancer Society's Relay for Life. As darkness fell, the word HOPE was spelled out with luminarias in the far grandstands at a local high school. "I felt, at that moment, to be touched by a higher spirit and certainly believe that Jay can have more good days ahead," Mike wrote.

Jay went to church camp in June and when he returned, he complained of weakness in his legs. By the next afternoon, he could barely walk, even with crutches, and the next day, he couldn't get out of bed by himself. Tests showed a new tumor in one lung and a more serious tumor on his vertebrae at the base of the neck.

"Holley and I look at each other and we know that our son is dying," he wrote. "We have for the past two and one half years passed off this condition or that suffering as something less than the worst. Now we gently remind each other that this is the end."

They told Jay together. He cried and apologized for being sick.

He asked if he had been a good son. He had, his father said, been the best son, the perfect son.

~

They took him home and put him in a hospital bed in the master bedroom. Hayley moved in, too, sleeping on a cot next to her brother while Holley and Mike shared their big bed. At first, Jay could play video games with his buddies Barrett Nelson and Thomas Knapp, but each day the enemy moved closer—crouching in the shadows, waiting to strike.

Mike and Jay often watched Cowboys games together, and Mike looked forward to the nights he and Jay had alone together when Holley went to a high school game to watch Hayley cheer. One night after a ballgame aired on television, one of Jay's buddies called to talk about the game. Mike handed his son the phone and stepped into the hallway. The boys exchanged words about the plays and the players. Jay was so weak he could hardly talk, but Mike heard him say, "Yeah, I love you, too."

Every night, friends brought a meal. One day, an unusual delivery came to the house. It was from the International Star Registry. The package was a framed certificate and a framed map. A business colleague had registered a star in Jay's name.

In late August, the spirits came. Jay told his mother he heard singing in the house. He often said his late grandfathers were in the room with him. Sometimes the children Jay and his family had met in cancer treatment came to him. Each day, he became more removed from this place. He spoke in whispers and suffered limb aches. His eyelids drooped. He couldn't use his arms. Once, his father asked him if his time was over. "No," the boy said, but Mike knew that hour was drawing near.

Now that Jay is gone, Mike has given up the postings and Holley has done more of them. In some regards, they have changed places. Holley, who was so tearful before Jay's passing, is now more often clear-eyed, and Mike is the one who must blink back tears if he is to spot Jay's star in the nighttime sky. They plan to register three more stars in the Libra constellation—one for each of them, a shining reminder of all they have meant to each other in this world.

Holley, Mike, and Hayley
Hendrickson face tomorrow
without Jay. Courtesy, the
Fort Worth Star-Telegram.

PART THREE
Star Crossed

Priscilla's Story 🕊 August 28, 1991

T H E   D R I V E R is gone now, as are the custom-made cars, the bodyguards, the art collection, the swimming pools, the posh condo overlooking Turtle Creek. There's no need to carry a gun in her purse anymore.

Once she was the principal witness in a sensational murder trial, and her testimony has never wavered—not once in fifteen years. She says her ex-husband, Cullen Davis, shot her and then turned the gun on her lover. She was, she says, an eyewitness to that killing. She did not know then that her twelve-year-old daughter was already dead, killed in the basement.

But an expert team of defense lawyers gunned down her testimony. They focused on her clothes, her friends, her jewelry, her conspicuous life on the fast track. The man was acquitted and charges for the murder of her lover were dismissed.

Life goes on.

Priscilla Davis says she's not bitter. But she is sad—profoundly so.

"I don't want to change. I don't want to be a cold person," she says, flicking the trademark blond bangs from her eye with the tip of a painted fingernail. But it is impossible to miss the sadness in her eyes.

She props her elbows on the glass breakfast table, tucks her bare feet under the sleek black lacquer chair and sips a glass of water. She's wearing white midcalf pants and a pink T-shirt. Daisies are painted on her toenails.

At fifty, Priscilla finds her life has changed. She says most of the $3 million plus she got in a divorce settlement is gone, used up in living and loans, legal fees, medical bills, and bad stock market investments. She's looking for work, but not just any job. She's got to have some flexibility. She wants to be home at the end of the school day to meet her seven-year-old grandchild. There are ballet classes and piano lessons, and she's determined the girl won't miss any of those advantages.

Priscilla lives with that granddaughter, also called Priscilla Davis or PD2, and two gay roommates who pay rent in her comfortable Highland Park two-story house. Grass pushes through the cracks in the sidewalk and there's a "For Sale" sign planted in the neatly trimmed lawn.

Inside, the house is spotlessly clean—bare hardwood floors, white furniture, glass-topped tables. She hasn't had a housekeeper in years but hired a one-day-a-week maid only two weeks ago. She splits the cost with her renters.

There are white gladiolas on the cocktail table and the living room walls are a fashionable high-gloss pale peach finish. There are few mementos from earlier days. On a bookshelf is a picture of Priscilla in a long white evening gown leaning against the ornate doors of the mansion where she once lived. A picture of her three children is displayed in the den. A childhood portrait of herself hangs above the fireplace in her bedroom and a bedside table holds a host of tiny photographs of her family and friends.

She picks up several of the framed photos, smoothing a finger over the tiny protective ovals of glass. Her face is soft, and she is smiling. Priscilla says her friends have stayed beside her in spite of the bad press, the vicious gossip, and the days of black depression.

"Oh, some fair-weather sorts flaked off, but my real friends stayed. You may not see them everyday, but they're there if you need them," she says.

Fort Worth friends Judy Rice and Linda Plemons have come to treat her to a birthday dinner. They say Priscilla is generous to a fault. They tell of the kindnesses she has shown them—the baby bed she sent over, the flowers when they were hospitalized, the lunches catered from Neiman Marcus.

Priscilla has chosen for the celebration the trendy Buffalo Club, an upscale restaurant in the Quadrangle in Dallas. Reservations are for 8:15 P.M. Priscilla opens the door to her home at 6:30 P.M.

A short, blue, terry cloth robe, her initials embroidered on the back, hangs open over a mid-thigh denim skirt and navy tank top. She carries a glass of Smirnoff and water, with lime. She'll order the same drink several times during the evening.

She quickly exchanges the robe for a white linen jacket and before dinner puts on a pair of black pumps with high heels and scuffed toes. She climbs into her 1986 white Cadillac. There are no vanity plates, only the license plate number followed by the letters MEG. Priscilla seems delighted to call the car Meg.

"We'll go in Meg," she says. "Meg and I've been through a lot together."

At the Buffalo Club, all the waiters and many of the diners know her. They call her name and wave. Some stop at the table and whisper conspiratorily in her ear. The place throbs with the noise of conversation bouncing from the black concrete floor striped with white travertine and the wall of glass overlooking a courtyard. It's almost impossible to talk. Priscilla smiles and sips her drink. She orders half a Caesar salad and an appetizer portion of crab cakes. She's on a diet. Picking at her dinner, she suggests having an after-dinner coffee at another vogue hangout and then changes her mind.

"I'll take you to my favorite place," she declares. "I've never taken anyone there who doesn't like it. I call it the Wrinkle Room … old fags," she says with a throaty laugh. It's a gay bar that caters primarily to older men.

After dinner, she sweeps into the tiny, 1940s-type bungalow on the outskirts of Dallas' Oak Lawn neighborhood. She smiles and greets friends. Most of the customers are in their forties and fifties. A singer croons old tunes from a postage stamp size stage. The place is quiet except for the music.

Priscilla warns her dinner companions not to talk too much because the patrons like to listen to the music. During a break, the singer pulls up a chair, and she and Priscilla joke and laugh easily.

Friends say Priscilla is waiting for a prince to rescue her, but Priscilla insists there is no special man in her life right now. The man she moved to Dallas to be near is gone, but there is a "man friend" she sees on Friday and Saturday nights. He's only a friend, she declares. They go to dinner or for drinks at the Mansion, maybe pull on jeans and hang out on Greenville or stop at some country-western place. Occasionally they end the evening at the Wrinkle Room.

It is, she insists, just a comfortable friendship. After all, he's got another woman in his life and Priscilla says she's got too much responsibility raising her daughter's little girl to make room for a heart-deep relationship.

It's clear her life revolves around little Priscilla, who'll start second grade this fall at Bradfield Elementary School. Friends say the child is Priscilla's second chance. The little girl is the daughter of Priscilla's oldest child, Dee, but Priscilla stepped in to take charge of the five-day-old baby while Dee was in prison for offenses relating to a drug problem. The two Priscillas have been together ever since. She is the only mother her grandchild has ever known.

They are a striking contrast. Priscilla's hair is platinum, her skin ivory, her brown eyes transformed to blue by contact lenses, but the little girl has black eyes and the dark complexion of her African-American father.

Priscilla calls the child "my little international beauty" and dreams of a life for her in the spotlight. "I hope she'll stay with ballet," she says of the girl. "I think she's really good. I want her to get into piano. She has a natural gift. I've thought about modeling for her, but I'm not sure. She may be too shy."

Clearly Priscilla enjoys the child's company. Typically, they get up in time to watch *The Young and the Restless,* Priscilla says. They take Meg out for a spin and have a late lunch in a cafeteria. Often they take in a movie matinee and then it's home for a short rest before happy hour at the home of friends, she says.

It's not the kind of childhood Priscilla had herself. One of three children, she says her memories of Houston are happy ones. "My brothers and I couldn't leave the yard," she remembers. "All the kids came to our house to play."

They spent summer days in vacation Bible school, and her mother was active in church and school programs. While Priscilla regrets not getting an education, she seems proud that her mother attended the University of California at Los Angeles, postponing a family until she was in her thirties. "Mother has college sense," Priscilla says, "but I have common sense."

Priscilla doesn't remember her father but has deep affection for her mother's brother, Uncle Guy. When her father deserted the family, Uncle Guy became a major family support. Her mother and Uncle Guy built a three-bedroom house. Priscilla shared a bedroom with her mother while her brothers bunked together. "Mother thought I was wild, but I don't know why she thought that. I wasn't," Priscilla says.

Still, she married for the first time when only sixteen. The marriage failed. She married again, this time to Jack Wilborn, twenty-one years her senior. They had two children and were divorced.

And then there was Cullen Davis, who was acquitted in the mansion shootings.

Priscilla sighs. "If I had it to do over again, I wouldn't marry any of them," she declares.

But Priscilla's not looking back. "Everything's going to be OK. We make our own happy endings. I'll make mine. I want to do a real good job of raising Priscilla. I've had so many things. God has been good to me," she says matter-of-factly.

"You think of all the pain and suffering, but I can't say 'poor me' by any means," she says, a shadow of sadness sliding over her smile.

Cullen Talks ℘ *October 9, 1991*

HIS DARK eyes intent upon the speaker, Cullen Davis sits perfectly still—listening.

Legs crossed, thumb stuck under his chin, an index finger pressed lightly against his lips, Davis is expressionless. It is a familiar posture, polished and refined through years of courtroom appearances, but now the words that shape his life are not spoken by a judge or jury.

He hears a testimonial and waits for word from God.

Davis is, he says, a soldier of the cross, often battling demons to follow a higher calling. He comes each Friday to pray and praise God with this group of Christians who make up the Fort Worth Chapter of the Full Gospel Business Men's Fellowship International, a worldwide non-denominational organization. Davis is their local leader.

At fifty-seven, he is a grandfather whose hair is streaked with gray. There are the beginnings of cloudy halos around his brown irises. Still trim in black slacks and an open-necked striped shirt, he blends into this gathering. He greets some members of the fellowship with an embrace and tells them he'll pray for them.

He says he needs for them to pray for him, too.

It's been a long time, fifteen years in fact, since Davis was exonerated in two bloody killings. He was acquitted in the slaying of his twelve-year-old stepdaughter, Andrea Wilborn. Charges against him in the killing of Stan Farr were dismissed. Farr was living with Davis' second wife, Priscilla, at the time of the killings.

Cullen chose to settle out of court when Bubba Gavrel filed a personal injury suit against him. Gavrel was shot and permanently disabled the night of the slayings.

Davis has always maintained his innocence.

When asked what would happen to a man if he were guilty of such crimes, forgiven by God, and delivered to a new and nobler life, Davis says such a man would still owe a debt to society. "If he was guilty," he says hesitantly.

He drums his fingers on the table while considering the question. He cocks his head sideways and gazes at the ceiling briefly. "Yes, he would still owe something to society." His voice is strong and resolute. He snaps his head forward in an affirmative motion. "That's what the Bible calls for, and I believe it," he says. "The Bible says, 'Vengeance is mine, saith the Lord,' but it also says we're to obey civil authority." He is sure and unflinching.

Davis has become something of a biblical scholar, devoting years to his study. He is, he says, so transformed by God's grace that he can hardly recognize the man he was all those years ago. "I'm entirely different. I recognize that," he says with the slightest smile tugging at his lips.

Once he was known as a shrewd, no-nonsense businessman, the head of an international conglomerate that generated revenues of more than $2 billion a year. He was ambitious, some say calculating, aloof and rich—very rich—but despite his wealth and apparent success, Cullen Davis admits that more than anything he was a man filled with resentment and obsessed with the love of business.

"I had a long list of people I loved to hate," he says. "I don't remember who was tops on the list. I was very resentful and bitter toward certain people. Some were family." But even as he recalls minor childhood injuries, he's quick to declare that business was once the most important thing in his life. "My idol or god was the business, was working," he says matter-of-factly.

But that was yesterday, he says.

Today, he is a new man, a happier man, a peaceful man—a man with a mission.

"My objective is to know God," he says. "To tell other people about God. To rid my life of conflict and to go where God shows me to minister to other people."

It isn't an easy objective to accomplish.

The road to success is fraught with doubters and demons. Davis shrugs. He is not disturbed by the skepticism of those who question the authenticity of his conversion experience, and he has learned to battle the devils.

"I deal with demons very frequently," he says. "In my own life, I deal with them [demons] almost daily. I have some kind of temptation or attack almost daily. It can come from anger or lust."

His eyes fill with tears, not from emotion, but from other irritations. It's a frequent occurrence, he says. "Lust is not just sexual," he says. "It can be for material things. I'm not much bothered by material wants. I don't have any sexual lusts. I just want to go places and do things."

Davis swears he's had it all: fine clothes, luxury cars, exotic trips, and, of course, a spectacular house. All of that may be behind him, too. The international financial empire he helped control has been shredded by the bankruptcy courts, and he is waiting to settle yet another bankruptcy petition filed in 1987. His wife, Karen, has recently been working for Manpower Temporary Services as office help at Johnson & Johnson Medical, Inc.

Still, there is enough money to take an occasional ski trip to Aspen or Salt Lake City, and he and his wife plan a month-long European tour soon.

"We're going with our pastor and his wife to visit churches," says Davis, his voice registering some excitement. They'll visit Hungary, Yugoslavia, Poland, Austria, and Germany. The pastor, Olen Griffing of Shady Grove Church in Grand Prairie, has been going for the past decade, according to Davis.

Davis is employed by Great Western Drilling Co., an enterprise held by his older brother Ken Davis, but he denies having real responsibility there. He says he's touched all the bases in the business world, and his focus has changed. "Along with my brother, I headed a company bigger than Tandy," he says. "I don't want to work that hard any more."

Davis says became a born-again Christian more than ten years ago with the help of television evangelist James Robison. He insists his conversion is genuine. As a matter of fact, he says he's delivered more than one soul from torment himself. "I spend most of my time counseling those in spiritual calamity," he says.

He quotes scripture easily and talks about God without hesitation. He also talks of Satan. "I need prayer all the time because Satan, not with just me, but you and me, is supposed to attack everybody," says Davis. "God created him [Satan] for that purpose. Someone in a ministry like mine comes under attack more than others. Satan comes against the family for this thing and that thing and he creates arguments."

Davis says he has learned to disarm Satan. "I've learned how to deal with all that," he says. "The best way to stop an argument is not to win it, but to ask the person to forgive you for starting it." Now he says he lives peacefully with his third wife, Karen; her twenty-year-old son Chesley; and four dogs in a house on the edge of the golf course at Woodhaven Country Club in east Fort Worth. Chesley suffered profound hearing loss years ago when a drunken driver slammed into a car his mother was driving. His brother Trey, now twenty-three, was also injured. Chesley is working, and his hearing has improved with a cochlear implant, the newest technical tool for the deaf. Trey is in Midland in a management training position. He works for Ken Davis. Davis has two sons by his first wife. Cullen Davis Jr. is twenty-eight and has a three-year-old daughter. Brian Davis is twenty-six and manages a club in Dallas.

Careful about how and where they spend their time, the Davises do not closet themselves away. Friends drop in for a game of pool. They go out. Sometimes they dine at the Swiss House or Edelweiss restaurants, but Davis says he never has a drink—not a beer, not a highball, not a glass of wine. There's no scriptural prohibition. He says he doesn't want his actions to cause "a brother to stumble."

Last year, Cullen and Karen hosted a high school foreign exchange student from Spain and even visited that family in Madrid at Christmas. The student attended Lake Country Christian School in Azle. It is a campus and a curriculum they are familiar with, according to Karen. Her son, Trey, graduated from the program a few years ago.

There is no question that religious training and study have become central to their lives. They often have Bible study sessions in their living room.

The contemporary, white brick house is several levels on a high sloping lot dotted with trees. Walls of glass stand above the manicured greens below the back door and the upper balconies offer a pleasant view. It is an attractive house, neat and impressive enough, with a porte-cochère that reaches across the circle drive to the front door. But it is not the spectacular multimillion-dollar mansion Davis built on the family farm on Hulen Street south of the Trinity River. That estate became a pivotal point in Davis' divorce from Priscilla and was the site of the two bloody murders.

With a contemporary design of white stone, an indoor pool and walls of glass, the house fit the lifestyle of the hard-driving, hard-playing, high-power, high-profile boss of an international business conglomerate. It was a house Cullen shared for a time with Karen, her sons, and Dee, Priscilla's daughter by her first marriage.

"I loved Dee and wanted to help her," Karen Davis says as she recalls that time in the house. "And really, there weren't any problems until she started going back to her other friends; then the temptations were just too much, I guess, and we couldn't keep her." But Cullen says all that's behind him now.

"The Lord gave me a different attitude about everything, about relationships with people, about forgiving everyone for what they've done to me during my lifetime," he says.

PART FOUR

The Benefactors and the Legends

A Treasured Life ✌ *February 11, 2007*

Fort Worth doyenne, Martha Hyder, poses for a photo with her dog, Shivi, in her treasure-filled drawing room. Courtesy, the Fort Worth Star-Telegram. © *Jill Johnson.*

MARTHA HYDER leans forward, her head cocked slightly to the side. She smiles, listening as a longtime friend regales her with a story from their shared past. She is known for her parties, her generosity to the arts, her international connections, her late-night hours, and her landmark home that bulges with antique furniture, Moroccan rugs, Italian angels, Russian icons, and other historic memorabilia. For most of her seventy-something years, she has traveled the world, buying beautiful things, and it is this devotion to acquiring handsome and sometimes rare objects that has landed her yet another accolade. On Friday, she will be honored at a champagne reception that marks the opening of the first Charity Antiques Show, benefiting Historic Fort Worth, Inc. She and her late husband, Elton Hyder Jr., filled their Fort Worth home and the house they own in San Miguel de Allende, Mexico, with colorful collectibles from putti to dueling pistols, candelabras to Cossack bronzes. They added decorative pieces to their children's homes, filled his office with art objects, decorated public rooms at Sweet Briar College in Virginia and St. Mary's College in San Antonio, packed the attic and a warehouse, and still they weren't finished.

Together, they transformed the Tarlton Law Library at the University of Texas at Austin into a treasure trove of seventeenth-century furniture, portraits, framed trial scenes and historic legal documents; the library's Elton M. Hyder Jr. Collection contains some 4,000 pieces. Even more legal memorabilia is on display at the Texas Supreme Court in Austin and at the Tarrant County Courthouse. But now there are too many treasure hunts behind her to recall them all, and besides, Martha, who is recuperating from neck surgery she had last year, leaves the remembering to others—and it seems that everyone who has ever met this doyenne has a story to tell about their time together.

"Don't you remember that road trip to Austin, when we ran out of gas?" asks Ken Blasingame, an interior designer who has worked with dozens of high-profile clients, including First Lady Laura Bush. He is one of several friends who have gathered at Martha's home on this February afternoon to help select items from her vast storehouse of treasures to illustrate this story. A housekeeper places a tray of cheese and grapes on the dining table and asks if anyone would like a drink. More friends arrive, and it begins to feel like a party.

Blasingame perches on the edge of the sofa in the cozy den as Martha toys with the triple-strand pearl choker at her throat. She tries to recall that day in the late 1980s, but the memory hides.

"What happened?" she asks.

"We had been working at the law library, and we were leaving Austin in a rented midsize station wagon," Blasingame begins. "We looked like 1930 refugees from the Dust Bowl. The car was packed full. We had the dog. The bumper was almost dragging the ground. We were going to leave really early, at one in the afternoon, then it was two, then three and finally, we got away after ten at night. We were supposed to have dinner with these people in Temple. Elton was supposed to put gas in the car earlier, but I don't think he knew how to do that . . . so we ran out of gas. Don't you remember?"

She thinks. No. No. She can't recall.

Interior designer Tara Tooke, who helped Martha select the jewelry she wears from a pile of baubles turned out on the bed, stands in the doorway chatting with another friend. Martha's daughter and a woman from San Antonio are in the dining room. Another friend arrives, and Blasingame stops his story, but Martha jiggles his knee.

"Go on, what happened," she says.

"Well, these truck drivers brought us a milk jug full of gas, and we finally got to Temple about ten minutes to midnight and had drinks with these people. Then they loaded us into a limo and took us to an all-night hamburger place. . . ."

"Oh, yes, I do remember that," Martha says.

Midnight gatherings and late arrivals are part of Martha's late-night life. Her longtime friend Nancy Holmes, who was a contributing editor for *Town & Country* magazine and does public relations work in San Antonio, recalls another missed dinner. The two met in the 1960s, in the lounge at London's swank Claridge's Hotel, and soon became such fast friends that they happily tottered to Mexico, New York, and Africa together.

"I remember being in Paris once and someone was giving a dinner for Martha, but she was in Spain," Holmes says in a telephone interview. "She showed up around midnight, all breathless. She thought nothing of it. She's always late, you know."

"I was never late on purpose," Martha says. "It's been about ten years since I was late."

But late or early, Martha always has been comfortable giving others advice on how to decorate their homes, fix their makeup, or improve their wardrobe.

"Martha is always saying 'You ought to' and 'That will never do,'" Holmes says.

"You can get in a fury with her . . . but she's the only woman I know who makes people mad and remains friends with them," she says.

Even those who get in a huff with her find her powers of persuasion irresistible. In the early 1960s, the Hyders bought a massive home on Fort Worth's west side that had been the home of Ollie Lake Burnett, mother of philanthropist Anne Tandy. Martha had dreamed of building a more contemporary home in the Ridglea area and found the 1916 mansion too dark for her taste, but Elton had always admired the place and snapped it up when it came on the market.

Martha launched a three-year remodeling campaign. In the end, the original Tudor-style house was molded into something akin to an Italian villa. Today, wide front doors reveal a classic floor plan with a generous foyer dominated by a broad staircase with carved balusters that rise to a landing where ancient wooden figures from New Guinea keep watch. A long living room is on the right and a gracious dining room on the left. From a small hallway behind the staircase, doors lead to an ample den and an impressive stoa, a grand two-story porch that has been the setting of many parties.

The family, which included her husband and three children, moved in before the construction was finished.

Things were so hectic that Martha couldn't work in her beauty-shop routine, and so each day, her hairdresser would come to the house to apply her false eyelashes. Soon, he told her she'd have to learn to do it herself. Instead, she persuaded her building contractor, Bill Taylor, to learn to apply the eyelashes. "She is something else," says Taylor. He recalls that one day she complained that the piano contestant practicing in her living room for eight hours a day was being disturbed by all the construction noise.

"I had six to twelve carpenters there, and she said, 'Have them hammer quietly,'" he says.

For years, piano contestants were part of Martha's life. She and others worked to bring the world's best pianists and the media spotlight to Fort Worth for a once-every-four-years competition now known as the Van Cliburn International Piano Competition, which then did not have its global reputation. Martha also threw herself into work for the Fort Worth Symphony, the ballet, and Fort Worth's modern art museum. She became an officer and trustee of the National Symphony Association in Washington, DC, and served on bank boards locally.

She traveled and partied all over the world, and no matter her obligations, she opened her home to every sort of cause. Even if she wasn't in town, she allowed nonprofit groups to use the house for fundraisers and parties.

"I've never given a party without Ruth, but she's given a lot of them without me," she says of her assistant, Ruth Ybarra, who has been with her more than thirty years.

As Martha's reputation for being a hard worker and a visionary spread, more and more accolades came her way. In 1985 she was pictured in *Town & Country,* along with Nancy Reagan, Brooke Astor, and Ann Getty, as one of the "First Ladies of Charity," and, in 1993, she and her husband were named Fort Worth's Patrons of the Arts by the Arts Council of Fort Worth.

~

Martha was born to an influential Fort Worth oil family. Her parents were Merle and Charlie Rowan. Her husband was the son of a Fort Worth lawyer. At twenty-eight, Elton was Texas' youngest assistant attorney general and among the youngest men ever to argue a case before the U.S. Supreme Court. He served as an attorney in the opening phase of the war-crimes tribunal of Japanese Prime Minister Hideki Tojo, who ordered the attack on Pearl Harbor, but when he was forty-five, Elton walked away from a skyrocketing legal career and turned his attention to real estate and investments.

Martha says she had never collected anything until they bought the house on the bluff, but by the mid-1960s, the Hyders were becoming a force in the world of collectors. They filled the house with whatever pleased their eyes: marble columns from Italy, wooden masks from Africa, carved skeletons from Mexico, a ram's head snuffbox from Scotland, antique toy dogs from England, a bronze elephant from Japan. Martha haunted London's antique shops. She became a regular at Sotheby's auctions in New York.

The Fort Worth house alone is a testament to a lifetime spent hunting and gathering. The first time Holmes saw Martha's Texas house, she was astonished. "Martha Hyder has never believed that less is more," she says. "It makes Martha nervous if there is a quarter inch of unoccupied space on her walls."

Antique daggers and pistols are carefully laid out on a living room desk along with a framed lock of Napoleon's hair and three skeletons of crabs. Soft light filters through the potted palms at the living room windows and rests on a seventeenth-century Italian table that holds an assortment of wooden angels from the seventeenth and eighteenth centuries. Antique Bibles are displayed on tall easels at the end of the room. In the den, an ottoman that doubles as a coffee table holds an assortment of miniature cannons and a Victorian lord high chancellor's purse once used in processionals at the opening of the British Parliament. The long dining table is covered with a kilim rug, and crowns that once belonged to Russian rulers Nicholas II and Alexandra are displayed as centerpieces. Russian icons surround a table at the end of the room, and a wooden saint once carried in processionals through a French village sits at the end of a chest in the dining room. A group of stuffed turtles occupies the steps outside the breakfast room.

The treasure-filled house is a wonder of Martha's devotion to acquisition.

~

If the house was the beginning of their collecting legacy, the law library came at the end. Blasingame remembers with fondness and laughter one of those law library trips. There was, he recalls, a large aquarium in the library's lobby. "We didn't think it fit with the dignity of the collection, and Martha decided we should move it to the faculty lounge on the fourth floor."

The facilities manager said he couldn't be a part of moving the fish tank, which apparently was highly prized by the staff, but as he left for the day, he did mention where they might find a flat dolly suitable for such transport.

Under Blasingame's direction, some student volunteers wrangled the cumbersome container onto an elevator and up they went, but when the doors opened, the elevator was at least an inch below floor level. The young men gave a mighty shove, hoping the heavy, water-filled tank would pop over the barrier.

It did not.

They shoved again, and this time, the weight of the water crashed against the glass and broke it, just as Martha rounded the corner carrying a bunch of decorative Chinese bowls.

"There was this cascade of water running down the elevator shaft. The hallway was flooded.... Fish were flopping.... Martha was scooping them up in the Chinese bowls," Blasingame says. "We were madly filling the bowls from the water fountain. Of course, the fish could not survive...." The next day, the faculty wore black armbands, he says.

~

According to curator Michael Horn, the law library's collection was complete—or nearly so—by the time Elton Hyder died in 1995. Martha planned an Irish wake, and he lay in state in the living room of their imposing bluff-top house, dressed in a black-velvet smoking jacket and red tie and surrounded by the collection of miniature cannons. His trademark gold bracelets winked in the dim light. Before the funeral began, his clothes were exchanged for his favorite outfit: white shirt, white Bermuda shorts, and tennis shoes with no socks. Family and friends tucked letters into the casket, along with treasured books and a toy telephone so his wife could keep in touch.

Ever the hostess, Martha opened the home to mourners returning from the graveside services. Valets parked cars, wreaths of fresh yellow lilies adorned the open doors. A Dixieland jazz band played on the stoa. The dining-room table held a catered lunch of tamales, grilled pork loin, shrimp, and vegetables. Even in times of grief, the house thrummed with life.

It seems quieter now as Martha recuperates from last year's surgery. "You know, she becomes an expert on everything," her friend Nancy Holmes says. "Since she's been sick, she's become an expert on television, and I just hate it."

The photo session is over, and Martha's friends kiss her cheek and tell her goodbye. Her dogs, Astor and Shivi, both Wheaten Terriers, huddle near her feet. She is looking forward to the dinner party she will attend that night with her close friend and traveling companion of eight years, Kurth Sprague of Johnson City.

At a time when some people find that life is losing its color, Martha confides that she has fallen in love again—this time with a Coton de Tuléar, a fluffy breed of lap dog. The new puppy will arrive from Italy before the end of February, she says.

"Now, what do you watch on TV?" she asks. "You must watch *Grey's Anatomy* . . . *Boston Legal* is outrageous . . . and you have got to turn on Larry King every night, and don't forget *20/20* and. . . ."

Her eyes flash with interest. She will not be bored; she will collect what she can and right now that includes television programs—and accolades.

Such a Lot Of Giving To Do ❧ December 25, 1994

THE EARTH trembled and there was a thunderous roar as a black geyser of oil gushed over the top of the wooden derrick. She was four years old—and just for luck she stood with her Daddy in the dark spray, letting the oil spatter her dress and cover her arms. That well, the Mary D. #1 drilled in the fields north of Burkburnett about 1917, was only the beginning.

~

It wouldn't be Christmas, they say, if the pilgrims didn't come, if there were no bells, no boys singing in practiced chorus, no shepherds, no angel choir, no wisemen looking for the star.

For too long they've depended on these friends to help them discover once again the joy of the season. Never mind that their vision is not as clear as it once was, their step a little less sure, or that now they must sometimes rely on Rolls and Royce, twin wheelchairs that they say "live in the entry hall at the house."

F. Howard and Mary D. Walsh, both eighty-one, fret and plan the whole year long, eager for the Christmas traditions to begin. They say they are happy to pay the pilgrims' hotel bills, delighted to host the dozen parties.

Such generosity is commonplace for the Walshes. Their unique partnership seems almost anchored in gift giving. Over the years, they have quietly given away millions of dollars to hundreds of causes, including hospitals, churches, and the arts. In a city renowned for generous foundations, the two foundations they head—the Fleming and the Walsh foundations—have combined assets that rank them among the top fifteen according to the Directory of Tarrant County Foundations.

A gift to Texas Christian University this year will help build a performing arts center as well as a sports rehabilitation and weight training complex bearing their name. And there would be no Dorothy Shaw Bell Choir, no Texas Boys Choir without them, but that only scratches the surface of their patronage. Each year they send the Fort Worth Symphony, the Texas Ballet Theater, the Fort Worth and Dallas opera companies, and the Van Cliburn Foundation a $10,000 Christmas present each—in addition to their other gifts to those organizations.

The Walshes say they don't consider themselves philanthropists, but they have always showered presents on each other and on their friends. Since their wedding day on March 13, 1937, they've exchanged gifts on the thirteenth of each month. "We call them sussies," Mary D. Walsh says.

But perhaps their most remarkable gift, their most special salute to friendship, is what they call the "Winter Pilgrimage," a four-day round of parties and celebrations early each December connected to *The Littlest Wiseman*, a Christmas pageant they've been producing in Fort Worth for the past thirty-four years.

Mary D. still sprinkles her hair with glitter for the occasion, dresses in her prettiest party dress, straightens Howard's tie—and dreams of dancing. And this year, at a square dance that has become a Winter Pilgrimage tradition; she did dance—just once more. A friend pushed her wheelchair through the familiar routines, and she flipped her skirt in time to the music while a host of friends, touched by the spectacle, smiled through tears.

The play itself has become something of an old friend. Written in 1917 by Dr. Lloyd Shaw, for years, *The Littlest Wiseman* was presented by the Cheyenne Mountain School in Colorado Springs, but in 1961 the Walshes brought it to Fort Worth. For a time it was staged at McLean Junior High School. Then in 1965, only three days before the play's opening, a U.S. Supreme Court ruling banning religious productions in schools threatened to shut the show down.

A compromise for a Saturday night production was reached, and the next year the pageant moved to the William Edrington Scott Theatre. "This was just a simple children's play. A school pageant," Howard remembers. "It's gotten a little more elaborate through the years."

Now the sets are expensive, eye-popping spectacles, and the Texas Boys Choir and the Dorothy Shaw Bell Choir have leading roles in the production. But this show is only the beginning of the Walshes Christmas celebration. As soon as school dismisses for Christmas vacation, the Walshes and thirteen sponsors load up the thirty-two-member bell choir for a tour they pray may be life-changing. They pay the entire cost for trips to such locations as Brazil, England, Asia, Hawaii, Germany, Austria, Italy, Ireland, or a cruise down the Mississippi River.

The young men are required to wear ties each day and the young women must wear dresses. Ranging in age from fourteen to twenty-one, the bell choir members must act respectfully and to display proper table manners. "I hope this gives them some advantages," Howard says. He is stopped suddenly by the memory of one young girl's remark, and he struggles for control as he tells the story.

He remembers the day the bell choir gathered for a meal in a fine hotel. "She looked around the table and said, 'Who would have ever thought I'd be here—and know what fork to use!'" he says. He covers his eyes for a moment before remembering his own childhood—and a time when he, too, fumbled with forks.

Both Howard and Mary D. Walsh came from strict Southern Baptist homes, with demanding parents. Howard's father, Percival Frank Walsh, was born in India of English parents who migrated to the United States early in the century. The elder Walsh married Maude Elizabeth Gage, and they began life together in Waco, but they soon moved, first to Dallas and then to Fort Worth, where they became active members at Broadway Baptist Church and involved with a number of civic endeavors.

Then, as the country slipped further into the terrifying years of the Great Depression, Howard remembers the family's financial struggle. "Now we always had plenty to eat. We had a place to live, but we sure didn't have any money," he says.

A tennis star who would eventually capture several titles, including Southwest Conference Champion, Howard was determined to get a college education even though it meant walking to TCU each day from his family's house near Our Lady of Victory on the far south side of Fort Worth. He snagged a job at the Armour plant on the north side, working for 16.5 cents an hour, but his skill with numbers and strong work ethic didn't go unnoticed, and soon he moved to an office job. Later, he would get into the oil business, first as an accountant for his future father-in-law, William Fleming, and later for himself.

Now the Walsh enterprises occupy two floors of the NationsBank building and employ 149 people. Oil and ranching occupy his interests and his time. "There's no work on a ranch," he declares. "It's all pleasure."

Howard says his proudest accomplishment is what he calls "the employee thrift plan," an employee savings plan with company contributions matching an employee's contribution. Under this remarkably generous plan, some employees have accumulated $1 million or more. He runs his hands over the savings plan's ledgers and remarks on the security the figures represent. The bleak Depression years when few people had money seem far away.

Mary D. says it was during the Depression that she realized her family enjoyed a privileged financial position. She was attending Southern Methodist University in Dallas and returning to Fort Worth each weekend as her father insisted.

"I suddenly saw that the word 'rich' might apply to us," she says. It was, she says, a disquieting notion. "I felt guilty."

Her father was William Fleming, a devout churchman who became president of the Texas Baptist General Convention. Fleming often entertained evangelist Billy Graham in his home and even commissioned a life-size wax replica of the Last Supper, which for years was displayed in a furniture store window.

Fleming spent much of his boyhood at Whitewright, a little town at the end of the Cotton Belt rail line where his father owned the livery stable and rented wagons and buggies. By the turn of the century, Will Fleming married Anna Maud Lewis, a milliner and the first telephone operator in Leonard. They had four children, but only the youngest, Mary D., would survive: one died of whooping cough, one of diphtheria, and one of "summer complaint," a condition brought on by drinking unpasteurized milk.

As automobiles began to take over the roadways, Fleming moved his family to Bonham and then to Sherman, where he opened car dealerships. He prospered and the family enjoyed a busy life in a comfortable home, but his wife was frugal with the household budget. "Mother was a saver. She knew how to put something back," Mary D. remembers.

And it was that little nest egg that gave Fleming a stake in that first oil well. Gusher followed gusher, and by 1930, Fleming moved his family to Fort Worth, the oil capital of Texas. The country was sliding into a depression. People did without the most fundamental necessities, but Mary D. had a car, a Cadillac her daddy had given her. She began to use the car almost as a taxi service taking people around town. About that time, she remembers wanting to help people anonymously.

After the Walshes married, they continued to give anonymously to all sorts of causes. "But I don't do that any more," she says. "I don't think it's right. It's easier to give anonymously, but you give away your influence when you do that and I think just giving money isn't the answer. Now that's good, all right. But I've got to give of myself, too."

The Walshes still live in the two-story brick house near TCU that Mary D.'s father gave them as a wedding present. They say they've never thought of moving. "We've never lived in neighborhoods like Westover Hills or Rivercrest. We don't fit well there," she says. Through the years, their house grew like Topsy, new rooms sprouting as each of their five children were born. It's a busy house even now with a staff of nine and sometimes more who show up each morning. A full-time cook prepares lunch each day for those at the house, but almost every night, the Walshes go out to dinner.

It's a house that has seen good times and bad, for, like all families, the Walshes have experienced sickness, depression, disappointments, misunderstandings, business worries, and regrets, but through it all, they say they've tried to fill that house with joy.

Of all the additions, the party room is central to their lifestyle. The bell choir rehearses there each week, square dancers promenade there on Monday nights. For at least the past thirty years, the Walshes have hosted birthday parties for their friends every month except December. There often are several honorees at these birthday parties.

The low ceiling is decorated for each occasion, and when the Birthday Club gathers, a narrow shelf that extends around three walls of the room is loaded with gifts. After dinner, Howard leads a game called "Draw." Each guest is dealt a card from a deck. When Howard draws a matching card from another deck, the guest holding that card selects a gift from the shelf, but not without a good measure of cat calls and funny remarks. "There's lots of hurrahing going on," Howard says with a wide smile.

Guests always arrive with a canvas "loot bag." They'll leave with a draw gift, a place mat, and often a bowl or cup or glass that was the service piece for the first course. They pick up "chore cards" left on the piano in the living room and happily set about filling glasses with ice or setting the table.

"I want people to feel at home and at ease here," Mary D. says. "I learned a long time ago that if people help out it makes them comfortable." The same chore rule applies when friends go to any of the other three homes the Walshes maintain: the house in Colorado Springs, the Northstar Ranch near Aledo, or the Lazy D Ranch in Oklahoma.

The party room accommodates only about forty-four people,

but more invitations than that are sent out each month with a note that the first forty-four who reply can be seated. Social prominence or financial strength does not influence whom they choose. "We have a wide circle of friends," she says.

It is this sharing of friends that Mary D. sees as her most important talent. "I can't sing. I can't play anything. But I know how to share my friends," she says, a thoughtful look crossing her gray eyes. "Some of these people think of us as family."

Hallmarks of a Marriage ✌ *Sunday, April 26, 1998*

NANCY LEE and Perry R. Bass seem to have lived charmed lives. They've made and given away fortunes, cultivated powerful friends, traveled the world, and raised four sons who have themselves become benefactors of the first order.

If there has been sadness in their lives, the usual disappointments that visit every family, the tensions that every long-term marriage knows, they find them unremarkable, and choose to focus instead on their good fortune.

"We've been lucky," says Nancy Lee, and Perry nods agreement.

At a time when many would choose a more sedate routine, the Basses lead spirited lives, fishing for salmon in Iceland or hunting quail on San Jose Island, the 32,000-acre family retreat on the Texas Gulf Coast. Always publicity-shy, they seem flattered that one of the last great performance halls built in America in this century is named in their honor: the Nancy Lee and Perry R. Bass Performance Hall. It is a salute to the indelible mark they and their sons have left on Fort Worth—a tribute advocated for by their friend and neighbor, acclaimed pianist Van Cliburn.

On a recent spring afternoon, Nancy Lee, eighty-one, and Perry, eighty-three, recalled the journey they've made together.

∾

By the time they met at the Ridotto Club's spring dance in the late 1930s, Nancy Lee Muse and Perry R. Bass were already leaving their mark on Fort Worth's social set. In 1937, Nancy Lee graduated from the University of Texas at Austin and returned to her father's house on Mistletoe Avenue. During those years, young women of a certain station, even if they were educated and capable, did not work. Instead, she made her debut with The Assembly, Fort Worth's oldest debutante organization, and joined the Junior League.

"I did a lot of charity work," she says.

Her father, Ewell H. Muse, the son of a Baptist minister, was not a wealthy man, but as the regional manager for a shoe company, he kept his family comfortable. Her mother, Roberta Maddox Muse, born in 1889 in Fort Worth, was part of a pioneering family with roots that go to the city's bedrock.

While Nancy Lee was close to her two brothers, Perry grew up an only child in Wichita Falls. His father, E. Perry Bass, an M.D. by training, gave up his medical practice and hitched his hopes to the oil fields early in the century. Perry was eighteen when his father died suddenly of a heart attack. It was 1933, the darkest days of the Great Depression.

"At that time oil was ten cents a barrel," says Perry. The elder Bass had traveled to Austin hoping to persuade legislators to address the problem of the oil glut but died before he got the chance. Perry's mother, Anne Richardson Bass, in her forties, never married again—never even had a date. Her bachelor brother, Sid Richardson, became her protector and a father figure to Perry.

Richardson was a flamboyant wildcatter who collected Frederic Remington's western art, made million-dollar deals on a handshake, and wore his celebrity as comfortably as an old hat. He had already made and lost two fortunes before he took his nephew as a partner in 1935. Perry was a college sophomore then and excited about the opportunities. Uncle and nephew drilled in West Texas' rich Keystone field and struck two dry wells—and then oil.

By 1937, when he visited Perry at Yale just before graduation, Richardson was riding another lucky streak. "He'd been to New York and he says—called me 'Son' until the day my daddy died and from then on I was 'Bass'—and he says, 'Bass, the Bank of

Manhattan wants to loan me one million dollars. Can you imagine? One million dollars.'"

Perry chuckles, then smoothes the crease in the trousers of his blue suit. "He'd come a long way," he says of his uncle.

Perry's mother had planned an around-the-world cruise to celebrate his college graduation, but Richardson had other ideas. In October, the old bachelor had bought the sprawling San Jose Island on the Texas Gulf near Rockport. He wanted a house on the island, and he thought his smart, Yale-educated nephew could build it.

Perry remembers the conversation in detail. "I says, 'Uncle Sid what are you going to pay me?' He says, 'Pay you! Good God. You ought to pay me. This is the greatest opportunity any young man has ever had. You'll learn how to plan materials and how working people think. It'll be the greatest education anybody could ever have.'"

The island was a remote paradise accessible only by boat. Perry first had to construct a barge to haul building materials from the mainland and a harbor in which to dock it. He built a power plant on the island to provide electricity, a barn for storage and a place to house the workers. Later that building became servants' quarters.

By spring, Fort Worth friends were hounding the old bachelor to let Perry meet some girls. The Ridotto Club, a men's dance club that still exists, was having its spring dance. Perry attended and danced with every debutante there.

"The next day, I was the only one he called," Nancy Lee remembers.

They married in June of 1941 at the First Methodist Church. She wore a lace-covered gown and carried a bouquet of white orchids, but there were clouds on the horizon.

∽

The Japanese bombed Pearl Harbor in December. Nancy Lee was in Fort Worth that day. Perry was with Richardson on the island.

"We were listening to the radio, and this shrimp boat came over from Rockport. This fellow came up to the house and said 'Mr. Richardson, the president is calling you,'" Perry remembers. We went over to our Rockport office, which really was a pay phone at a filling station, and Uncle Sid answered the call to the president [Franklin D. Roosevelt]. The president said, 'I want you to have lunch with me next Sunday and tell me where we stand on petroleum. I don't trust any of these major company bastards.'"

Perry—who as a teen had built a sailboat from plans in a magazine—was pressed into service as a naval architect, designing patrol torpedo boats. By the time America jumped into the war, Perry was "ready to put on a blue suit." But his friends in Washington wouldn't let him join the navy. Instead, they wanted him to design a fireboat; a small, quick craft that could extinguish harbor fires after an air raid. Perry's simple design won a contest sponsored by Uncle Sam, and the government asked for delivery of three boats a week.

During the war, President Roosevelt, a visitor to the San Jose Island compound, appointed Richardson to the National Petroleum Council. About that time, Richardson made another important friend—a soldier named Dwight Eisenhower who was destined to become president of the United States.

When Ike stepped into the oval office, Richardson stayed at the White House so often, some joked that it was his second home.

As Eisenhower prepared to leave office, Nancy Lee and Perry attended one of two farewell dinners. It was the first of many visits to the historic residence.

When good friend Lyndon Johnson was president, the White House door was always open to the Basses. "I remember the last time we went," Nancy Lee says. "We'd just gotten in the hotel and the phone rang and it was the president. He said, 'Get yourselves over here. You're not supposed to be in a hotel.'"

One night, after most of the dinner guests had gone, Nancy Lee and Perry lingered, talking with Lady Bird Johnson. Soon the president appeared in his pajamas. Nancy Lee remembers the exchange between the Johnsons.

"I just felt like something like this was going on," he said.

"Lyndon, you need your sleep," Lady Bird scolded.

"I need this more," LBJ declared and sat down to talk.

Other first families extended invitations too, including Barbara and George Bush.

Nancy Lee and Perry's first son, Sid, was born in 1942. During the war years, housing was scarce, and the family moved from one rental property to the next. When Ed was born in 1945, they moved to a small house on Pembroke Drive. By 1948, when Bob was born, Perry was eyeing a lot that his uncle owned. It was a finger of land surrounded by a deep ravine, adjacent to Kay Kimbell's gracious Westover Hills estate. Nancy Lee wanted a home. Perry thought this the perfect location—but there were obstacles. Dotted with huge boulders, the lot was assumed to be solid rock that would have to be blasted away to level a building site. Worse, there seemed no easy way to reach the land.

Perry didn't believe the lot was solid rock, and he figured he could haul in fill dirt and create a drive for access. All he had to do was persuade Richardson to sell. The old bachelor finally relented and, in 1950, the Basses began construction on the gracious Georgian home where they live today. They thought it was a house they'd never outgrow. There were three bedrooms in addition to a master suite. There was a large game room with a basketball hoop for the boys. A tennis net was painted along one wall for practice. An ice cream and cold drink bar held refreshments. Then in 1956, son number four, Lee, was born. Sid and Ed began sharing a room. The next year, Sid went to prep school.

Nancy Lee was in charge of the house and the children. "I would not do club work or anything else while our boys were small. I was not going to do any charity work for someone else when I had my own charity at home," she says. "But I wasn't sacrificing. I was doing what was my pleasure."

After church each Sunday, there was always fried chicken and cream gravy. Nancy Lee's mother, her bachelor uncle, Web Maddox, Perry's mother and Richardson always showed up.

Nancy Lee set high standards for the boys. She demanded polite behavior—and As in citizenship. She used travel as a teaching tool. Once when they sailed to Europe, Ed remembers that she handed each of the boys an itinerary. The cover sheet read, "Mother's Trip, Paid for by Daddy."

Ordinarily she didn't think an allowance necessary, but when they traveled, she gave the boys money to buy souvenirs. "Ed always spent all of his and had to borrow from Sid," she recalls with a smile. She remembers that on one trip, Ed ran through his cash and Sid's—and needed more. "He'd found a drugstore in the hotel that had a lot of things that he wanted to buy as Christmas presents. This was August, but he bought everyone's Christmas present." She laughs. "It was darling."

In 1959, life in the Bass house changed. Richardson died in his sleep while at the island compound. He was sixty-eight and reported to be one of the nation's richest men. Many of America's most influential citizens flocked to Fort Worth to pay their last respects.

Billy Graham conducted the funeral service. President Eisenhower sent a white floral cross that adorned the pulpit at Broadway Baptist Church.

As the sanctuary filled, it was clear that Perry had lost more than a father figure and business partner. He'd also lost a friend. In no time, he was battered by financial storms. Three years earlier, Richardson, then in poor health, had passed the baton to Perry.

"He called me into his office one day and said, 'Bass, you take it and head for shore.' And I took it and I headed for shore and I got halfway to shore and Uncle Sid passed away. Then I had a fantastic problem of inheritance taxes."

According to a 1991 report in *The New York Times,* Richardson left each of Perry's four sons trusts of $2.8 million each, with the bulk of his $105 million estate going to the Sid Richardson Foundation, which supports education, health, human services and the arts in Texas. Perry retained his share of the partnership, but to settle the estate he had to borrow $30 million. In 1960, Perry used his four sons' inheritances—totaling $11.2 million—to form Bass Brothers Enterprises, increasing its assets by the end of the decade to about $50 million. It had been a grueling, decade-long struggle, and he was tired. He turned the business over to his oldest son, Sid, then only twenty-eight, and went sailing.

For three years, Perry immersed himself in the demanding sport of ocean sailboat racing, winning the World's Ocean Racing Championship and raising funds for the America's Cup race. Sailing had always been his passion. Racing became almost an obsession. "He didn't know what it was to get in the sailboat and just go out relax and have fun," Nancy Lee declares. "He was racing against nothing."

Meanwhile, the Bass' oldest son, Sid, began to steer a new course in business. He seemed to have the Midas touch, turning investments into gold, but he seemed to hunger for something more. Looking out his Fort Worth office window one day, he determined to clean up Main Street. He began buying up property and, with Charles Tandy, started to transform the north end of the central business district. All the Bass sons have left a mark on Fort Worth. Ed built the Caravan of Dreams nightclub, led a campaign to put a movie theater downtown, and became the driving force behind Bass Hall.

As their sons took over the business, Nancy Lee and Perry traveled more, hunted more, fished more. "He is lucky he married a girl who can keep up with him," says their sister-in-law, Lucy Muse. In 1991, to celebrate their fiftieth wedding anniversary, they gave away $50 million to a variety of causes and medical research—and they slipped quietly into a new chapter of their story.

In January, they cruised through the Panama Canal on a luxury ocean liner. They found the ships' movement through the great locks fascinating. "We were the only two people who stood on the bow of the boat for the last hour, just watching," she says.

"Just like the two of them on the front of the Titanic," he says with a chuckle.

They look at each other and smile. "We've been lucky," he says.

A Midnight Conversation with Van Cliburn ❧
May 18, 1997

I T I S almost two in the morning as Van Cliburn settles against the pillows piled on the couch in the library of his Westover Hills home. Baby Chops, a tiny white Maltese, has lost one of the pink bows that decorated her ears; the remaining bow sticks haphazardly to her fluff as she climbs into the nest of pillows and heaves a sigh. This room, like all others in this baronial estate, bulges with photographs and memorabilia of Cliburn's life as one of the world's most celebrated concert pianists. He twists a cigarette into a white holder and lights it, pressing it between his thumb and index finger, palm up, European fashion. Blue smoke curls upward in graceful rings.

Cliburn, famous for his late-night schedule, carefully guards his privacy and is reluctant to talk about his accomplishments, but tonight, on the eve of the tenth Van Cliburn International Piano Competition, he considers his remarkable career, his music and his future.

When he won Russia's Tchaikovsky Competition in 1958, some thought the lanky twenty-three-year-old an overnight success. In fact, Van Cliburn had been playing for twenty years by then. An ambitious child, he made his debut with the Houston Symphony at twelve, graduated from Kilgore High School at sixteen and Juilliard at nineteen, pushing himself through summer terms as if it were all a prerequisite to life. He was just twenty-eight when the first Van Cliburn International Piano Competition, named in his honor, was held in Fort Worth.

Cliburn seemed born under a lucky star. Everyone appeared to love him. He hobnobbed with the likes of Greer Garson, Rosalind Russell, Merv Griffin, and Ingrid Bergman. When he learned that actress and longtime friend Arlene Dahl wanted a piano, he sent her one from Steinway Hall as a gift.

At sixty-two, the now silver-haired Cliburn has become the unofficial dean of classical music, a beloved citizen of the world, and one of Fort Worth's favorite citizens. Friends note that he is an old-fashioned man with a sense of elegance who doesn't own a pair of tennis shoes and always dresses in a suit and tie, even as he practices his art into the small hours of the morning. He is, they say, sentimental, generous and kind, with a childlike trust in people and a deep faith in God. They say he is simple—unaffected by his fame—and almost always late.

A lively raconteur, he often leaps from his chair to illustrate points of his stories and laughs easily, often at himself. He delights in people, the famous and the unsung, and is as happy at the corner sandwich shop as at the 21 Club. On the other hand, he admits that he is moody and very fussy about his recordings. He says he has a temper but doesn't hold a grudge—and he never sets out to be late.

He says he enjoys intelligent wit but doesn't care for comedy. He is devoted to opera and adores old movies. He owns hundreds of films; *Random Harvest* with Ronald Colman and Greer Garson is one of his favorites. He likes *Jeopardy* and sometimes watches soap operas.

He prays, writes poetry, walks late at night, and is composing a sonata. He doesn't dwell on life's disappointments, has no time for jealousies or betrayals, and believes in the fundamental goodness of people. He was, he says, old when he was young.

"In some ways my life has had no turning points," Cliburn says. Not the Levintritt Award that won for him national attention? Not the 1958 Tchaikovsky Competition that catapulted him into the international spotlight? Not the crushing years of concert schedules? Not the almost decade long respite from the stage? Not the 1985 move from New York to Fort Worth? Not his return to the concert hall? Not the loss of his mother, his staunchest ally, mentor, and friend?

All are merely milestones, he says, markers along life's highway. "Oh, there have been bends in the road," he declares, clapping his long hands together and weaving them through the air like a fish swimming through the lamplight. "There have been moments of insight—times of great inspiration—but when you have a great beacon, things are put in perspective so you never lose sight of the beacon. The transitory flows are measured against the real beacon."

The light of Cliburn's life—the soul of his existence—has been music. It is, he says, the fabric, the very fiber of his heart. He could not live without it. "Music is architecture, mathematics, philosophy, narrative, and spirit," he says, ticking each word off on his long fingers. Music is everything he needs to know. It is, he says, his calling.

He was bewitched by music at an early age. He learned piano at his mother's knee when he was only three. She was Rildia Bee O'Bryan Cliburn, a gifted pianist in her own right and the pupil of Arthur Friedheim, the virtuoso who had been a student of the great pianist Franz Liszt. Born in 1896, the youngest of the six children of Judge William Carey O'Bryan and his wife, Sirilda McClain O'Bryan, Rildia Bee was encouraged to study music—but forbidden the life of a concert performer.

Instead, she became a dedicated piano teacher who delighted in her pupils' achievements and prayed for their success. Van, her only child, became her most celebrated student. It was at dinner one night that Van announced he would be a concert pianist. He was only five. His father, Harvey Lavan Cliburn, an executive with Magnolia Oil Co., frowned. He accused his wife of planting such a notion in the boy's head, but Cliburn says his mother was just as surprised. Soon, however, the elder Cliburn became his son's most ardent fan and protector.

"I just knew," Van says now of his early conviction. "I could see it."

Before Cliburn was old enough to go to school, his mother had been part of a committee that brought Russian pianist Sergei

Rachmaninoff to Cliburn's hometown of Shreveport, Louisiana. She'd given her young son several of Rachmaninoff's records and talked enthusiastically about meeting the great musician backstage. Cliburn holds out a tattered playbill from that time. He smiles, remembering the night he'd listened, enraptured, to the radio broadcast of the concert.

As a child, he was equally interested in Russia. Once when he was very small, his parents gave him a picture history of the world. Cliburn was mesmerized by photographs of Moscow's Church of St. Basil and the Kremlin. The colorful onion-topped towers reaching to the heavens were magical. He told his parents he wanted to go there. He had his chance in 1958. He agreed to compete in Russia's Tchaikovsky Competition just so he might see those landmarks. "Everything else was ice cream," he says, waving aside his stunning victory there.

～

When Cliburn was about six, the family moved from Shreveport to Kilgore, Texas. Music moved with him.

His childhood was spent playing concerts and recitals of every stripe. "I enjoyed my contemporaries," he recalls. "But most of them couldn't remember what they wanted to do yesterday. I was having, even then, to think about what I would be doing in three months or a year. I wasn't worried about fitting in. My wonderful parents saw to it that I was exposed to all the great music. I sometimes say I grew up on Highway 80, because we were always rushing up and down to Dallas or San Antonio or wherever a wonderful performer was playing."

Cliburn's young life was marked by an older generation. He talks adoringly of older friends he found so interesting—but none more than his mother. He laughs now, remembering what he calls the biggest "spat" he ever had with his parents, shortly after he began touring as a concert pianist. "It seems I was always old. I felt the parent to my parents. I was always checking on them. Hovering really. Once they didn't let me know where they were for a forty-eight-hour period. I was absolutely insane. I was calling everywhere. You would have thought I was looking for my children. It was crazy, but I just loved my parents so."

Rildia Bee had carefully directed Cliburn's performance schedule during those early years, but in the early 1950s he signed with Columbia Artists of New York. There, Sol Hurok, the illustrious impresario of the music world, noticed the young pianist. Hurok was the most important presenter of the day, and in 1959 he began to represent Cliburn. It was a long and happy relationship that lasted until Hurok's death in 1974.

Sometime in the early 1960s, Rildia Bee began working for Hurok as her son's personal manager. They set out together on the touring circuit, with Cliburn performing an astonishing 100 concerts each year. His mother became ever more important to Cliburn's life and career as she took on the role of counselor and confidant. "I don't know just when my mother became my friend," he muses.

In 1974, Cliburn suffered a double loss. His father died and was buried in McGregor, Rildia Bee's birthplace. Hurok died less than two months later. The loss was stunning—but suddenly, Rildia Bee was her son's only manager. The mother-son team could often be found at the suite of fourteen rooms Cliburn kept at New York's Hotel Salisbury. The rooms were filled with what Cliburn calls "his junk"—silver pieces, paintings, and photographs that chronicled his career. He kept the rooms for decades, but never had a lease, paying instead from month to month.

In 1978, his soul weary from the grind of touring, Cliburn stepped out of the spotlight. "I felt I was losing contact with my friends. I wanted to go to the opera more often. I wanted some time off." It was a planned but unannounced intermission, as he calls it. He had no idea the respite would last almost a decade.

It was during this intermission that he and his mother began to look at houses in Fort Worth, the headquarters of the Cliburn competition and the home of many of their friends. She thought the eighteen-acre estate once owned by grain magnate Kay Kimbell, benefactor of the Kimbell Art Museum, "had possibilities."

One of the first houses built in the exclusive residential enclave of Westover Hills, the Tudor Revival-style home commands a bluff-top site with impressive views of the river valley. Cliburn parks his Lincoln Town Car in one of the six bays of the garage. The lawn rolls away to a tree line just below the bluff. There are well-kept rose gardens with fountains and statuary, stone walkways, and a large swimming pool and cabana on the main grounds.

Cliburn says he will at some point live at the Worthington Hotel, but for now he finds this large home "cozy." All his "junk" fits perfectly. There are six pianos—one in every major room of the house—three upstairs and three downstairs. He strolls through the great living room, lighted by two large Baccarat chandeliers and an assortment of lamps. It is jammed with antique furniture, paintings, polished candelabras, silver bowls.

The Steinway in this room is his favorite practice piano. Like the piano in the library and the one in the sunroom, the top of this piano is covered with silver-framed photos of friends and celebrities. A bust of Rachmaninoff sits on a pedestal nearby.

"This is my office," he says. Every night, he closes the doors and sits down at the piano. "Oh, sometimes you don't want to work. But you must, every day, seven days a week," he says. And so he toils through the night working through complex passages. The notes stir his memory, touch his heart, remind him of ageless beauty, everlasting lessons.

"Working at the piano, working out passages that are difficult for you, is an analogy of life," he says. He spreads his long fingers wide, then folds them like a tulip. "No one has perfect hands. Everyone must work with their own limitations. To play isn't release—it's consolation."

The test of his skill always comes in the spotlight—and always with anxiety, even after thousands of performances in more than fifty years. "Every time I go onto the stage I'm nervous. Every time is like the first time."

He works wearing a coat and tie, and when he is finished, he puts a little plate of pasta into the microwave, then sits down to a small supper. His favorite is garlic ravioli from La Piazza. It is not the glamorous nightlife people think he enjoys. "Oh, you give one party and everyone thinks that's how you live all the time," he says. "This life is very solitary."

He has no set bedtime. He may work until four-thirty or five in the morning. Once in bed, he might watch an old movie or read a historical novel. He likes the history of England, France, and, of course, Russia. He gets up about one-thirty in the afternoon, after eight hours' sleep.

"The minute I get up, I do a few stretching exercises," he says. "No more than five or ten minutes."

He downs a cup of hot water with a squeeze of lemon and then has breakfast. "I love poached eggs on whole wheat toast." Sometimes he prepares them himself. Sometimes he goes to Denny's or the Ol' South Pancake House.

He works on his concert schedule as well as his business and real estate interests in the small sunroom on the west end of the house. It is a more intimate arrangement than the great living room and not as cluttered as the kitchen table. Two Teddy bears, a gift to Rildia Bee some years ago, occupy a chair by the door. A silver bowl filled with red Christmas ornaments sits atop a pedestal. He is amused that the Christmas ornaments have become a permanent display. The piano top holds the usual jumble of photos, plus several elaborate flower bouquets made of sugar that once decorated Rildia Bee's birthday cakes. "Oh, they're beautiful and last forever," he says.

Cliburn was living here in this comfortable house in 1987 when he returned to the concert stage after almost ten years away from the spotlight. He recalls meeting his old friend Emil Gilels, the famed Russian concert pianist, in New York in 1983. Gilels complimented

Cliburn on having the courage to take time away from performing, but by then Cliburn was thinking of ending his long sabbatical.

"He was known for his predictions, so I thought I'd test him," Cliburn says of Gilels. "When do you think I'll play in public again?" he asked his old friend.

"Don't even think about it. Just feel like you have endless time," he told Cliburn. "But I do feel that the next time you play will have something to do with Russia."

In 1987, Soviet leader Mikhail Gorbachev was at the White House for a summit meeting with President Ronald Reagan. Cliburn was invited to play a recital after the state dinner. He began what was to be a twenty-minute program with the Russian national anthem, followed by "The Star-Spangled Banner," followed by classical selections. Raisa Gorbachev was taken with the performance and asked if he would play something else.

Protocol officers panicked. In a moment charged with spontaneity, Cliburn turned back to the piano and began to play "Moscow Nights," a popular Russian ballad, as the Gorbachevs sang along.

It was a private concert, but everyone knew Cliburn was back.

No one could have been more delighted than his mother. Rildia Bee was in her nineties then but still interested in every concert her son played. Before Cliburn left for any tour, the two would pray together. As he prepared to go to New York for a performance at the Met in 1994, mother and son prayed aloud together, as was their custom.

"Let Van be brave," Rildia Bee said. Cliburn recalls that he was troubled by the prayer and thought of it as he winged his way to New York. His mother called later and said she'd like to attend the performance so he brushed his apprehension aside.

"We'd always had such a wonderful time at the Met," he says. "I was delighted that she wanted to come, but the next day she had a fatal stroke."

He says he'd had a premonition at least two weeks earlier. He remembers arriving at the house on his birthday, July 12. "I was alone in the house except for Mother upstairs. I had such a strange feeling. I knew it would be over soon. It was a horrible birthday. She was stricken on July 28."

As Rildia Bee clung stubbornly to life in Fort Worth, Cliburn tried to finish the performance at the Met. "I had an excruciating pain in my head during the concert. There was terrible trouble in my right arm. I knew she was going."

He rushed off the stage and to a waiting charter flight that whisked him back to Texas. He was with his mother as she stepped out of this life. It was August 3, 1994. She was two months shy of her ninety-eighth birthday.

"I was holding her," he says. "She went oh so peacefully. Oh so beautifully."

He wouldn't allow the shades to be drawn, nor her face to be covered. He stayed with her for several hours before he left her.

Now, more than two years after her death, he feels her presence in the great house. "Oh, I know she's here," he says. "Sometimes it feels like I could step out to the kitchen and speak to her."

There are times—just before sleep—when the longing overtakes him and he pleads for her counsel. "When I wake up it's as if we've spoken," he says with a smile.

Once he awoke in a hotel room to the secret knock they shared. "It was our knock," he says, demonstrating a series of rapid taps on the coffee table. "I opened the door, but no one was there. But I knew. I knew."

Baby Chops stirs, and Cliburn strokes her silky fur. He talks about the dogs that came before her: Spotty, Konstanza, and Joy. He considers what waits around the bend in life's highway.

"I don't think I'll ever have such a busy schedule as I once did," he says, but his voice is tentative. He controls his concerts carefully now, accepting only a dozen or so invitations a year. Then he laughs, his face alive and animated. "But who knows. I might. Sometimes in the eleventh hour an artist eclipses everything he's done before."

Preserving a Western Birthright ℘
November 28, 1993

THE COOK quit—just walked off the job—and the foreman's wife refused to get in the kitchen. So the fourteen-year-old heiress known as Little Anne tied on an apron and prepared beans and beef stew all summer long for the eight or ten cowhands at the Four Sixes Ranch at Guthrie.

"Well, they had to eat," Anne Windfohr Marion said, remembering the men who crowded around the table that summer in the early 1950s. "They threw a lot of hard biscuits at me before the summer was over, but I finally mastered a few things and it wasn't so bad after all."

That take-charge, no-nonsense approach to life has become a Marion trademark. The great-granddaughter of ranching impresario and oilman Burk Burnett, who counted presidents and American Indian leaders among his friends, Marion is known as an arts patron and savvy businesswoman, but she says she is first and forever a child of the land.

Now, because of her passionate devotion to the land and her stubborn determination to preserve the western heritage that is her birthright, she will receive the Charles Goodnight Award on Wednesday night at a gala benefiting the Texas Christian University Ranch Management Program and celebrating the National Cutting Horse Association Futurity.

A multimillionaire who is among the state's wealthiest residents, Marion, fifty-five, is a cosmopolitan and complex woman. She's comfortable in the elite environs of art collectors and museum directors, serving on the boards of the Kimbell Art Museum and the Modern Art Museum of Fort Worth, and she is a past trustee of the Museum of Modern Art in New York. But she has also earned a reputation as an astute businesswoman who understands power and is a shrewd judge of character.

As president of the Burnett Ranches, Ltd., the largest individually owned ranch property in Texas, and the Burnett-Tandy Foundation and as chairman of the Burnett Oil Co., she isn't timid about making business decisions either.

Still, Marion is more than art and oil, boardrooms and roundups. She's a tangle of traits, a woman with a sense of humor who never forgets her sense of purpose.

She reads "trashy" novels at bedtime, rents movie videos, loves country-western music, likes to cook, and hates to talk on the phone. "My friends say I'm abrupt on the phone," she said.

Clothes, she said, are an indulgence. "I'm the worst. I buy them and then I feel guilty," she said. "I spend half my life in jeans anyway."

She doesn't like big parties, says she's no good at small talk, and prefers small dinners with eight guests. "That way you can really talk," she said.

She counts Kay Fortson, niece of Kay Kimbell who established the Kimbell Art Museum, as a close friend. Each is an only child reared in comfortable circumstances. "We adopted each other as sisters," Fortson said.

And Marion is shy. With all her business acumen, philanthropic pursuits, board positions, social standing, and very direct approach, it is difficult to see Marion as shy, but she and her husband of five years, John Marion, chairman of the premier auction gallery Sotheby's, say that she is shy and sometimes self-conscious.

She is also sentimental. She cried when she read *The Bridges of Madison County,* a best-selling love story by Robert James Waller. And when the Phillips Ranch north of Dallas dispersed this fall, she carried that sentimentality a step further by moving Dash for Cash, a champion racehorse she once owned with her former husband, the late B.F. Phillips, to the Four Sixes.

"There's not much call for a twenty-one-year-old racehorse stallion," she said. "I couldn't stand to think of him just spending the rest of his life in some barn where no one would care about him."

On a recent afternoon Marion settled in a comfortable sitting room at her contemporary Fort Worth home, surrounded by modern art and custom-designed rugs. She sipped Evian water from a bottle and remembered her formative years on the expansive, fabled Four Sixes Ranch, which is about 200 miles northwest of Fort Worth.

"If I wasn't at school or camp, I was at the ranch," Marion said of the childhood summers she spent on the Four Sixes, where the cowboys call her Anne.

Time and time again, Marion has invested herself and her money in efforts to protect and promote the ranching way of life. She was an industry leader when she made medical insurance and retirement plans available to the ranching staff, said J.J. Gibson, a former manager of the Four Sixes and now vice president of Burnett Ranches, Ltd., but Marion waves that accolade aside. "I may have been one of the first, but now big ranches everywhere offer employee benefits," she said.

Always the rancher's advocate, Marion chose to serve on the Board of Regents of Texas Tech University instead of the more prestigious University of Texas board. "I wanted to be involved with Texas Tech because that's where a lot of our kids who grow up on ranches go to school," Marion said. "I thought I could do more there than at the University of Texas."

That resolve to do more is a key to understanding Marion. "I have a tremendous sense of responsibility," she said. She is credited with ensuring the success of the National Cutting Horse Association Futurity, which begins Monday at the Will Rogers Equestrian Center.

"If it hadn't been for Anne, I don't know how we'd have got the cutting horse futurity started," said Zack Wood, former executive director of the NCHA.

Marion said that the success of the futurity may be traced to a single fateful conversation in 1967. She recalled talking with the late W.R. Watt Sr., then president and general manager of the Southwestern Exposition and Livestock Show, at a cocktail party. "Annie, if you'll get out and sell the boxes for the futurity, you'll make a success of this," she remembered him saying. Now a two-week show with an international following and a purse of $1.3 million, the futurity was then only a two-day competition. Cutting was a sport in its infancy, struggling to attract fans.

"For three years I sold boxes," Marion said of her campaign to sell the box seats. "And after that time, there was a waiting list for the boxes and there still is."

Friends recall other examples of Marion's ability to get things done. Local attorney Dee Kelly remembered once when only a word sent Marion on a campaign to improve the chancellor's box at TCU's Amon Carter Stadium. "I remember telling Anne that the chancellor's box was an embarrassment. He had an elevator that went about five miles an hour and the box was really shabby," Kelly said.

Marion said she'd look into it and when she did, she was appalled. She paid for a remodeling project through the Burnett-Tandy Foundation and insisted the box be enlarged.

"Well, now he's got an elevator that goes 100 miles an hour and a box that's better than the best at Texas Stadium," Kelly said.

Marion is amused by the story. "Since that's where Chancellor Tucker entertains visiting dignitaries and alumni, I thought it was important that he have a first-rate facility," she said.

~

Reserved by nature, Marion also has a mile-wide streak of playfulness that often surfaces at the ranch. An accomplished bird-hunter, she had a dozen friends to the Four Sixes for a quail hunt a few years ago. She said that it wasn't the first time there had been a competition between the men and the women to see which team could bag the most birds.

The women almost always won. Small wonder. They'd scoot

up the road to a commercial quail farm, purchase birds, and shoot them before returning to ranch headquarters at day's end.

"I did it lots of times," she said. And the men were always impressed with the kill. "But this once we forgot to take the leg tags off. So we got caught," she said.

Growing up on the ranch, she was a prankster as well. "I was a tomboy and a pest," Marion said. "I was awful. I'd put nails under the saddle blankets and the cowboys would spank me."

Once she tried mimicking the tough talk used by the ranch hands, but she found the men wouldn't tolerate such a display. "I cursed and got my mouth washed out with soap by the cowboys," she said.

Though Marion divides her time between homes in Fort Worth, Santa Fe, and Palm Springs, she considers herself a steward of the land. "That love of the land is in her blood," said Gibson, the former ranch manager, who wears a gold buckle with the famous 6666 brand that was a gift from Marion. Her feeling for the land is a legacy left by her forbears.

She is the daughter of Anne Burnett Tandy and her second husband, James Goodwin Hall, who helped establish the American Quarter Horse Association. Hall and Marion's mother divorced and Marion was adopted by her mother's third husband, oilman Bob Windfohr. Eventually "Big Anne," as her mother was known, married Tandy Corporation's founder Charles Tandy.

Friends say that Marion was never pampered by her strong-willed and gregarious mother, and she remembered an affection-ate relationship with Windfohr, her stepfather. But Marion said her grandmother, Ollie Lake Burnett, provided the most emotional support. "She's the one who told me the old stories. She had the background of the Depression, and she kept telling me that I was lucky to have all that I do and not to waste it."

Marion's grandfather was Tom Burnett, founder of the Triangle Ranches near Iowa Park and Paducah. He was the son of oilman and rancher Burk Burnett, a larger-than-life character who was close friends with Quanah Parker, the last war chief of the Comanche Nation. Burk Burnett acted as a liaison between the cattlemen and the Indians and even entertained President Teddy Roosevelt.

Marion said that the old story that Burk Burnett won the original ranch in a poker game with a hand of four sixes isn't true. Actually, Burk Burnett bought a herd of cattle branded 6666 when he was just nineteen. He purchased the brand along with the herd. The origin of the brand is unknown, she said.

Marion owns a huge piece of West Texas: the 245,000-acre Four Sixes Ranch in King County and another spread at Dixon Creek in Carson and Hutchinson counties that measures more than 100,000 acres. She also owns 3,000 acres near Granbury.

She recently sold the Triangle Ranch that had been her mother's primary interest. "Her father left that ranch to her and she always spent more time there than at the Four Sixes," she said. "My great-grandfather really left the Four Sixes to me before I was even born," she said. Burk Burnett's handwritten will provided for two trustees to manage his estate. He died in 1922, and Marion, his great-granddaughter, took over in 1980 after her mother's death.

Educated at Miss Porter's School in Farmington, Connecticut, and then at Briarcliff Junior College in Briarcliff Manor, New York, Marion attended the University of Texas at Austin and the University of Geneva in Geneva, Switzerland, where she studied art history.

Friends said that Marion found a soul mate when she married John Marion in 1988. Three previous marriages ended in divorce.

John Marion, an urbane Easterner with an easy laugh, seems enormously proud of her. "It's fascinating to see her at the board table talking about oil and cattle," he said. "But she has another side, too. She's a very astute art collector. Very cultured. Very refined."

Her husband said that she resigns from boards that don't keep her active. She finds time to champion the American Quarter Horse Association Scholarship program, for instance.

"I'm real involved in that program because I really believe that children learn a lot by dealing with horses," she said. She's also honorary vice president of the AQHA.

She developed an interest in horses early when she spent summers at the Four Sixes.

"I rode from daylight 'til dark with the cowboys at the ranch. I did what they did," she said. She no longer rides, however, because of a stiff back.

Gibson said that she's done more for the Four Sixes than anyone since Burk Burnett and it's clear he likes her management style.

"She always respected my judgment, but she had her own ideas, too. She was a real hands-on type. Sometimes we'd have our board meetings in a pickup truck as we looked over the herd," he said. Gibson's son, Mike, now is the ranch manager.

Marion often travels with her husband and goes to the Four Sixes during hunting season, at Thanksgiving, and during roundups. "Sometimes I'm there for a month. Sometimes I don't go for three months," she said.

No one in the family ever lived at the Four Sixes year-round, Marion said. Not even Burk Burnett. He built a big house in Fort Worth and traveled to Paducah by private railroad car, where he kept a horse and buggy for the thirty-mile trip to the ranch. In 1917, he invested $100,000 in a fine headquarters house that he shared with the ranch manager.

Marion's grandmother maintained a grand house on Crestline Road where Elton and Martha Hyder now live. Marion keeps her mother's Fort Worth residence near Shady Oaks Country Club, but her city life hasn't diminished her interest in the ranching way of life.

She endowed a professorship at TCU's Ranch Management School, serves on the executive committee of the Fort Worth Stock

Show, and is a director of the Texas and Southwestern Cattle Raisers Association. She also is director emeritus of the National Cowboy Hall of Fame, where both her great-grandfather, Burk Burnett, and her grandfather, Tom Burnett, have been inducted.

When she remodeled the Four Sixes ranch house in 1980, she donated the American Indian shields, beadwork, and other artifacts that had belonged to her great-grandfather to the Ranching Heritage Center at Texas Tech. She said that she wanted to share the artifacts and the history of the Four Sixes with a wider audience.

"The most important thing that ever happened to me was growing up on that ranch," Marion said. "It kept my feet on the ground more than anything else."

Who Was Martha Sue Parr? ❧ March 5, 2003

Ms. Parr was a financial wizard who lived a mysterious life and left millions to a Fort Worth hospital. Courtesy, the Parr Family.

MOST neighbors called her "the cat lady" and gave her plenty of space, but children sometimes took fallen birds to her, hoping she could make them fly again. Children, it seems, had a special affinity for Martha Sue Parr. Little ones rushed to her—hugging her legs or stretching up their arms, begging to be held. Perhaps they understood her shy reserve and accepted her idiosyncrasies in ways that so many adults could not.

When Martha Sue died in October, she was seventy-six. She did not provide for the two dozen or so cats that lived in her greenhouse and prowled her estate. Instead, she had focused on human needs and left multimillion-dollar life insurance policies payable to All Saints Health Foundation, Baylor All Saints Medical Centers, and the Cumberland Presbyterian Children's Home in Denton. It is the third-largest single gift from an individual that the foundation and the medical centers have received, and perhaps the largest for the children's home, but that is only the beginning of her largesse.

Her will established a charitable trust that will distribute millions more from an estate that could measure from $16 million to

$20 million, with at least half those assets in real estate, primarily ranch land ripe for development. The foundation, the medical centers, and the children's home will benefit again, but few people guessed that she had such resources. A Fort Worth native who lived an inconspicuous life, she is being honored posthumously Thursday night by All Saints Health Foundation at its annual Heritage Awards dinner, along with Iranian-born heart surgeon Dr. Manucher Nazarian. Nazarian is recognized as a pioneer in cardiovascular procedures, but few know Martha Sue Parr. However, in years to come, she will be remembered as someone who provided for hundreds of children and enhanced the medical centers' healing missions—but for many the question remains: Who was Martha Sue Parr?

Some say she lived in the shadows, a puzzling woman with a bright smile who was clever with investments. Yet she was a paradox: a frugal soul who once told a luncheon companion that the sugar snap peas on her plate were so expensive she had to grow her own, and a "shopaholic" who bought dozens and dozens of knit caps and afghans at senior citizen fairs and purchased antiques and art from a trusted dealer.

Born at All Saints Hospital in 1926, she was an only child who never wed. For most of the last twenty years of her life, she lived alone, tending her gardens and working out ways of paying the smallest tax bill allowable. She was an attorney with a photographic memory who never practiced law; a voracious reader who gobbled up five newspapers each day and was none too eager to throw them out. She kept a large library, collected first editions, and was interested in grassroots politics.

"Some might have called her an eccentric," says insurance agent Don Woodard Sr. "But I always called her Martha Sue Parr, Mighty Special Person." Martha Sue and Woodard were Democratic Party faithfuls who sometimes worked on campaigns together. (Later his son, Don Woodard Jr., handled her insurance policies and some of her investments.)

"She knew more about high finance than I'll ever know," says Woodard Sr. But if he was the political fire starter, he counted on her to keep the spark alive.

"She was always there licking envelopes—an important worker bee in the hive," he says, but her financial gifts were modest. "She never gave me thousands, but $100 here, $200 there."

Martha Sue didn't get her political interest from her father, but she did learn about finance at his knee. H.G. Parr was president of the Well Machinery and Supply Co. and a big shot with the Fort Worth Chamber of Commerce. He was a man devoted to business.

About 1930, just as the Great Depression began, he moved his family into an attractive arts-and-crafts-style house on South Adams Street on Fort Worth's near south side. It was a good address, and the brick home built in 1923 had a glazed-green-tile roof and an imposing covered porch that measured 12-1/2 feet wide and 48 feet long. The original two-bedroom, 3,000-foot single-story home was solid but modest compared to the gracious two-story mansions that lined Elizabeth Boulevard just two doors away.

Over the years, H.G. Parr bought and sold other properties, including the Katy Lake tract that became the site of Seminary South Shopping Center, but he held on to the South Adams Street house. Like her father, Martha Sue enjoyed baseball and fishing, but her mother, a retired schoolteacher, focused on social acceptance. She took Martha Sue to the opera and hosted teas at their South Adams Street home, and in later years, at Colonial Country Club. As Parr became more successful, he made generous donations not only to the Cumberland Presbyterian Church but also to the schools where its ministers were educated.

Martha Sue enjoyed her own success at the University of Alabama, where she studied law. She had at least two articles published in the *Alabama Law Review* before she graduated, but when her school days were over, she came home to South Adams Street to live with her parents. She was as attached to the house as her father had been and even after she bought a million-dollar property in the 1980s, she would not part with the house.

For more than twenty years the place sat empty, stacks of *Life* magazines molding in the basement and the rooms bulging with keepsakes. The north wall was collapsing and the roof was in need of rebuilding when she sold the place only a year before she died.

Around 1980, Martha Sue was ready for a new home. She looked for big rooms and land and she found a low, rambling house on Briarhaven Road on the east side of Hulen Street. The 8,100-square-foot house was surrounded by 4.5 acres that encompassed a small lake that was perfect for fishing. She moved into the house with a maiden aunt, Septima C. Smith, her mother's sister, an amazing woman who had earned a doctorate and retired as professor emeritus from the University of Alabama's department of biology.

The women quickly hosted a small dinner party and invited their new neighbors, Virginia and Melvin Diggs and the Reverend James Gilbert and his wife, Freda. The women gave other dinner parties, entertained at the Century II Club, and attended the opera and symphony. But when Aunt Seppie died in 1984, Martha Sue's world began to shrink. She became reclusive and soon let almost no one, except for the Gilberts, into her house. If she did allow anyone over her threshold, it was only into the servants' quarters, a three-room apartment under the same roofline.

When Don Woodard Jr. went to her house for business, she sat him on a stool in the six-bay garage. She always met Norris Williams, her stockbroker of more than thirty years, on the back porch. "It could be hot as blazes and we'd sit on that back porch and drink Coca-Cola. We'd walk around the grounds, too. She had all these cats, but she didn't have names for any of them except the one that she let in the house. She liked the general idea of cats, but not individual cats. I never saw her pick one up or pet one, but she saw to it that they were fed and cared for," he says. She also insisted on buying PetSmart stock. "She said she was buying all that cat food . . . so she better own some stock."

Williams always called her "Miss Parr," and she always called him "Mr. Williams." This formality extended to Gilbert. He was her senior by only a year, but he had been her father's pastor and later director of the Cumberland Presbyterian Children's Home. "She always called me Mr. Gilbert, even in private. I called her Martha Sue," says Gilbert.

He'd also befriended Martha Sue's mother, a devout Episcopalian, who lived the last two years of her life in a single room at All Saints Hospital. The Gilberts became Martha Sue's most trusted companions. They took her to the post office and to dinner, had her over on holidays and saw that she went to the doctor. She gave them trips and antiques, and her thoughtfulness extended to the very practical. When one of the Gilberts' grandchildren died in infancy, she gave gravesites not only for the baby, but for the entire Gilbert family in the Parr family plot.

One of the only individual gifts in her will went to the Gilberts' eight grandchildren. "We were surprised no end," says Gilbert.

For more than forty years, they had been Martha Sue's true friends. It was Gilbert who found her body on that rainy morning. He had the cats picked up by the Humane Society. He made the funeral arrangements and gave a eulogy. He is thoughtful when remembering her life. "We were her family," he says. "My goodness, we've been undone since we lost Martha Sue."

PART FIVE
Classic Characters

ॐ ॐ ॐ
ॐ ॐ
ॐ

A Deb Goes to Boot Camp ❧ March 5, 1997

EVERYONE always knew she had a mind of her own. Sassy and smart, sometimes arrogant, often funny, Lenore Long Moncrief— known to friends and family as BB—made her social debut in 1992 just as expected. She wore an elaborate white gown with a billowing skirt and bowed low to Fort Worth's old guard. She attended the rounds of parties: the black-tie soirees, the afternoon teas, the mother–daughter luncheons. She raced up and down the red bricks of Camp Bowie Boulevard in a maroon Delta 88, lunched at River Crest Country Club, or met friends at the toney Michael's restaurant on Seventh Street. Sometimes she finished the night with pals at the SuSu Lounge or J&J's Hideaway. BB flounced through that debutante year with little care—and then she went right out and joined the marines.

If eyebrows shot up and society matrons clucked their tongues, BB did not notice. She was determined to prove herself in an arena far from the quiet, winding streets of Fort Worth's west side. She willingly traded Escada for camouflage, twisted her wheat-colored hair into a French braid each morning, gave up gossip about the latest bride-to-be, and trusted that grenades would make the biggest explosion of the day.

"It was a shock in lifestyle," she says.

Born to prominence, BB knew the life of privilege. Her family is respected, powerful, and wealthy. Her father and grandfather are successful oilmen. Her great-grandfather was an oil patch legend. Her mother came from Texas pioneer stock. BB's most fanciful wishes could easily become reality—but what she wanted most was the opportunity to become her own woman. Now, almost three years after enlisting in the marines, BB, twenty-five, is a corporal. She is the only woman in artillery electronics maintenance. She repairs artillery radar—and she's good at it.

Her immediate supervisor at Camp Pendleton, Gunnery Sergeant Richard Frank, is generous with praise. "Tenacity is first and foremost her strongest characteristic," he says. "She's not afraid of anything. Her willingness to learn makes her valuable. She's popular. She knows how to get along—but she isn't the kind of woman who would stand for sexual harassment."

Regardless of her apparent capabilities and willingness to shoulder responsibility, because she is a woman, BB wasn't allowed to go on field maneuvers with her unit. When the men went out for the two-week-long desert drills, BB had to stay with women from other divisions at the headquarters camp. Never mind that she was trained to do the same thing the men were doing.

"There's nothing much to do in the rear. You can only sweep the floor so many times," she explains. But all that changed when the men in her unit insisted she be allowed to go to the field with them. "The radar team said, 'We're not going out to the field without her,'" she says with a delighted laugh.

It was an enormous commitment. "They knew we'd all be under a microscope because I would be the only woman there. They said they'd do whatever it took to be sure I had the privacy I needed—they'd put up a tent for me; they'd all congregate on one side of the camp to allow privacy. They were willing to do whatever it took. They made a list of the special arrangements they'd make for me. I got to go. It was so exciting," she says. "Not once did I feel uncomfortable."

If BB is enjoying success, she is the first to admit that life in the corps has not been easy. The rigorous physical demands are eclipsed by the need for mental stamina.

"It's very hard to be a woman in the marines. There are lots of men who don't believe any woman deserves to be here. Sometimes it's depressing—overwhelming, really," she says.

In those moments of self-doubt, she says she most often turns for support to her father, oilman Charlie Moncrief.

"I'd reach for my phone and call my dad," she says. "He'd always know the right thing to say. He'd tell me I could do it—that I was mentally tough. He'd tell me he had no doubt in his mind that I could overcome this."

Moncrief is clearly proud of his daughter's hard edge—and not in the least surprised by her decision to join the marines. "It's not for most girls, but most other girls aren't tough like she is and adamant about doing something out of the ordinary. It didn't surprise me in the least," he says. "How classic."

Perhaps BB comes by her strong will honestly. She is the product of at least two legendary Texas families. Her great-great-grandfather on her mother's side was rancher and businessman Andrew Jackson Long, who survived early tragedy to emerge as a prominent citizen of Fort Worth. When he was just fourteen, Long witnessed his younger brother being scalped by Indians and left for dead. The boy clung to life for two days after the attack, then died. Long carried the memory of that terrifying afternoon to his grave.

Only two years later, his father died. When his mother sold the homelands near San Antonio, Long, then sixteen, became a cowboy. Soon he started acquiring ranch land of his own and built a herd of cattle. He eventually became a banker and finally moved to Cowtown's elite Elizabeth Boulevard in his later years. His daughter, Lenore, made her social debut with The Assembly in 1919. BB and her mother, Lenore McLeland, are his daughter's namesakes. Long sold his OS Ranch near Post, Texas, in 1901 because he broke his leg and could no longer ride his pastures—and because "it smelled funny," says McLeland. Apparently, he didn't recognize the scent of money.

BB's great-grandfather on her father's side, W.A. "Monty" Moncrief, was never put off by the rank odor of the oil patch. He forged his oil company into one of the largest independents in the nation with a long string of discoveries—but it was not an easy victory. It's said that during his early years, the wildcatter drilled more than twenty dry holes. Even with a string of worthless wells, he kept going back to the oil fields. His persistence paid off with important strikes in Louisiana, Florida, New Mexico, Colorado, Wyoming, and other fields across the country. Handsome and engaging, Moncrief became a celebrity in his own right, often entertaining presidents such as Dwight Eisenhower, Lyndon Johnson, and Richard Nixon. He rubbed shoulders with luminaries such as Jane Russell, Bob Hope, Bing Crosby, and film star Randolph Scott, even bringing them into some of his oil deals. Control of the company eventually passed to his oldest son, W.A. "Tex" Moncrief Jr., who has drawn his sons—including BB's father, Charlie Moncrief—into the family enterprise.

BB is proud of her family and now wants to make them proud of her, but things were not always so clear. Her parents divorced when she and her sister, Michelle, now an interior-design student at Texas Christian University, were very small. It was a tumultuous time as each parent remarried and started another family.

"Michelle clung to me and BB clung to Charlie," says Lenore McLeland, BB's mom. BB lived first with her mother and later with her father. By her teen years, BB admits that she was often belligerent and rebellious. She says she pushed the limits of her family's endurance.

"I didn't have the right attitude about almost anything," she says. "I was spoiled. I was a brat. I was self-centered and thought of no one but myself. I would do whatever I wanted to do." That included running up big charges at places like Neiman Marcus without permission. "It wasn't that Dad wouldn't buy me a nice outfit if I asked. I just didn't ask," she says. Her father insisted she promptly return the merchandise. It was, she says, the right approach. "He shouldn't have put up with that behavior—and he didn't."

She appreciates Moncrief's no-nonsense approach. "I'm more like my dad than my mother," she declares. "Mother is so liberal. Dad's rules are very clear, very defined, very black and white. With Mother, everything is gray," she says.

BB flourished in a regimented environment. Her turbulent teen life became easier when she enrolled at Indiana's Culver Military Academy, a college prep school attended by her father, grandfather, and other family members. She excelled under the narrow rules. Her grades shot upward. When she finished Culver she looked forward to college and a more relaxed environment. Her father had other ideas. Even then, he says, he felt a stint in the military would be good for her. He went so far as to take her to the recruiting office. "I think we got material from the marines and the navy," he says. Both say there was no pressure to enlist.

But BB wasn't about to trot off to the military. Not then. She had other plans. She enrolled at Southern Methodist University but didn't fare well. "The alarm clock just didn't go off," she told friends. Apparently she kept that same clock when she moved the next year to TCU, for she did no better there.

"Every once in a while I went to class," she explains.

Her cavalier attitude confounded her family. "Dad was very upset. He said there was no reason for him to pay for college if I wasn't going to do well," she says.

She took the next year off to make her social debut with The Assembly, Fort Worth's oldest and most prestigious debutante organization. "I hung out, did the deb thing, went to parties, got really, really bored," she says with a laugh.

Finally it was time to pay the piper. "I knew Dad wasn't going to pay for college again. I'd really lost his trust. That's when I remembered the military," she says.

One afternoon, with her sister Michelle and another friend in tow, BB visited a recruiter at Ridgmar Mall and took the preliminary test.

"I thought she was crazy," says Michelle. But BB knew what she was doing. She aced that pre-test. A few days later, she says, she secretly slipped away to Dallas for the more extensive exam and the mandatory physical. She signed up for a five-year hitch before she returned to Fort Worth that day. She waited until the ink was dry on the contract before she told her mother.

Now supportive and proud of her oldest daughter's accomplishments, McLeland was astonished by the move. "I couldn't believe it. Oh, there are so many other options. I told her to go to Aspen and work at something for a year. Kids do that all the time—take a year off. I could not see her in that situation. Was she going to go to boot camp and say, 'I can't possibly come out, I'm doing my nails?'"

She thought she'd spend her military career in the intelligence field. "I was promised intelligence. They wrote it on the contract. I would never have enlisted if I hadn't gotten that assignment," she says.

But boot camp brought a disappointing turn of events. BB remembers the life-changing interview well. "They asked me lots of questions about my family. They wanted to know if there was someone who could help me or hurt me in the military. I said, 'No,'" she recalls. BB didn't think her father's first cousin, State Senator Mike Moncrief, or her stepmother's first cousin, then-U.S. Representative Pete Geren, had anything at all to do with her military career.

"I wasn't lying," she says in amazement. "I never thought they had anything to do with me."

The marines saw things differently. BB was disqualified for the intelligence field. She got the news on her twenty-third birthday. "I was open contract. I could have gotten anything. I could have been a cook," she declares, rolling her blue eyes in disgust.

When she was notified that she had been tapped for communications/electronics, she was very disappointed. "It wasn't until I got to my first school that I realized that this is important and you have to be smart to get in." BB decided to tough it out. The decision has earned her respect in a rugged arena.

She isn't sure where this military duty will lead. She has no plans to re-enlist when her tour is complete in about two years. She'll definitely finish college, she says. "I regret that I didn't live up to what my family expected of me. I pretty much wasted two years of my life. I have the intelligence and the capabilities to do well in school and I blew it off. What was I thinking?"

Her sister, Michelle, believes BB will marry. BB laughs. "Who would I marry? I've never been in love," she says.

Childhood friend Courtney Rainwater Poth can easily visualize BB as a businesswoman. "She's so smart. She can learn anything and she's got the edge for business. She's empathetic, but not sympathetic," she says.

BB's dad would welcome her into the oil business—but he has other dreams for her. He thinks she'd be an asset to the FBI or the CIA.

BB agrees. "I'm lucky. There are so many doors open to me, so many options. I have to just sit down and figure out all my possibilities." It's been said that with the reins of power comes the harness of responsibility. If BB were indifferent to that equation before, she says she is no longer. But for her, the first step to full accountability is going it alone.

"I have to prove to myself I can do it on my own," she says.

No one is surprised. Everyone always knew she had a mind of her own.

She was a POW ?? *April 16, 2003*

JEFFERSON—Once the sharp edges of those memories gouged at her dreams, but now the years have polished away so many of the horrors. Looking back, she knows only that she wouldn't change a minute of her life, not the childhood spent on a farm near Jefferson, Texas, not her time as an army nurse, not even the desperate years she was held as a prisoner of war by the Japanese.

Retired Lieutenant Colonel Hattie R. Brantley—called H.R. by friends—is part of an elite sorority of American women who have been POWs. In the Civil War, both World Wars, Vietnam, the Persian Gulf War, and the current war with Iraq, women have been imprisoned by the enemy. They were missionaries, civilians, and military women. Many lost their lives.

Brantley, like so many other World War II captives, never talked much about that time. In those years, government officials advised against it, and Brantley took that advice to heart.

It was, she says, the worst possible advice, and she hopes that Jessica Lynch and Shoshana Johnson, the army women recently rescued in Iraq, will tell everything. "Spill the beans," says Brantley. But in the 1940s, people did not openly fret about the circumstances of life. Counselors were not called in to help citizens cope with the realities of war or its aftermath. The idea was to get on with living, and that meant putting unhappy experiences away. To do otherwise would be the weakling's road.

Just two days past her eighty-seventh birthday, Brantley settled into a comfortable chair in the brick house she owns in Jefferson and tried to recall memories forged some sixty years ago. She is one of only a handful of survivors left to tell the story.

In 1941, Brantley and the other army nurses stationed at Fort McKinley, just a few miles outside Manila, enjoyed a life that to their farm-bound sisters sounded more like a romantic dream than a job. The military personnel in the Philippines spent their days in an almost country-club atmosphere of bridge games and polo matches. The nurses lived in bungalows tended to by Filipino houseboys who brought them fresh juice for breakfast and kept the floors polished by strapping coconut shells to their feet and scooting across the expanse. Better yet, the hospital work was easy and left plenty of time to swim or read or catch a game of golf or tennis.

If rumors of war in Europe drifted in on the tropical breeze, it was easy to dismiss them. The war was far away—it would never touch the Philippines.

Brantley had always craved adventure. She didn't want her mother's life as a farm wife with half a dozen kids pulling at her skirt while she washed and cleaned and hoed the garden. Brantley decided early that she would be a nurse and ride horseback through the country, dispensing medical treatments. That fantasy had been replaced by this wonderful reality, and Brantley could hardly believe her luck.

Then one bright morning, news that the Japanese had bombed Pearl Harbor reached the Philippines. No one could believe it, but when the nurses were issued gas masks and helmets, the reality was impossible to ignore. Ever the optimist, Brantley went to play golf that morning. But even as she stepped onto the first green, Japanese bombers were targeting other American strongholds.

Wake Island, Midway, and Guam were attacked, and then the bombs began to fall near Manila, demolishing planes on the runway at Clark Field and Fort Stotsenberg. Suddenly, it seemed the entire world was at war.

Soon Brantley and other military personnel were moved to Manila. The nurses were quartered in a posh town club called the

Spanish Club, but before the end of December it was clear that Manila, too, would fall as the U.S. forces retreated south along the Bataan Peninsula.

On Christmas Eve 1941, Brantley and more than twenty other army nurses and a number of Filipino nurses climbed aboard buses headed for a field hospital in Bataan. The nurses relied on humor to get them through, says Brantley. In radio broadcasts, President Roosevelt was often heard to say "I hate war. Eleanor hates war." Now the nurses turned those words into a joke meant to bolster sagging spirits. Pronouncing the word war as "wah," they'd say, "FDR hates wah." When things got really ticklish, they'd say, "Help is on the way" and believe it. But things went from bad to worse.

The Japanese bombed the convoy. At the sound of approaching planes, the nurses took cover in the ditches, but their white poplin uniforms made them good targets, Brantley remembers. Eventually, the buses inched their way down the narrow jungle roads.

The nurses expected the hospital was already operational and they were ready for the work at Bataan, but they were surprised that Hospital No. 1 was a primitive camp with long barracks constructed of bamboo with grass roofs. Windows consisted of flaps that could be lowered when it rained. "Set up? Ready to go? In a pig's eye," says Brantley with a disgusted sniff. The nurses scrounged up metal cots, bedpans, and other provisions that were stored in sheds. These relics of World War I were wrapped in newspapers dated 1918, Brantley recalls.

The sick and wounded poured in. Doctors cut and stitched and sawed through bone. Nurses assisted and saw to those who were sick with malaria and dengue fever. Arms and legs had been blown away. There were too many head wounds to count. The bloody bandages piled up as one after another of the wounded took a turn on the operating table. The hours seemed unending and the nurses, at first shaken by the extent of the injuries, became anesthetized to so much suffering. A second hospital was set up a bit farther down the peninsula, and soon both medicine and food were in short supply. Brantley hid tubes of morphine in the hem of her skirt and parceled it out to those in the worst pain.

The patients called the nurses angels—the "angels of Bataan." But by spring it was clear that Bataan could not hold. On April 8, the eve of the surrender, Brantley and several dozen others from the Army Nurse Corps were sent to Corregidor, an island in Manila Bay called "The Rock." They moved to the piers at night and were packed onto a small launch. Bataan burned, and the sky was orange with the glow.

Once on Corregidor, word circulated that some nurses would leave on two planes that had just delivered supplies. "I'm proud that I wasn't on that list," Brantley says. Those who stayed behind felt they'd been chosen because they'd already proved their courage and dedication—but they had no idea what was coming.

Corregidor's Malinta Tunnel complex offered refuge for the medical personnel and patients alike. This maze of concrete tunnels, built in the early 1900s, had many branches called laterals. The nurses lived in one lateral. One was used as an operating room, another for a recovery room, and still others served as wards, but the tunnels were dank catacombs with sweating walls and no air conditioning. Thousands of patients were jammed into the oppressive tunnels and as the Japanese bombing increased, the ceilings shook and the laterals filled with dust. Rations were short, and the list of wounded and dying grew longer each hour. Everyone hunkered down, knowing that the worst was still to come.

Then, on the morning of May 6, 1942, word circulated that the commander would surrender at noon. The nurses were shocked. Some were outraged. In one of the tunnels, a nurse cut a square from a rough bedsheet and at the top wrote "Members of the Army Nurse Corps and Civilian Women who were in Malinta Tunnel when Corregidor fell." Brantley, along with sixty-seven others, signed the sheet.

Even as a white flag of surrender was raised, Brantley was

optimistic. She thought now they could bake some bread. She was wrong, of course. She was a prisoner of war, and she wouldn't taste bread again until 1945.

The nurses stood in a line as the Japanese commander inspected every patient. Then the soldiers turned their attention to the women. The Japanese were unaccustomed to seeing women in uniform and apparently they did not know what to think of them. Perhaps that is what saved them, Brantley muses. Through the three long years of captivity, none was molested, she says.

After the surrender, the medical staff stayed on duty tending to the wounded in the tunnels, while outside, dead bodies bloated in the tropical sun. One day, the women and patients were ferried to a freighter where the patients were lifted into the ship's hold and the nurses, suffering from malaria and other jungle fevers and weak from a lack of food, climbed a rope ladder to the deck three stories above them. The Japanese were moving everyone off "The Rock."

Brantley remembers with amusement that the Japanese served tea and cookies on the short voyage back to Manila. When they reached shore, the sick and wounded were loaded into trucks and the nurses were put on other vehicles. At a fork in the road, the patients' truck turned one way and the nurses went the other. The women protested loudly, demanding that the driver follow their patients, but the Japanese had other ideas.

Santo Tomas Internment Camp was a large compound in the northern section of Manila. It was built as a university in 1611, and its lush grounds were surrounded by high stone walls. The Japanese had installed barbed wire on top and turned the sprawling campus into a prison camp. Almost 4,000 souls were imprisoned there. At first the nurses were quartered in a convent outside the prison grounds, separated from other prisoners. This isolation worked in their favor. Like many other nurses, Brantley had dengue fever and a 104-degree temperature. Others had malaria, dysentery, or hepatitis. All were exhausted and malnourished. They concentrated on getting well, but when that was done, the women wanted to get back to nursing. The convent was turned into a hospital, and the women were transferred to the main prison camp and assigned rooms in a dormitory. Brantley and thirteen other women shared a room. She came to think of them as family.

Santo Tomas was not a military prison camp but a civilian one, and a civilian committee organized work details and provided some semblance of order. There were many children in the camp and so a school was established. Internees used the library. A choir was formed. There was a drama club. Brantley took Spanish classes several times a week. But it was a prison still, a place with guards and gates and short provisions. The women struggled to keep their sense of balance—and their sense of humor.

When the women passed through the main gate in a group to report for hospital duty, they bowed to the guard and he bowed back. One day they decided to pass through the gate individually so the guard would be obliged to bow to each of them. The next day the guard moved to another station and later turned his back on the women. That small bit of fun did not change the realities. Food was always scarce, and if a nurse was lucky enough to get a banana, she ate it skin and all. The women talked incessantly of food and traded recipes. Malnutrition took its toll, but one of the worst things about prison life was the total lack of privacy. There was never a moment to be alone, Brantley remembers.

She would have welcomed a bit of solitude one day in 1944 when the camp accepted a mail delivery. She received a card from her mother—the first word from home in years, but the news was not good.

Brantley learned that her father had died in 1943. He had been her biggest supporter. Now he was gone and she was shaken to the core, but she hoarded the grief, keeping it totally for herself. "If I told anyone, I was afraid I'd break down," she says.

And then the tide began to turn. American planes dropped leaflets on the camp. "Hang on. Your Christmas is coming soon," they read. The Japanese tried to confiscate all the fliers, but

Brantley hid one in a can of foot powder. It, like almost all her other war souvenirs, was lost in a fire years ago.

The prisoners hung on, but every day, dozens died of malnutrition and disease.

Brantley was on hospital duty that February evening in 1945 when an American tank rolled through the gates at Santo Tomas, but she remembers the perfume of gasoline and American cigarettes. More tanks followed. People cried for joy.

All the army nurses had survived the nightmare. They were free—but they weren't home.

The nurses flew to California, where most were met by their families and where they had a little time to recuperate. Brantley's cousins met her. The other nurses were eager to get home, but Brantley, knowing her father would not be there to greet her, delayed the trip as long as she could.

Waiting for the plane that would take her to El Paso, she felt more alone than she ever had before. "I'd had someone right beside me every minute for years," she says. "All of a sudden I was sitting beside people who didn't know me—people I didn't know."

In El Paso she planned to kiss the soil, but she didn't have to. When she stepped off the plane, the blowing Texas sand slapped her in the face.

Finally she made it back to Jefferson in far East Texas, but she says there was no parade, no grand homecoming, as there was for some of the women. She closeted herself away at the farm. Her family was happy to see her, but no one asked any questions about her war experiences and she volunteered little. Once she told her mother that a Japanese soldier stopped to watch her as she showered. "What did you do?" her mother asked. "I put a washcloth over my face," she said.

She stretched her leave to ninety days, and then she knew it was time to go back to work. She reported for duty and drew a post in Arizona. After the war, she went to Germany and Italy and finally finished more than thirty years of service at San Antonio's Fort Sam Houston. She never married.

Her mother came to live with her and when Brantley retired in 1969, the women moved back to Jefferson together. Brantley worked in a hospital for a time, and she still raises bees with her brother. She keeps jars of honey in the trunk of her white Mercedes so she can sell a quart to anyone who wants one.

Now she has only casual contact with the other prison camp survivors. Most have died, and only a few are left. News comes through the grapevine, she says. The war memories are far behind her now. The wounded never call to her in her dreams anymore, but sometimes she hears her mother's voice.

Two for the Show ❧ *August 25, 2002*

Rudy Eastman (left) and Joe Rogers were an unlikely team who celebrated African American life. Courtesy, Fort Worth Star-Telegram.

RUDY EASTMAN didn't feel lucky that day in 1988. The piano player was sick and the timing couldn't have been worse. Eastman was smack in the middle of a new musical revue for Jubilee Theatre—impossible to do without a keyboardist.

"My brother-in-law plays piano," piped up skinny Eddie Dunlap, a master percussionist who played drums for the show. Inwardly, Eastman rolled his eyes and thought, "Oh, Lordy," but he was desperate. What the hey? Maybe Eddie's brother-in-law would be OK for one night.

So Joe Rogers showed up to tickle the ivories, and Eastman knew immediately that this man had unusual talent. That meeting was a lucky break for both of them, but neither knew it right away.

Most people think Luck dances down the street in a shiny red dress. In fact, Luck is sometimes hard to spot. "You never know when you're being lucky," the old folks used to say. Rudy Eastman would probably shout "Amen" to that now. Back then, he was a schoolteacher with a full-time hobby—make that a full-time dream—that kept him up nights and weekends.

He wanted to build a theater to showcase African-American talent and tell the story of the "black experience" in all its many forms. By 1988, he'd been plugging away at it for seven years, teaching school by day, and producing, directing, and sometimes writing shows by night. Who knew that the white guy who played piano for one performance would become his most important collaborator and his creative soul mate?

Fourteen years later, Eastman, fifty-eight, and Rogers, forty-nine, have become famous in Fort Worth's theater circles, and now other theatrical troupes from places such as Ohio, New York, Illinois, and Missouri are asking to produce their shows. Recognized for their imaginative, original musicals that transcend race and economic status, they have settled into an unsettling routine they say works for them. A three-week-long creative blitz each year leaves them with an original script, written by Eastman, with music and lyrics for as many as eighteen innovative songs from Rogers.

It's certainly not the only theater work they do. Eastman produces and directs at least five other Jubilee shows each season, and Rogers provides the music, but the original plays are their most rewarding efforts.

Last night, the final curtain fell on their *Alice Wonder,* an original musical inspired by Lewis Carroll's *Alice's Adventures in Wonderland.* In this version, the Queen of Hearts is a drag queen who can't sing the blues, and Alice is a mom with a demanding boss and more work than she can do. The show filled Jubilee Theatre's 105 seats almost every night of the run and left patrons wanting more. Eastman and Rogers mean to give theatergoers what they crave. Their next original show is already in the planning stages. It will close next year's season.

Eastman calls it *Roadshow* and has a general idea what it's about. In a few months, he'll start to bounce his ideas off Rogers—who will mostly sit and listen. Then Eastman will draft a rough outline, suggesting the story line and musical numbers to be written. Rogers will mostly sit and listen.

Eastman might change his mind. He'll spend hours researching his subject. He'll talk with Rogers—who will mostly sit and listen.

Rogers doesn't write music that's not performed. He waits for Eastman to finish his creative gyrations. That takes about six months.

The men will talk informally about the show many times. Or rather, Eastman will talk. Rogers will listen.

Late in the spring, the men will have formal meetings. Then a couple of months before the show opens, Eastman and Rogers will go their separate ways. Eastman will sit down in his cramped office behind Jubilee's stage, sharpen a No. 2 pencil and begin to write the "book" on a yellow legal pad. He'll work each afternoon from one to five P.M., and in three weeks he'll have the show. If it takes longer than three weeks, he knows it won't work.

Rogers may wait longer to start. He's a deadline man. Once he knows that rehearsals are only days away, he'll get busy. He can't write at the piano—he gets his best ideas when driving, so he'll slide behind the wheel of his blue 1996 Mazda and head for the winding lanes around Lake Worth, stopping occasionally to jot down a lyric.

He can write at least one song a day; maybe two—three if he's lucky, he says. He usually has a couple going at once in various stages of progress, but if the words or music won't come to him, Rogers doesn't fret.

"I've learned that if you put yourself under a lot of pressure, you hurt yourself. I've got the confidence to know that the songs will come. Something's going to happen and the song is going to pop out. If it doesn't come to me today, I'll get it tomorrow," he says.

When Rogers and Eastman come back together, even they are amazed. It's as if they've been talking every day, says Eastman. "My lead into the song is exactly the right words and the things that come after the song are exactly right. It's like we're completing each other's sentences," he declares.

The first show they wrote together was *Midnight Walker,* but it might not have been if the first guy Eastman asked to do the music hadn't turned him down. What a lucky break. Eastman remembered Rogers and offered him the job. Rogers took it. A year later, Eastman learned that Rogers had a master's degree in music composition from the University of North Texas.

They say they can't recall the exact number of shows they've done together, but the list includes productions such as *The Book of Job,* based on the Old Testament account of a man whose faith is tested. In this version, Satan is a jovial character rather than a menacing devil, and a group of gossipy "sisters" demands a list of Job's sins in a finger-pointing ditty called "Can't Get to Heaven."

Coop DeVille: Time Travelin' Brother, a sequel to the troupe's 1986 hit, *Negroes in Space,* kept the audience laughing as visitors from another planet observe Earth's greed, politics, and pop culture. One reviewer said that Eastman and Rogers' version of Shakespeare's *Tempest* had some "Motown moments." Characters got modern costumes—and modern names. Miranda is Mandy. Antonio, the duke, is Tony. Ferdinand is Lil' Freddy. When *Travelin' Shoes* opened in 1999, audiences were introduced to the sounds of the gospel quartets of the 1930s and 1940s.

No matter what the show, Eastman's scripts drive home a lesson about love or injustice or the longings of the human heart. The themes are universal but always presented from the African-American point of view. Rogers' music matches the pace and covers a wide range of styles, from blues to rock to gospel. He's been preparing for this part for a long time.

Joe Rogers has been busy with music his entire life. Even as a boy, he wrote music and played in bands. Once he went to New York to seek his fortune but decided the big city wasn't for him. He loved music, but he hated the music business. When his two little girls started school in the late 1980s, he was still playing in bars, staying out until two A.M., taking every gig that came along and even then never making a decent living. He'd had enough—not enough of music, but enough of that life.

He learned about computers, landed a job as a computer programmer, and now heads the computer department for a Grand Prairie-based business. Even so Rogers always knew he'd find a place for his music, but he never gave musical theater a second thought until Eastman called.

Eastman has always been fascinated by theater, but when he graduated from Waco's Paul Quinn College in 1966, he had a degree in history, not drama. That fall, he landed a teaching position in Fort Worth, and as luck would have it, he was quickly tapped to co-sponsor the drama club. Later, he taught drama.

On his own time, he joined the Sojourner Truth Players, an amateur troupe based at a local church. There, in 1972, he met his wife, Marian, who had signed on as stage manager for a show he was directing. Marian, fifty-seven, grew up in Fort Worth, a part of its vibrant black community. She remembers Evans Avenue in the early 1960s as a busy thoroughfare crowded with people shopping at businesses owned and operated by African Americans. There was a shoe repair shop, a barbershop, a beauty salon, and dozens of black churches.

A trip to Flint's Drug Store with its marble counters and soda fountain was a real treat. Ordering a cherry Coke made you a big person, says Marian; a banana split meant you were a somebody, with money to spend.

Eastman came from a different sort of place. In 1961, he was the only black kid in the junior class in Hereford, Texas. No one made a fuss. There wasn't any attempt at any sort of formal segregation. Everyone went to the same school; everyone enjoyed the same picture show. There were no "colored" water fountains, no section of town where blacks were forced to live.

There was also no one for him to date; no group of teens to hang with, no way to belong. Worried that he might not finish school, his parents sent him to Tulsa, Oklahoma, to live with an aunt for his senior year.

Eastman pushes up his glasses and straightens his baseball cap. Deep lines crease his forehead as he tries to remember those unhappy years and the way the people of Hereford treated him. "I'd call it benign neglect," he says with a wry smile.

Eastman's daddy was a tenant farmer, and in 1956 the Eastman family moved to Hereford, a small farming community in the Texas Panhandle south of Amarillo. The first African Americans had settled there only three years earlier. Eventually the black population numbered about 120 souls, but Eastman says now that in that remote place he didn't really have a sense of what the larger black community was all about.

If his classmates were indifferent, and his teachers insensitive to the point of telling racist jokes in class, he still did not experience the same level of animosity his urban brothers took as a matter of course. "It was real hard to be there," Marian says of those early years in Hereford.

Oddly it is this insulated environment, this detached and separate existence, that she sees as the seedbed of one of Eastman's strongest attributes. "Rudy's view of black people has always been from the outside. This is a real strength," she says. "He sees things a little different."

He admits that his early work might have been angry. "I may have felt it important to make a political or social statement," he says. Now the shows may make the same point, but the tone is more satirical, softer edged, more humorous, simply good theater.

Eastman thrives on what he sometimes calls "the musicality" of the language and other times he refers to as "black speak." Marian proclaims herself the expert on dialect, and the shows are full of it.

They are also fun, fresh, insightful—and black. It's exactly what Eastman meant to do all those years ago when he set out to create a place to tell the story of the "black experience," but there were times it seemed an impossible dream.

In 1981, Eastman organized the Jubilee Players, and the troupe opened in an old church on the corner of Vickery Boulevard and Riverside Drive. The audiences seemed appreciative enough, but Eastman and his actors couldn't keep up with the rent, and the show closed after only five performances. It was community theater then, and the company became a traveling band that roamed from stage to stage, hoping the audience would follow. They did, but the company needed a home.

Then in 1987, Eastman found an empty storefront on Rosedale Street across from Texas Wesleyan University that he thought would make a dandy playhouse. It was in the heart of Polytechnic Heights, one of the city's oldest neighborhoods, a district with a largely black population that Eastman hoped would become his faithful audience. He also hoped the university, which was clearly in sight, would give white patrons the confidence to attend.

He had the backing of a dedicated group of patrons and support from the Amon Carter Foundation, so he signed the lease on Martin Luther King Jr.'s birthday and called the place Jubilee Theatre. It had been a long time coming, but for Eastman it was only one more step in a long journey of self-discovery.

Marian Eastman is his most trusted critic and ardent supporter, but by 1991 she had reached overload and he, too, was approaching burnout. Marian laid down the law. "You cannot do two eight-hour jobs in a day. You decide which way you want to go and then I'll support you," she remembers saying.

Eastman went to Jubilee's board of directors with the idea that he would leave teaching. Jubilee would become his livelihood. It had long ago become his life and the only child he and Marian would ever have.

He got a thumbs-up from the board and took, not a step, but an enormous leap of faith. The timing couldn't have been better, but things were about to change again.

The next year, in 1992, Jubilee Theatre found a new home in a tiny space on Main Street. It's so small that actors sometimes exit into a narrow hallway that leads to the lobby. Theatergoers must walk across the stage to reach the seats against the west wall, and those on the front row actually sit on the stage, but its size is exactly the thing that gives Jubilee its energy.

～

Rogers and two other white guys—one of them his brother-in-law Eddie Dunlap, the other bass player Chris White—provide the music. They can see the stage and the audience from their second-story perch behind a scrim, but the audience can't see them. Lucky. They're usually dressed in their grubbies and swigging imported beer. Rogers likes Chinese beer best, but Mexican will do.

"They're exactly opposite from what people think," says Marian. "Rudy is all about following the rules. Joe is a rule-breaker. Rudy is on time. Joe is on CPT, you know that means 'Colored People's Time.' He's always late."

Eastman won't tolerate tardiness in anyone else, and those who arrive late for rehearsals are fined $5 or $10.

Rogers may be easy-going about most things, but he's serious about his music. When an actress suggested that one song should have a faster tempo, Rogers didn't argue; he just kept speeding up the music until it was impossible for the singer to keep pace.

He made his point.

Rogers isn't a man who has to make his point often. Easy-going and non-confrontational, he doesn't usually insist on his way. He likes to see what the singers bring to the music he's written, but it is first his music.

Rogers grew up in Fort Worth and graduated from Southwest High School. His world was segregated, his friends were white, but when he started working with bands, he was sometimes the only white musician in an all-black group. He liked those men, liked the bluesy sounds that were the hallmark of black music, but truth to tell, he was sometimes uncomfortable. All that is gone now. "Lots of times I'm the only white guy in a group, but I don't even think about it anymore," he declares.

No need. Rogers is an important and accepted fixture at

Jubilee, says Eastman. Rogers is a man who has left his thumbprints not only on the piano but also on the theater's productions. "Joe has made me more daring," says Eastman. "I used to be more conservative. I go a little farther than I used to, but it's more sophisticated now."

And for Rogers, Jubilee has become a chrysalis, a warm, protected place where his creativity is recognized, even cherished and where his music has wings. The discipline, the routine, the challenge of creating for the next new show have given him a stability he craved. Since he and Eastman began their collaboration, his twenty-five-year marriage crumbled. He divorced, remarried, and had two babies who, like his older children, think Rudy and Marian are family.

"I'm real happy where I am. I feel like I've got the talent to do what I want, but I like trying to please myself. I like what I do, and I'm proud of it. I don't need people from somewhere else telling me I'm good."

Eastman nods and smiles. Oh, it would be wonderful if Broadway came calling, but if that doesn't happen, he's still a lucky man.

"I occasionally feel guilty," Eastman says. "My life is so good."

Rebel with a Cause ৡ *August 10, 2003*

Gary Gardner is one ornery farmer who uses racial slures one minute and defends justice for all the next. Courtesy, the Fort Worth Star-Telegram. © *Rodger Mallison.*

MAYBE this story really began in 1906, the year his granddaddy, an Indiana carpenter, came to the Texas plains to build a combination store and hotel at Vigo Park near Palo Duro Canyon and stayed to frame up a life. Never mind that he was a Yankee, a Republican, and a Methodist in a southern state that leaned heavily to the Baptists and Democrats.

Or maybe it started long before that in some tangle of DNA that, through the generations, has demanded not only blue eyes and a ruddy complexion but also a certain single-minded contrariness, a pronounced distaste for conformity, and an intense respect for fairness—not to mention a distrust of the practiced rules of order.

But if Gary O. Gardner had to name the moment it began, he would point to the day in 1999 when a black man named Joe Moore was sentenced to ninety years in prison. From then on, Gardner was hell-bent to fight the justice system of Swisher County.

In 1999, a now-discredited Swisher County sheriff's deputy ran an undercover drug sting that landed forty-six people in jail—thirty-nine of them black. Gardner heard the talk about how "fine" the lawman was and how "sorry" and "no-account" the accused were, but when he saw television footage of some of the suspects herded across the courthouse lawn at Tulia handcuffed—

some of them rousted out of bed and wearing only their under-wear—his blood boiled.

"They stripped those people of their dignity and for what?" Gardner demanded. "I don't care how heinous the crime, when you arrest someone, you treat him as a person, a human being. There's no honor in humiliating your fellow man."

He grew angrier when he learned that even those who had never had any brush with the law drew hefty prison terms. But for Gardner, the absolute last straw came when Moore, now sixty, was sentenced. Moore was a one-time roadhouse operator, a bootleg-ger in a dry county and a man with a record that he said was earned with trumped-up charges. But by 1999, Moore said, he was a hog farmer who kept his nose clean. From time to time he'd done farm chores for Gardner.

According to Moore, they weren't friends—just friendly, but Gardner didn't believe Moore was guilty of drug trafficking. At first Gardner was alone in his showdown with the law. Then oth-ers joined him, and in June, after a four-year battle, all forty-six defendants were released. The story made national headlines, and those close to the situation say it might never have happened if Gardner, fifty-seven, had kept quiet. Instead, he did all he could to put the spotlight on the cases.

So who is Gary O. Gardner, and why did he care what hap-pened to those forty-six people?

On a recent summer day, Gardner and his wife, Darlene, sipped iced tea in the shade of a tree on the lawn at Southwestern Baptist Theological Seminary in Fort Worth, where one of their daughters is studying for a master's degree. He admitted that he's cantankerous, bullheaded, controlling, and hot-tempered.

He didn't say that he's politically incorrect. He didn't have to. He demonstrated it in almost every sentence. "Some of those n——s might have been guilty. Some of them might have used recreational drugs. Some of them were probably addicts—but they wasn't *all* guilty," he said. He talked about "pickaninnies" and "dark town" and "sons of a b——s" without apology, then grinned, showing off a row of teeth stained dark since childhood by the minerals in the West Texas water. He wore bib overalls, and when the camera came up, he plopped a $10 straw hat on his round head, clearly aware of the impression he makes.

"He likes to exaggerate things," said Charles Kiker, a retired minister who grew up in Tulia. "It's his way of saying you can say the n-word and still take up for people of color."

Kiker and his son-in-law, Alan Bean, were among the first to join Gardner in his fight to free the Tulia Forty-six. Gardner and his wife, convinced that local coverage of the bust had scuttled any hope of a fair trial, wrote letters to all the prisoners and urged them to ask for a change of venue. The Beans and the Kikers contacted Gardner after Bean's wife, Nancy, spotted one of Gardner's letters to the editor. Soon they were laying the groundwork for the Friends of Justice, a grassroots organization that advocates criminal-justice reform.

Although Kiker, Gardner, and Bean are sometimes called the KGB, Gardner insists he is not a member of the Friends. "I'm not a joiner," he said.

He did, however, help contact the League of United Latin American Citizens and the National Association for the Advancement of Colored People, said Bean. It didn't take long for word to reach the American Civil Liberties Union. Then in September 2000, Gardner and the Friends of Justice took about fifty people to an Austin rally. Suddenly, television cameras focused on the children of those incarcerated, and newspapers began sending reporters to Tulia for the story.

Word spread that Tom Coleman, the undercover police officer, had manufactured the charges and doctored the evidence. There was no other witness, no video, no audio surveillance, nothing but one man's word. Coleman had entered drugs into evidence, but defense attorneys argued that there was no proof the defendants had ever touched those drugs. While residents of Swisher County organized a rally to thank the sheriff for keeping them safe from drug dealers, the ACLU pushed for a criminal investigation of the undercover narc.

In May of 2003, Governor Rick Perry signed a bill that freed the defendants pending an appeals court review of the cases. Last month, the Board of Pardons and Paroles recommended that Perry pardon thirty-five of the defendants. Coleman faces perjury charges.

"Taking those pickaninnies to Austin was the most exciting thing," Gardner said proudly. "We had those kids out front on the steps of the Capitol. Television cameras were everywhere. We were getting the word out."

While Friends President Thelma Johnson, a black woman who is also Moore's longtime girlfriend, said she is unperturbed by Gardner's language, other African Americans are offended.

"The Gardners were always people who stood for what was right, much like Gary," said Freddie Brookins of Tulia, whose son was one of those jailed. "I'll always love ol' Gary because that man stood up for truth, but racial slurs do hurt. That doesn't go around me, and Gary knows it."

∽

For all his posturing and political incorrectness, Gardner is no rube. It's true that he's had little formal study beyond high school, but he considers himself an educated man from a family that values schooling. His mother was a teacher, and his aunt studied music at Juilliard. His sisters earned college degrees.

"I've probably got a better education than most; I just don't have the papers to show for it," Gardner said.

Part of that education came in 1965 when he spent six months in the army's Officer Candidate School. "They kicked me out. The sons of b——s said I wasn't tactful," he said. But the training he got there, and later in noncommissioned officers school, made an enormous impression on him.

Honorably discharged as a sergeant a few years later, he went home to farm—but that was the year "the green bugs hit the milo." He cast about for something else to do and decided he'd make a dandy highway patrolman. He soaked up that education, too.

He's proud of his service but pokes fun at it. "Lack of tact and ugly was exactly what the DPS [Department of Public Safety] was looking for," he said. Then with a sly smile he added, "I was really looking for a date. You know, a girl will give her phone number to a highway patrol officer."

"Oh, he was really handsome in that uniform," said Darlene, the woman he married in 1970 and still calls his partner. They've raised five children of their own, and from 1991 to 1995 they served as foster parents for nine others—many of them black—placed by Catholic Family Services.

Gardner was never shy about punishing his kids. He sometimes administered a well-placed pop to their backsides—but more often he demanded that they read him poetry or sing hymns to him.

"He'd have us read to him for hours. We hated that," said his daughter, Kimber Gardner. "But as we got older, we really kind of liked it. We began to argue about who would get the book: A *Treasury of the Familiar* edited by Ralph L. Woods."

He insisted the children read, among other things, Mark Twain's *Advice to Youth* speech, Frank R. Stockton's *The Lady, or the Tiger?*—and Martin Luther King Jr.'s *Letter from Birmingham Jail.*

⁓

Gardner doesn't drink and only occasionally smokes a pipe. He seldom goes to church, prays when he needs something, thanks God when he gets it, and sleeps in fits and starts. He said he's dyslexic but reads ravenously. His sisters say he can do anything he sets his mind to. He plays the harmonica and taught himself to fly. At one time he owned four crop-dusters.

Gardner is also an insulin-dependent diabetic whose heft is too much for his five-foot-nine-inch frame and whose knees are giving out under the weight. He takes medication for depression, and laughs often, his sky-blue eyes crinkling at the corners, but underneath the comic exterior of a redneck farmer is a man who is a knotty jumble of mind and heart. A man doesn't simply wake up one morning and decide to confront community leaders or argue with his neighbors. It takes a lifetime of practice to do that, and Gardner learned early to exercise his contentious nature.

"They're all contrarians," said Kiker, who knew Gardner's father. "They're not just contrary. They're contrarians."

West Texas tolerates—even encourages—characters and non-conformists such as Gardner, but he admits that this time, he was uncomfortable with the stand he said he was compelled to take. He knew that challenging the verdict placed on the Tulia Forty-six might cost him friendships, damage his reputation, and even hurt his income as people went elsewhere for the water well service he provides to some of the community.

You don't grow up in a tiny place like Vigo Park without knowing how to gauge your neighbors' reactions. After all, there are only 8,000 souls in all of Swisher County's 896 wind-swept square miles. About 5,000 of them live in Tulia, the county seat some sixty miles from Amarillo. A few hundred sit down to supper in Kress or Happy or Claytonville.

Vigo Park, with a population of about thirty, is a wide place in the road twenty-five miles from the middle of nowhere—big enough to support a Methodist church at one end of town and a Baptist church at the other. Locals eat chicken-fried steak at Mom's Place and discuss the weather, politics—and dogs. Gardner often takes a bloodhound and a Chihuahua with him as he ranges over the county in a '93 Chevy Lumina with folding chairs filling the trunk and legal papers spilling over the dusty back seat.

Vigo Park residents drive to Tulia for school, the mail, or a haircut. Gardner lives in one of the few houses scattered about this outpost—but now he goes to Amarillo when he wants his hair trimmed. It got back to him that the Tulia barber didn't like Gardner's stance on the Tulia Forty-six.

Folks in Swisher County weren't about to tolerate drug dealing. Gardner wouldn't abide that, either—but for him there was a bigger issue. He wanted a justice system blind to color, economic standing, and social class. He wanted a system that would fero-ciously protect a person's dignity and his presumption of inno-cence. It didn't, he said, and he couldn't turn his back on what he believed was divine guidance to put things right.

"If I'd have been a stranger in town it wouldn't have been a problem," he said. "Some of those people in Tulia who I had to oppose had prayed for my family when we needed their prayers."

Gardner rubbed his thick hands together remembering those hard days.

In 1996 the Gardners' son Charlie died of a brain tumor. He was almost seventeen. The boy's sickness, and finally his death, changed Gardner in important ways. For more than three years, Gardner did all he could to hold the cancer at bay. When the tumor stole control of Charlie's right side, Gardner fashioned a lefthanded shotgun stock for the boy. Then he rebuilt Charlie's pickup, installing controls for everything on the left side. But in the end, the cancer won.

Then Gardner built Charlie's casket himself from black wal-nut, waiting until the last minute to make the first cut in the lovely wood. Hospice workers paved the way for Gardner and his other sons to dig the grave themselves at Vigo Park Cemetery.

On the day of the funeral, the casket was set on hay bales. A piano was moved under the windmill, and Charlie's Sunday school teacher played the old hymns while hundreds of mourners crowded into the yard. Gardner sang.

They carried Charlie to the cemetery in the back of a pickup and the boy was buried beside his great-granddaddy. When it was over, Gardner had to find a way to go on.

"That was the first time he didn't have control of things," said his son, Craig Gardner, thirty-two, of Bryan.

Charlie's illness gave Gardner a profound awareness of how feeble his attempts at control really were. It deepened his empathy for those who are powerless to direct their own destiny. It also left him time to fight for the Tulia Forty-six.

Gardner is grieved that he had to clash with those who had

supported him—and sorry that Tulia got a bad rap from the media, but he is not sorry for what he did. In fact, he and his family are proud of the part he played in freeing the Tulia Forty-six, pleased that the justice system of Swisher County was examined in a more public arena and found flawed. Gardner likes the role of advocate for the underdog, savors the correctness of the law—the drama of litigation. But when this story is finally over, when the fate of the Tulia Forty-six is only a memory, Gardner and his wife will be left with neighbors they've had for years in a place his granddaddy pioneered—a place now marked by his own brand of stubborn determination.

Of Like Minds 🍂 *May 28, 1995*

THE SHRUNKEN head, with its tightly sutured eyelids, coarse hair and shriveled skin, was real. A grim treasure owned by their older brother, it fascinated and repulsed the twins' thirteen-year-old friends—so they were sure of its commercial value.

They were inspired.

It was spring in the mid-1950s and the brothers needed money. The pheasant farm they started as a hobby boasted seventeen kinds of ornamental pheasants, but it was costing more than the boys ever dreamed it might. It would have to be subsidized with the sale of remarkably authentic-looking shrunken heads they created from modeling clay and squirrel skin and marketed through the Princess Pawn Shop on Main Street.

Turns out Scott and Stuart Gentling couldn't make the heads fast enough. Almost as soon as Earl, a friend's chauffeur, would get them home, the pawnbroker was on the phone asking for more.

The Gentling twins were adventurers, confederates of the heart sharing a magical childhood created, they say, as a refuge from a more turbulent world. Now at fifty-two, the artist brothers still complement each other's curiosity, indulge their wide interests and avoid the more frantic pressures of humanity. Since they were boys, they've made their way by their art and originality and unlike so many other creative people, they are never afraid the well of inspiration will run dry.

Many of their drawings and dry brush watercolor paintings of American Indians appeared in a documentary film called *500 Nations*. Produced and hosted by Kevin Costner, the first part of the film aired late in April and the last segment will be shown at eight tonight on CBS (KDFW/Channel 4).

Some call the Gentling twins Renaissance men who are never afraid to indulge their interests and trust that their talent will always pay the bills. The list of their projects is long. The Gentlings won't talk about design details, but they say they are also coordinating the art that will appear inside and outside the downtown performance hall, which is scheduled for completion in 1998. They are designing art for the dome, mosaics for the exterior, and murals for the interior. Groundbreaking for the hall, said to be the last great performing arts center to be built in the United States in the twentieth century, is planned for Thursday.

Together, the Gentling twins have produced an enormous forty-six-pound bird book dedicated to the memory of John James Audubon, whose work they copied in their beginning years as artists. They are working on a second volume about Tenochtitlan, the Aztec capital as it was before the Spanish conquest of Mexico. Their efforts have already earned them recognition by the Mexican government, film-makers, and museums.

They've spent years accumulating wooden masks, prints and art from India, China, Nepal, and Japan. They collect eighteenth-century stringed instruments as well as eighteenth-century men's clothing, including military uniforms and royal court dress. They love history and Elizabethan poetry, stories, and storytellers. They are, they say, romantics who avoid the computer age.

Friends say the brothers have spent a lifetime developing the art of being interesting. And even those who grumble that the pair are too self-absorbed concede that at the very least the twins are interesting.

Dr. Benjamin Spock, the acclaimed baby-raising expert of the 1950s, thought the boys remarkable, says their mother, Barbara Smith. Spock was doing a study on twins and concluded that the toddlers were exceptionally lively. Smith still lives in Fort Worth, only a few blocks from the frame bungalow her sons share.

Fraternal twins with almost identical interests, the men are very different in temperament. Stuart is as much a gregarious public relations man as a painter. He is the protective front-man who loves to talk and travel.

Scott seems more driven, introspective, and reclusive. He is precise in his language, and paints, with compelling detail, birds, landscapes and still lifes. He is a sought-after portrait artist. Most Gentling works are in private collections, but Scott's portrait of naturalist Jane Goodall has been acquired by the Modern Art Museum of Fort Worth.

The twins were about five when their father, a doctor at the renowned Mayo Clinic, moved his family to Fort Worth. He became head of anesthesiology at Harris Methodist Hospital, and the family was quickly accepted into the prominent west side social circle.

The Gentling brothers remember that their parents encouraged their many interests. Stuart took a taxidermy course when he was only ten. Scott practiced his art but was never forced to take a lesson. Their bedroom bulged with their projects: train models, eggs hatching in an incubator, stuffed birds, a box of silkworms, paintings started by Stuart and finished by Scott.

But Stuart says their parents' passionate relationship was sometimes explosive. Although they had an older brother, Peter, who is now a physician living in North Carolina, and a younger sister, Suzanne, who is also an artist, the twins turned to each other for comfort. Their parents divorced in the early 1960s after twenty-five years of marriage. Their father died in 1976.

"It wasn't an overnight divorce. There was a lot of tension," Stuart says. "In a way, the tensions our parents were going through stuck Scott and me together even more. I think in a way that's why there's such magic in our relationship. It was an escape from the tensions."

As the twins grew older, they avoided some of that strain by spending more and more time at friends' homes. "We had lots of friends and so many of them had equal interests," Stuart says. A look passes between the two and Scott smiles slyly. "I do say we put most of the kids up to these things," Scott says as the two remember their childhood.

The pheasant farm was an extension of the boys' interest in nature and birds in particular. It was set up behind the home of their boyhood friend Tom Loffland, who lived in the heart of Westover Hills, then Fort Worth's most exclusive neighborhood.

Early one Sunday morning the three decided the pheasant cages needed gravel. Perry Bass' long, curving driveway held the mother lode. The boys had already helped themselves to one wheelbarrow full, when Bass, patriarch of the wealthy, philanthropic Bass clan, motored around the bend.

He was not pleased to see the boys with shovels and a wheelbarrow half full of his driveway. He sent them packing, but Stuart says that the next day a huge truck rolled slowly down the Lofflands' drive and dumped a mountain of gravel near the pheasant farm. The driver staked a note to the haul.

"This should be enough gravel to last you a lifetime. Leave my driveway alone," Stuart remembers. The note was signed "Perry Bass."

It seems the fourteen-year-old twins and their pal, Tom Loffland, were always scavenging. Bass' neighbor, Kay Kimbell, the grain and grocery mogul whose art collection provided the foundation for the Kimbell Art Museum, raised quail. He liked to see the birds roaming the green valleys of Westover Hills, so when birds reached a certain age, he set them free. When he learned that the boys were catching the birds and caging them, he summoned the two to his estate.

Stuart recalls that Kimbell presented the boys with five pair of quail. "These are good birds," he told the boys. "They're healthy breeders. Leave my birds alone," he said.

The boys built a "fort" behind the Loffland house complete with a tower for defense against the little girls who attacked each week after the Bluebird meeting. The nineteen-foot-tall guillotine they built in a friend's yard when they were about fifteen wasn't quite so harmless. It would neatly chop a 2x4 in half. "Marguerite Gordon swore we tried to cut off her head," Stuart recalls. "But of course we didn't." Her father made them dismantle it anyway.

Perhaps their most dangerous creation was a tiny three-stage rocket made of soda straws coated with a hard shoe polish, weighted with copper wire, and fueled by black powder, a quick burning, highly volatile explosive. They wanted to shoot a rocket half a mile. "The rockets went farther and farther. Finally we actually made it half a mile. But then we almost went half a mile too," Stuart says. They recall a beautiful spring day in the late 1950s. The Gentlings were about seventeen and restless. Soon-to-be Texas Governor John Connally, living in Fort Worth at the time, sat on his porch across the valley watching the little puffs of smoke as boys fired the tiny rockets into a blue sky.

A rocket misfired, and rather than waste it, the boys just pinched off the burnt end. Tom Loffland did not finish pouring the powder fuse when the smoldering soda straw set off the explosion. Connally saw the huge cloud of smoke and heard the thundering report. The house shuddered. The windows trembled. He knew the boys were in trouble and rushed to help.

"I remember a flash of gray and red. I couldn't hear the explosion until it began to ricochet off the buildings across the valley," Stuart says. Their clothes were blown away, hair and eyelashes singed. Change in their pockets became red-hot, permanently branding them.

"I didn't know I was burned, but I knew something was wrong," Stuart says. "I went to the bathroom and put water on my face and my skin began sliding away."

The boys were rushed to the hospital where their father had specialists waiting.

News of the explosion flashed around the world. European papers picked up the story warning of the dangers of launching homemade rockets, but the fiery ordeal didn't extinguish the Gentling brothers' curiosity.

In high school, they worked with Tom Loffland again, this time to build a 750-pound cannon from Civil War plans. They were, they say, surprised at the enormous recoil of the cannon when it was fired.

~

After finishing at Arlington Heights High School in Fort Worth, Stuart struggled with career decisions, flirting first with the notion of becoming a lawyer, but Scott says he had none of that confusion. For him there were no turning points, only a gentle slide into his solitary life as a painter.

"I painted very naturally without the slightest intention of becoming an artist," he says of his early years. "I wanted to visualize something, to capture a record of it."

In the beginning, when they were still in grammar school, Stuart would often start a picture and Scott would finish it, perfecting his skill and technique with each project. By the time the boys were fifteen they were earning money with their art. "I'd work six weeks on a painting and it would sell for $150—a fortune to me at the time. But even from an early age, I had money. I was making my way in the world as a painter," Scott says.

Both brothers went from high school to Tulane University, but after only a year, Scott was invited to study at the Pennsylvania Academy of the Fine Arts in Philadelphia.

Stuart enrolled in law school at the University of Texas. "The first week I was in law school, I knew I didn't want to be a lawyer," he says. He too was accepted at the Pennsylvania Academy but only stayed a year. "I went with Tommy Loffland on a tiger hunt. Scott was my (art) teacher," he says.

Perry Bass offered to pay for Stuart's education if he'd study geology and oil and gas law and one summer he did work for Bass. Stuart remembers getting all dressed up and stepping into the impressive office of the man who was to conduct the mandatory interview.

"How many years of geology have you had?" the man asked a bit gruffly.

"Well sir, actually I've never had any geology. It seems a fascinating subject and maybe I'll take a course in it one of these days," Stuart offered nervously.

The gentleman took a long puff on his cigar. "Well, the job that is being offered is in the graphics department. How many years of mechanical drawing and drafting of maps have you had?"

"Actually I've never had any. I read road maps though. I mean I've traveled around," Stuart said.

"No mechanical drawing you say?"

"No, sir."

"No maps?"

"Just road maps," said Stuart.

The man took a long draw on the cigar. "Do you know anything about oil leases?"

"No sir. I don't know anything about leases," Stuart confessed.

The man took another studied drag on his cigar. The smoke circled lazily above his head. He flicked the ash off the cigar and gazed briefly out the window. "You'll start Monday," he said.

Stuart enjoyed the summer, but he knew before school started in the fall that he wouldn't take Bass up on his offer to pursue a career in geology and oil and gas law.

"Frankly I wasn't even tempted," Stuart says. "I wanted to be an artist." But he says he knew that an artist's life is difficult. Part of that dilemma, he says, were the decisions he knew he would be forced to make.

"I felt eventually I had to decide between a family or a career in art. Quite honestly, one of the difficulties of my life has been problems with women. I like them. But I've never cared about having a family with kids," he says.

For years, Stuart has dated Nancy Ferguson, who is an accomplished artist. He says he was immediately taken with her the day she came to buy one of their bird books for her grandfather. He and his brother keep a little brown house near the Rivercrest neighborhood. Neither has ever married. Unlike the gallery they own on the edge of the cultural district with its orderly exhibits, their house is bursting with their collections and projects. The harpsichord Scott had made and taught himself to play sits in a corner of the living room. He once composed a piece of chamber music show-casing the instrument. Stuart paints at a low table in the same room. He admits only friends who know the secret knock.

While Stuart dashes off to Mexico with friends, attends parties, and keeps business interest in their work alive, Scott seldom leaves home. Sometimes beginning work at four-thirty A.M., he puts in incredibly long days. Scott often writes early in the morning and paints in the narrow twin bed in which he sleeps.

Sitting cross-legged in shorts, he bends over a board that holds the portrait of a young girl in a wicker chair. She sits gazing dreamily at a green landscape. Like most of his work, the subject has a romantic quality and the detail is staggering. Every shadow cast by every line of wicker is captured. Every strand of hair teased by an unseen breeze is frozen in time.

A white cat sits purring in the bright circle of light cast from a floor lamp that stands beside the bed. The orb of light is trained on his work. The walls are brown and the dim room is stacked with books and magazines. A television set in front of the window flickers and smoke from his cigarette drifts to the yellowed ceiling.

"I'm a faster painter in the morning, wiser in the afternoon," Scott says dipping a tiny brush in color. "I am fearless as a water-colorist," he says. "I know how to remove what I've put on. It's penitence, real penitence, but if you make a mistake you pay for it with the sheer effort and the time it takes to remove it."

Stuart admires his brother's technique and respects his opinion. "Artistically, Scott almost always helps me curb my overly romantic impulse," Stuart says. "He has me pull back just a little."

The brothers talk often about style and symbolism and analyze the effect of a certain piece on the audience. They are, however, careful never to criticize works-in-progress.

But there was a time when their life as artists was threatened. When the brothers were about thirty-eight, both discovered that they had cataracts. It was the early 1980s and they were deep into the bird book project. Stuart says the two were never too concerned about the condition. Cataract surgery was improving by leaps and bounds, and they were confident the cataracts would be successfully removed, says Stuart. Eventually their vision was restored. But they found that because of the yellow tint of the cataracts, many of the pictures they finished before the operation had to be redone.

"The colors weren't true," Stuart explains. "The blues were just real blue."

The brothers have settled into a comfortable camaraderie, a magical alliance based on lifelong association and heart-deep understanding. "Scotty and I do what we like to do. We have a rapport that started in the womb," Stuart says. "We really are the best of friends."

Trend Tycoon ✍ *September 4, 1994*

I T ' S 10:40 A.M.—twenty minutes to opening—at the newest 8.0 Restaurant & Bar, this one in Sundance Square, and owner Shannon Wynne is barking orders. He tells a waiter to adjust track lighting to illuminate tables just pulled together for a party of ten and then turns up the music. Everything has to be just right. Wynne is as much showman as restaurateur, with an affinity for high-tech design and a drive to explore entertainment frontiers.

He has a celebrated knack for anticipating trends that keep the see-and-be-seen crowd waiting in line to get into his 8.0 restaurants in Dallas and Houston. And he says that the Fort Worth location, which opened in August after a long pursuit by Sundance Square management, is cranking out higher sales than either of those.

An early riser who almost never stays up past ten-thirty P.M. and who hates to eat out, Wynne wears the attitude of old money as casually as last year's Armani jacket, but those who know him well say Wynne at forty-two, is a complicated man, a romantic, an artist—a seeker.

He says he is an old soul who has lived many other lives and learned many lessons. This time around he's working on patience, control, and honesty. A believer in reincarnation, he goes so far as to say he thinks his only child, Sam, nine, may indeed be a reincarnation of his father, Angus Wynne Jr., the flamboyant land developer who built several Six Flags amusement parks and made and lost big money as easily as a bird builds a nest.

Those who know Wynne, talk about his creative nature. He makes jewelry and ceramic tables. He designed and crafted the whimsical pictures in the restaurant's terrazzo floors. He also pilots powered parachutes (a type of ultralight) and occasionally slips away to his private fishing camp at Caddo Lake.

Now a teetotaler who admits to once having had problems with alcohol and cocaine, he dreams of directing films or acting, but more than anything else, Wynne says he wants to look in the mirror without blinking, to be a good husband, a good father, and an enlightened man.

~

"My father didn't know me like I want to know my son," he says. "He didn't have a lot of time for me. I'm trying to fix that with Sam." Wynne makes it a point never ever to miss one of Sam's soccer, basketball, or baseball games and practices with him before school. Oddly Wynne says his father, Angus Jr., was very close to his father, Wynne's grandfather. "They talked every day," Wynne says.

Wynne's grandfather, Angus Wynne Sr., was a dynamic East Texas attorney who made his mark during the early days of Texas' oil bonanzas. Known as the King of the Boom Town Lawyers, he traveled the state sealing deals with a handshake. Always in the center of the action, he was one of the founders of the Dallas Cowboys. He was also a founding partner of the Dallas law firm of Gardere & Wynne.

Wynne's father, Angus Jr., staked his future and his fortune on land deals. He built one of Dallas' first tract housing developments, a place called Wynnewood, just after World War II. But he quickly moved on to develop entertainment parks, including Six Flags Over Texas in Arlington, Six Flags Over Georgia in Atlanta, and Six Flags Over Mid-America in St. Louis.

Attractive and urbane, Angus Jr. and his wife, Joanne, who was once the Camay soap model, were popular figures on the Dallas social circuit. They traveled and entertained and made all the right contacts. Powerful friends such as Texas Governor John Connally and President Lyndon Johnson thought Angus Jr. was the only man to stage the Texas Exhibition at the 1964 World's Fair in New

York. He got the concession, but it became a financial catastrophe. Even as Six Flags Over Georgia was being built, the family was forced into bankruptcy.

Wynne says his parents didn't miss a beat. With unflinching panache, they threw a bankruptcy bash. "Friends brought groceries, and all the waiters wore hats that said Soup Kitchen," Wynne remembers. He was just fourteen at the time.

"They were F. Scott and Zelda," he says of his parents' Gatsby lifestyle. And while it may have looked glamorous from the outside, Wynne says things inside the Highland Park home were not ideal.

By the time Wynne's older brothers, Angus III and David, and sister Temple moved away, the tension between his parents was almost unbearable. The strain was made worse by their daily drinking, he says. "I was worried. When I was in college I'd pour the gin out and fill the bottles with water," he remembers.

Finally his father, an insulin-dependent diabetic, stopped drinking. "He just didn't stop soon enough," Wynne says. The older Wynne had a stroke. Soon after, the thirty-six-year marriage ended in divorce. Angus Jr. died two years later in 1979, but not before he and his youngest child had a life-changing confrontation. Wynne was twenty-one then.

His eyes fill with tears as he picks his way though a tangle of regrets. "I was a liar," he says at last. "I lied all the time about everything. I could lie circles around anyone . . . and one day my father and I got in an argument and I called him a liar. He hit me. It was one of the first times he'd ever hit me, and I was shocked. I was grown, but I was crying and screaming. He picked up the telephone and called my grandfather and he said, 'Dad, Shannon called me a liar. He wants to know why I hit him.'"

Wynne's voice drops almost to a whisper and he struggles for control. He remembers picking up the phone. "My granddad didn't miss a beat. He didn't even hesitate. He started telling the story about how when he was growing up . . . everyone would do deals with a handshake. He said, 'I've taught your father that if you're going to call someone a liar, hit him, because he's going to hit you. That's the worst thing you can say. Your entire life depends on your word. If you tell lies, you're going to have to pay the consequences.'"

Wynne pauses. "I decided right then I was never going to lie again, but it was incredibly hard to turn it around. It's not OK to lie about anything. It's not a question of will it come back to you; it's how hard will it come back."

~

Wynne says he didn't set out to make a place for himself in the nightclub industry. In the beginning, he wanted to be a veterinarian. When he wasn't accepted at Texas A&M, he turned his attention to the film industry, aiming for a career as a director.

Even after graduating from Trinity University in San Antonio with degrees in biology and film production, Wynne couldn't find the opportunity he wanted. "I felt like I was beating my head against the wall," he says. Then, his favorite Dallas hangout, the Stoneleigh P, burned to the ground. It was later rebuilt, but not before Wynne decided he'd open a "gin joint."

It was 1979, and he told his mother he wanted to open a nightspot called The '80s. She shook her head. "Everyone will be tired of the '80s in three months. Why don't you call it 8.0, then all the matchbook covers could say, 'I done ate there, and, oh, it was good,'" she said.

The 8.0, with its ceiling-high murals and high-tech atmosphere, was an instant success. Wynne followed with a string of Dallas bars including Nostromo, Rocco Oyster Bar, Neemo, The Rio Room, Mexico, and Tango, which was known for its giant rooftop dancing frogs. With the high pressure and high rollers came high times.

Wynne doesn't flinch when he acknowledges his years of drug use. "Cocaine was the accepted social lubricant," he says. "More so than alcohol." But that, he says, was a long time ago.

Wynne's mother died in 1986. Her death and the birth of his son marked a turning point. The hot nightspots were cooling.

Businesses were folding. Sam was born in December 1984. Wynne and his wife, Patti, divorced the following spring after less than a year of marriage. He says alcohol played a part in the breakup. Wynne became the child's major caregiver.

"I've got to hand it to him," says older brother David Wynne. "He lived through all that self-indulgent stuff in the '80s. He learned from his mistakes. When Sam was born, he did an about-face."

Wynne began a spiritual quest that eventually led him to Father Albert Taliaferro (pronounced Tolliver), a controversial Dallas cleric who died last year. A one-time Episcopal priest, Taliaferro organized his own church more than twenty-five years ago, melding teachings from the world's great religions into a New Age doctrine that embraced notions about reincarnation and karma. Until this year, Wynne's son has attended the St. Alcuin Montessori School founded by Taliaferro.

When Wynne wed Brycie Hoecker eighteen months ago, Taliaferro officiated. It was a marriage a long time in the making. Wynne declares that he loved Brycie, thirty-one, the first minute he laid eyes on her five years ago in the second 8.0 restaurant in Dallas' Quadrangle, just north of downtown.

Once a model, she is tall with black eyes and thick dark hair. She wears little makeup and has a fresh-scrubbed look that Wynne found irresistible. Better yet she says she was interested, too.

"But Shannon's past is sometimes bigger than his present," she says. Brought up in a Catholic home in Danville, Illinois, she is a graduate of Southern Methodist University with degrees in business and finance. Now she works at Perot Systems in Dallas.

Brycie drinks little alcohol and says she never used drugs. Naturally, she didn't like the stories. "I was scared of him," she says frankly. Still she couldn't deny the attraction.

They dated for a long time. Then she broke things off, even began dating another. Months went by with no word. And then one day, an exquisitely wrapped package was delivered to her high-rise apartment. "Inside there were twelve small boxes each ornately wrapped and each with a card. The big box had a card attached that said, 'These are things that were in short supply during our relationship. I love you.'

"Inside each box was a card. One said 'honesty.' One said 'love.' Another said 'support.' " Her voice cracks with emotion, and she laughs self-consciously. "I'm still touched by it," she says.

That romantic gesture reeled her back in. Now if he leaves before she does, he sometimes draws a lipstick heart on the bathroom mirror.

Wynne admits to having a hot temper but says he never holds a grudge. His wife says he is sometimes a terror. Still, he tolerates her five-foot-long iguana called Kravis who lives in a six-foot-by-six-foot cage off the breakfast room in their Dallas home—and he's become a master of compromise.

She wanted a big dog. He wanted a small one. He gave her a blue heeler, a medium dog. She wanted a traditional four-poster bed. He wanted something modern. For Christmas he had a sleigh bed made of recycled aluminum.

"I've become more considerate, more sensitive, I guess, to other people," he says.

Yet, he declares that he can't abide laziness and admires those who can be true to their own artistic inspiration. He doesn't hesitate when he says he wants to raise his son to be the sort of brave person who follows that inner voice. "Creative choices—and life choices for that matter—are too often based on who's watching," Wynne says. "I'm not free of that by any means ... but I'm working hard to do what's right."

PART SIX

Heart of the Matter

Destination: Heaven ℘
Sunday, December 16, 2001

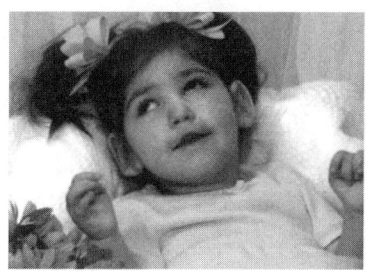

Caroline Tew was an unlikely bless-ing—an angel who went home to heaven. Courtesy, the Fort Worth Star-Telegram.

THE WIND blew up from the south, whispering across the brittle Texas pastures, dancing up the ribbons of highways that blistered in the August sun. It was really little more than a breeze when it coasted over Fort Worth and flittered through Hurst and up to Colleyville. In Southlake, it rattled the leaves in the oak tree outside the kitchen door of a spacious home where a woman and two little girls stood holding hands.

One of the children, the oldest of the two, with a single long, blond braid and dark, serious eyes, clutched a green ribbon attached to a brightly colored Mylar balloon. A letter encased in plastic swung from the end of the ribbon. The girl released the balloon, and they all turned their faces upward, watching as it drifted up into the cloudy afternoon. But before the wind could catch it, the letter was snagged on the oak branches and the balloon bobbed and rolled, tethered to earth while still reaching for heaven.

The Blessing Wind blew harder then, pulling at the balloon until it broke free and sailed lazily north toward the Red River. Behind the little wind, more powerful currents drove thunderheads full of rain and lightning across the land, and soon a storm washed across the countryside.

In the morning, a brilliant rainbow arched across the sky and five-year-old Brittany Tew knew beyond doubt that it was a sign. The angels had received their letter. "Look, Mommy, that means Baby Caroline is in heaven," she said, and her mother, Kristi Tew, knew it was true—but how she ached for something more.

That something came in September, packed in a padded envelope and stuffed into the Tew's curbside mailbox along with the usual bills, catalogs, and circulars.

Caroline Bailey Tew was born four weeks too soon on February 5, 1999, the third child of Kristi and Todd Tew of Southlake. She was a pink bundle with a mop of dark hair. The pregnancy was uncomplicated, even easy, says Kristi, now thirty-two. Nothing in any prenatal test indicated anything unusual. To Kristi, who has a Ph.D. in child counseling, and to Todd, an attorney who is now thirty-three, the sonograms were pictures of a perfect baby.

Still, little Caroline did come into this world sooner than expected—and with a mild tremor in her arms. The doctor wasn't alarmed. Caroline weighed a good six pounds-plus. The tremor would go away, he said. Give it a month.

But the tremor did not go away, and the once-peaceful baby grew more difficult by the day. She ate little, slept even less, and screamed constantly.

The Tews consulted a neurologist. Tests were performed. Kristi and Todd held hands in the doctor's office as they heard the results. Baby Caroline's brain was shrinking. Pieces of it had already calcified. She had a degenerative brain disease. She would not get better. She would get worse. She would die before her first birthday. She was, in fact, dying right there in her mother's arms.

The family wept and prayed and consulted other doctors, but nothing changed the facts. The Tews' last baby would not survive.

For a while they were eager to name the mysterious affliction. They longed to know the why of it. At last, one doctor put a long name to the disease, but tests were not conclusive and the Tews weren't completely convinced of the diagnosis. In the end, Kristi says, the name came not to matter.

The baby didn't simply cry, she screamed; a frightening wail that filled her every waking moment. She slept in fitful snatches. The entire family was stretched as tight as a piano wire ready to snap. Kristi says the family begged specialists for help, but doctors insisted that nothing could be done to quiet the baby's distress. Caroline's piercing screams continued.

Before the baby's first birthday, Kristi developed a stress tumor. She packed on weight and teetered on the edge of emotional and physical collapse. Doctors cut into Kristi's brain, believing the tumor had invaded the pituitary gland, but it was not there. Exploratory surgery followed and doctors finally found the tumor hiding on her lung. They cut it out, but by then Kristi was certain that she was dying, too. She believed that she would beat the baby to the grave.

She called for hospice care. Hospice workers took one look at Kristi and knew she wasn't dying, but they also heard Caroline's painful screams and knew something had to be done. They persuaded a pediatrician to prescribe small amounts of morphine.

"Within half an hour, she stopped crying," Kristi says. "It was the most glorious moment." In no time, Caroline was smiling. "For the first time, she began to see us," says Kristi.

Caroline began to eat. She even slept. Soon she was laughing. She made funny little noises, and the family called it singing. Her older sisters, Brittany, who was then five, and Victoria, who was four, carried her around, dressed her up as if she was a baby doll, played "beauty shop" with her, painted her toenails, and kissed her often.

Caroline learned to kiss back. "We held her almost all the time, because we knew she wouldn't be with us long," Kristi says.

And so it was that the baby who would never see her first birthday celebrated her second in February—but by July her time was over.

Friends came. The First Baptist Church of Keller prayed—and finally Kristi's and Todd's families gathered to say a last goodbye.

On Sunday, July 8, 2001, Kristi cradled little Caroline in her arms all day. She read to her from a little book called *What About Heaven?* hoping the words would comfort the dying child. The older children kept running downstairs to kiss little Caroline and then running back to their play.

Caroline grew weaker and weaker. Her pulse became nothing more than a timid quiver. Kristi crooned "Jesus Loves Me" to her—and waited.

Late on a Sunday afternoon, the weary family members began to leave. "We'd already said our goodbyes," Kristi remembers, and then, as if called by some unseen visitor, the family drifted back to the den where Kristi sat with Caroline. They stood in a circle holding hands. Todd began to pray.

"Dear Jesus, she's yours … ," he said—and in that moment Baby Caroline's spirit slipped away.

"She's gone," her mother said.

They buried Caroline on a Tuesday. She was barefoot because her sisters had painted her toenails. The Tews had experienced one terrifying year of tribulation and one beautiful year of love. They'd learned to count this small, imperfect child as a perfect blessing, and in the coming days they all missed her with an unexpected and ferocious yearning.

As days stretched to weeks, Brittany began to fret. At first the questions crept out shyly and then they came in a bold rush. "Is Baby Caroline in heaven?" she asked. "Is she happy? Is she all right? Is she with Jesus?"

In August, Kristi suggested writing the letter. Todd was leery. "I thought it was testing God at a time when my faith had already been shaken," he says, but he did not stop the plan. Now he is thankful for what he calls "the miracle of the circumstances."

Kristi gathered the girls around the computer and wrote:

Dear Caroline,

Hi, sweet baby sister! We want to write to you since you passed away from your brain disease and tell you how much we love you! We want to hold you again, and cannot wait to see you in Heaven. We will never forget you or your smile or your laugh.

All our love,

Brittany and Victoria

And then, almost as a postscript, Kristi added something on the back: *The girls want to get a sign from you that you are with Jesus and that you know that we love you.*

She attached a return address sticker and signed all their names before laminating the letter and attaching it to the balloon.

The wind carried it across the Texas border, over the flat, brown land and the small towns, past the place where the Cheyenne and Arapaho live, until after many days and more than 200 miles it came to rest in a pasture just outside El Reno, Oklahoma.

It was September.

Except for the time he attended Oklahoma State University in Stillwater, David Griesel has spent his entire thirty-nine years in the region just west of Oklahoma City. He lives in El Reno, a community of 14,000-plus; a place where people eat chicken-fried steak at a cafe called Tokyo Flavor and "onion fried" burgers at Johnnie's Grill. The Griesel family operates a car dealership just up the road in Okarche. David is the sales manager there, but it's not his only business.

He's a never-married man who has his fingers in several lucrative pies, everything from waste disposal to a mother-cow-and-calf operation he runs with his grandmother. Looking after the small herd is as much pleasure as business for David. Ordinarily he doesn't check on the cows until evening, but on that September day he went early.

It was only about three in the afternoon when he drove into the pasture. The cattle were strung out along the sloping banks of the North Canadian River, a wide, shallow waterway that cuts through his 420-acre spread, but it was not the herd that caught David's eye that day.

On the far bank, just below a bend in the river, he saw a glint and then a bright reflection of something he'd never seen before, something that had not been there the previous day. "The sun hit this and it was all lit up. Shining. Very bright. But even with my binoculars, I couldn't tell what it was. I looked, but all I got was this glare," he says.

David couldn't drive across the river with its deep sandbars, but he could go back to the road and loop a mile or so around to the far gate. And so it was that on a perfectly still, windless afternoon that he found the balloon, its ribbon tail tangled in a cedar tree.

The letter stopped him cold.

He knew immediately that he was meant to help those little girls, that wounded family, but for a few days he did nothing. Then on Friday, September 7, he took the Mylar balloon and the laminated letter to his office and showed it to Milea Gundlach, who works for the family's Ford dealership in Okarche. At twenty-one, Milea is small and blond with round blue eyes and porcelain skin. She is a married woman who struggles with asthma, loves dogs, volunteers at the Loyal Fire Department, and says green is her favorite color.

Like David, she was raised in the Lutheran Church—and like David, she knew immediately that they must answer the letter. They began the hard work of finding the right words. Milea's mother, Liz Cox, joined the project, making suggestions, writing out a rough draft. She even offered to pick up a children's book when she went to Oklahoma City and send it along with the letter. A friend recommended one book, but standing there in the bookstore, Liz was drawn to a little tome called *What About Heaven?* by Kathleen Bostrom. She bought it, never guessing that the book would become a profound comfort to the Tew family.

All weekend, Milea worked on the letter, and on Monday, September 10, she wrote the carefully chosen words on a sheet of notebook paper with a green crayon.

Dear Brittany and Victoria,

I found the balloon today that you sent to me in Heaven. I was so excited to get it. Jesus and I are having lots of fun in Heaven. He knows all my favorite games that I love to play.

I know that one day we will all be together again ...

God's Blessings,

Jesus and Caroline

She tucked it into the little book and mailed it.

David sent a separate letter on business stationary to Kristi and Todd.

The Tew family,

I found the balloon earlier this week that your family sent to Heaven. I was touched by your story, so I decided to take it to work with me to share it with the others. I asked an employee of mine, Milea Gundlach, to help with the response to you. She took your story to her mother who has worked with pre-schoolers for the past five years at St. John's Lutheran Church.... We pray that your family can hold on to the thought that Caroline is in Heaven with Jesus and that she is smiling and running.

God be with your family.

David K. Griesel

Kristi quickly sent a reply.

Dear David,

Thank you so much for your response to the balloon as well as the book and letter "from" our precious Caroline. We deeply appreciate your thoughtfulness in deed, your compassionate prayers, and your resourceful employee. When our daughters wanted to send the balloon to Caroline, we did not think we would get a response at all, much less one that was so wonderful or so appropriate. God truly answered our prayers in bringing that particular balloon to you.

Caroline has so far had over 150 memorials in honor of her ... but few things have been this thoughtful and touching to our family. ... The book you sent was the exact book that I read to Caroline and the girls on the day that she passed away. . . . God truly sent us an unmistakable sign of His love and His care for Caroline through you. Todd and I were both surprised and delighted. Thank you.

This unexpected spirit of gratitude, this feeling of thankfulness is now a common ribbon lacing these strangers together by what they each say is a blessing.

"I am convinced 100 percent that the balloon went exactly where it was supposed to go. I don't think it was by chance. I think it was orchestrated by a higher power," says Todd. "The Lord works through circumstances and through people. That they signed Jesus on the letter doesn't lessen the miracle of the circumstances."

Kristi agrees. "I believe David was sent by God to help us," she says.

David and Milea believe that for one September day they were instruments of divine providence, messengers of hope for a family that trusted the wind to deliver their most earnest and tender longings to the very hands of God.

The Tew Family must face all the coming Christmases without little Caroline, but they shall never forget. Courtesy, the Fort Worth Star-Telegram.

Trial by Fire ✌ *December 20, 1998*

"I believe that man will not merely endure; he will prevail.
He is immortal not because he alone among creatures has an
inexhaustible voice, but because he has a soul, a spirit capa-
ble of compassion and sacrifice and endurance."
                                        —William Faulkner

SOMETIMES, just when he's found some sense of peace, Jamie
Cashion catches someone staring at him and he knows that forever and always he will be different. For almost half his life, he has
lived with the prying eyes, the questions, the uneasiness of his
journey. Ask him, and Jamie will tell you that life isn't about getting a good hand, but about playing a bad one well. He'll say life is
precious, family matters, and there's no time to waste. Life goes
on, he'll say. You must go on, too.

At thirty-one, he likes fast cars and expensive watches, kids,
dogs, dancing, old jeans, tennis shoes—and people, most of all.
He'll tell you he's been lucky. He married his childhood sweetheart, runs a successful Fort Worth insurance agency, owns a new
two-story home, enjoys volunteer work, and goes to church on
Sundays. He could be the all-American boy next door, the fun-
loving class favorite, the guy who seems always to win—except for
one fateful afternoon almost fifteen years ago.

His mother, Pam Harrison, wasn't worried when she signed
the consent forms for Jamie to register as Joshua's youngest volunteer fireman. Her own brother had been a firefighter and a police-
man, and there was never a concern. What could happen? She
thought Jamie would be safe—and he might have been, if the
wind hadn't turned.

The minute the fire signal sounded, an ominous tingle rocketed up his spine, raising the hair on his neck, and he knew that this fire was different from all the rest.

Ignoring the faint alarm ringing somewhere deep inside his head, Jamie rushed to the Joshua Fire Hall, where he joined other volunteer firemen preparing to fight a ferocious fire that was racing across a rolling grassland west of Crowley. Jamie was only sixteen that February afternoon in 1984, a happy-go-lucky high school sophomore, the life of the party, a kid with boundless energy, and a mile-wide streak of mischief. Before day's end, he was barely clinging to life, writhing in pain, his face, hands, and legs gouged by the flames.

Jamie and his mother have the same brown eyes, the same sense of fun—the same understanding of calamity. Jamie isn't old enough to remember the car crash that put his mother in a wheelchair. He was only a toddler then. She was twenty-three, with two little kids and a marriage that was ending. She was alone and driving too fast on a dark road. The curve must have been a surprise. One miscalculation. One error in judgment. A lifetime without useful legs.

After the accident, she cried if a stranger looked at her. She withdrew, she says, sat and watched life rush past, a dizzy kaleidoscope of color and lost opportunity.

She wouldn't accept her predicament, refused to use her wheelchair. Friends carried her from place to place in their arms, but Jamie is different, she says.

He throws himself at you. He wants to touch you. He wants you to touch him. He's in your face and smiling, making a joke, demanding attention—affection, too, if he can get it. He chases after life with an enviable verve. She told him not to let it get away.

∽

The pain was excruciating, raw and throbbing. Jamie fidgeted and gritted his teeth, his burned hands excavated to the bone were swathed and hanging from netting above his hospital bed. The sheet was tented above his cooked legs, and his face—his face was a swollen blob, blackened and bleeding.

Every day, masked attendants hoisted him into a stainless-steel tub brimming with bleach-treated water and scraped the dead tissue from his burns. He screamed and cried and cursed them. He bit and kicked and tried to make them stop. Every day, his mother tried to comfort him, her voice low and soothing, but Jamie grew more agitated, more demanding, more recalcitrant.

Jamie's aunt, Mickie Tigner, watched one day as Pam pulled herself up out of the wheelchair and dragged herself onto Jamie's hospital bed. She crawled closer and closer until she was only inches from her son's scorched face.

"You thank God for your pain," she whispered, tears spilling down her face. "I can feel nothing."

Such powerful admonitions became so common, Jamie can't remember that particular incident. Mickie says she'll never forget it.

Other things are burned into Jamie's memory.

~

By the time Jamie got to the fire hall that Saturday afternoon, he was pumped; ready to go. His friend Duwayne Capps jumped behind the wheel of truck No. 7724 and Jamie got on the back. Duwayne, thirty, was the father of two small children. He liked Jamie's spunk. He had arranged for Jamie to join the volunteer team. Larry Stephens ran from the feed and veterinary supply store he operated next to the fire hall and offered to drive one of the trucks. Pat Clark drove another.

When they saw the white smoke rising into the winter sky, they knew this fire was like none they'd ever seen before. More than a dozen fire departments from all across Johnson and Tarrant counties were racing to the blaze with sirens screaming.

Pushed by a forty-mph wind, the flames roared across 2,000 acres of grassland south of Farm Road 1187—and then jumped the road. The heat was intense. The trucks coughed and sputtered, choked by the thick smoke.

Jamie stood on the back of the truck, spraying water, but a squirt gun might have been as useful. The eighteen-foot-tall flames rolled through the high grass like ocean waves. Pat's truck stalled, and he jumped out and ran. Terrified, Jamie ran, too. In that instant, the wind shifted.

A wall of fire rolled over the trucks. Suddenly, Pat was on fire and running. Somehow, Duwayne got him into the cab. "I'll never forget the smell; burned skin, burned hair, and the burned-rubber smell of his boots," Duwayne says now. Frightened and fighting to keep the sputtering truck moving, Duwayne had no idea Jamie was lost in the inferno.

Jamie smelled his own flesh burning, felt the flames sear his skin.

He thought he was dying. "Oh, God. Oh, God, don't let me die," he screamed. Let me live, he prayed. Let me live. Don't take me today. Not today. I'm only sixteen. For one black moment, there seemed no hope.

"Then I rose up. I rose up out of those flames. It was like a great hand—the hand of God—pulled me up out of that fire. I could hear people shouting 'This way. This way.' I was running then, and I could see shadowy figures on the other side of the flames."

Jamie broke through the fire, and Duwayne and another fireman grabbed him and smothered his burning clothing with their bare hands, but his life had changed forever.

$\sim$

At Huguley Memorial Medical Center, his mother, frantic to see him, tried to push past hospital personnel, but only banged her wheelchair into the doorjamb. She tried again and again, calling to Jamie over and over as hospital employees tried to quiet her. Jamie called back, and she knew he was alive, but his words were unintelligible. Jamie was airlifted to Dallas' Parkland Memorial Hospital burn unit. For days, his eyes were swollen shut. He communicated by wiggling his toes. Visitors tied on sterile masks and gowns before entering his room. He felt isolated and adrift and worried that something might happen to his family, and he'd be left all alone.

He begged his mother to kiss him. Afraid to remove the sterile mask, afraid she'd cause him harm, she refused. But Jamie pleaded all the more. Finally, she relented. She kissed him then and every day after that.

Jamie was moved to Shriners Burns Institute in Galveston, and his father, insurance executive James Cashion, chartered a jet for the journey. Shriners was, for Jamie, its own life-changing experience. Who could forget the children there? Some had no ears, no feet. Little fingers had been burned away. Faces were twisted into grotesque masks. Doctors wanted to amputate his fingers, but his mother wouldn't allow it. His fingers are misshapen now, twisted by the fire, but useful. Any idea Jamie had about beauty and bravery was challenged. He saw that some people were forced to live a life they hadn't chosen. He was one of them.

The town of Joshua didn't forget the wounded firefighters or the one they lost, Larry Stephens, who died a few days after the blaze. Three Crowley firemen were also burned. At a blood drive, 400 people stood in line to give; there were benefit dances and bake sales. Volunteers waited at the stoplight, holding out firefighters' boots for donations.

When Jamie returned to school, he was something of a celebrity. Everyone knew what had happened. Joshua was like a warm cocoon. Duwayne went by Jamie's house and even helped change his bandages, but he didn't go often. It was too hard to see Jamie that way. Jamie's stepfather, Jim Harrison, shouldered most of the responsibility for Jamie's daily care. Each day, Jim left his job at the convenience store and came home to bathe Jamie's hands, pull off the dead tissue and re-dress the wounds. Then it was back to work.

Life outside Joshua was harder. In order to graduate with his class, Jamie had to attend a summer session at a Fort Worth school. As he stood in the registration line, pretty girls stared or looked away. He didn't know these people. They didn't know him. He called his mother in tears. "You've got to come and get me," he demanded.

"If you come home today, you'll have to go back tomorrow," she said. She might as well have said, "Life goes on, Jamie. You go on, too."

Now he can't remember the exact number of corrective surgeries he endured—between seven and ten over the next year and a half. Some released his fingers. Some freed scar tissue so he could open his mouth wider. Some improved the appearance of the burns on his face. He was stoic about the results.

"It happened, and nothing's going to change it," he says. "I know I have to make the best of what I've got. I'm lucky I've got a face there."

Jamie tried not to think about his appearance. He got busy. He volunteered in political campaigns—a sheriff's race, a senator's bid for election. Then Texas Governor Ann Richards appointed him to the Governor's Committee on People With Disabilities. He discovered he had a talent at karate (he has just earned his third-degree black belt), and he began teaching karate classes at a Fort Worth recreation center in a tough neighborhood. He's been at it more than six years now. He loves the kids but says he's not ready for children of his own—not yet, anyway.

Jamie first saw Summer Rich at a ball game. She was in the sixth grade, his cousin's friend. Summer grew into a blond beauty, a high school cheerleader who could have her pick of beaus. She picked Jamie.

She says Jamie's scars never bothered her. Theirs was a long off-again, on-again courtship that began when she was just fourteen. Jamie proposed during his grandparents' fiftieth wedding anniversary party at Joe T. Garcia's in 1995. He called Summer to the microphone, read a poem he'd written, and slipped a ring on her finger. He had ordered more than 300 roses. The waiters arranged bouquets of them in a heart shape on the floor. Jamie and Summer were in the center, dancing slowly to "Unchained Melody."

They married in September of 1996. She was twenty-six. He was twenty-nine. Like most young married couples who haven't established their own traditions, they fret about where they'll spend the holidays: his parents' house or hers. They try to balance time together and time alone. Jamie's mom always thought he'd go into politics. So did Duwayne. Jamie laughs, but sometimes behind the lively brown eyes, there is a veil of sadness.

Occasionally, he thinks about trying plastic surgery again to improve the facial scars. He shrugs. It's painful. It takes so long to heal. He doesn't like to be out of the game. "I think at this point I'll just keep what I've got," he says. But who knows? Maybe. Someday.

No Man's Land ✌ April 28, 2002

Texas ranchwoman Randee Fawcett loved the wide rocky stretch of West Texas that had been her inheritance but wondered what would happen to her legacy. Courtesy, the Fort Worth Star-Telegram. *© Carolyn Bahman.*

SONORA—Sometimes it seems as if barren lands have an extra measure of gravity; some mysterious pull that anchors people's hearts in the rocks and thin soil as surely as the wind stirs the sand. People fight savagely to defend these waterless places, and deep in some pool of knowing they are persuaded that it is only here that they belong. For them it is the very center of the earth.

Texas rancher Randee Fawcett is a veteran of stony ground. For more than 100 years her people have owned the rocky 17,500 acres near Sonora that she calls the Encino Ranch. An only child, she inherited the ranch from her mother. Once, she was certain that she would be just one more in a long line of ranchers who would care for this thirsty land, but now she can't see the future so clearly.

She expected drought, tornadoes, and hail to visit her property. She knew predators and the killing bitterweed would take a toll on her herds of cattle and flocks of sheep and goats. At fifty-four, Randee has faced down all those calamities and more. Raised to stand by her decisions and trust her instincts, she is a woman with a no-nonsense reputation for getting the job done, a plain talker who doesn't whine and is proud of her heritage. She has always known that the ranching way of life takes a gambler's grit and an evangelist's confidence—and she's got plenty of both.

Still, she could not guess all that was coming to test her spirit. There are hundreds of female ranchers in Texas. In some ways their stories are all the same—but in important ways they are not.

This is part of Randee's story.

Randee puts the new sand-colored Cadillac Escalade's heavy-duty grill smack against the bump gate as she has a thousand times before and steps firmly on the gas. The luxury SUV muscles across the cattle guard as the gate swings open. The wide gate slap-slap-slaps the chilly air as it rockets shut on a tight spring hinge.

Randee's hands are small on the wheel; her fingernails painted red. There's a large green tourmaline ring on her right hand, a souvenir of a South American vacation, and a small diamond tennis bracelet on her wrist. She wears a green T-shirt, jeans, and sneakers. Tennis shoes are easier than boots now.

She doesn't ride horseback anymore, either—not since the wreck; not since her legs were mangled, her heart broken. It's been nineteen years since that fateful day, nineteen years to remember—and forget. Trapped in a month-long coma, suspended between the here and the hereafter, she didn't know then that there had been a funeral.

She couldn't understand that Keyes, her only child, had been lost forever in the rubble of the overturned car. Her marriage was already unraveling that summer day. She and Keyes were at San Angelo's edge when the car lurched out of control and tumbled wildly across the median. Earth and sky, life and death curled together—but she can't remember why. She was told that there was no other car involved. Did it matter? Her baby was gone—and at only ten. Almost two decades have passed, and she just recently sold his horse.

The insulin pump under her shirt clicks occasionally, feeding a pre-programmed dose through a tiny shunt in her abdomen. She doesn't think about it or about the ambulance ride to a San Angelo emergency room only a few days earlier where doctors said she had sudden-onset glaucoma, a potentially blinding condition that was arrested with laser surgery.

Randee has been insulin-dependent since she was diagnosed with diabetes as a child. She's coped with the frustrations and the consequences her entire life, but there's no time to think about that now. The truckers are on the way and the work isn't finished. Randee is selling her flocks of sheep and goats. With the help of two black-and-white sheepdogs called Seis and Mack, four riders are driving more Rambouillet ewes with their lambs into the corrals that everyone calls the "new pens," even though this collection of metal chutes and enclosed yards is at least thirty years old.

Some 800 lambs born in the fall have already been sold to a buyer in San Angelo who, in turn, has already sold them to someone in Colorado. This sale of sheep comes earlier than usual—an entire month earlier than sheep are ordinarily sold. It is a thirty-day gamble that Randee and her husband and business partner, Bobby Doran, hope will pay off.

The lambs weigh less than they will in a month—only about eighty-five pounds each—but those pounds must be measured against the cost of feed. It's the sort of wager many Texas ranchers are forced to make as a killing drought turns south Texas pastures into wastelands. There is no grass to feed their stock.

Droughts are always punctuated with stingy rain here and there, but it's never enough and seldom at the right time or in the right place. The last time the Encino felt the cooling splash of rain was November, months away from the growing season. For days before the roundup, an evil wind punished the earth, dropping a veil of sand over the land and driving everyone indoors.

Then, just as Bobby and three cowboys begin to herd the sheep into traps, a cold, drenching rain fills the bar ditches, leaving puddles on the caliche road and muddying the ground around the house and barns. Randee worries that the livestock trucks won't be able to get in, but there is no need to fret. It is not enough rain; not enough to stop the trucks, and not nearly enough to bring back the grass.

"I've worked my whole life to improve the stock. I've bought better bulls and cows, kept better rams and ewes. Now I have to sell these animals, because we just can't keep feeding," she explains.

Sheep buyer Bill Weatherby sits in a metal rocking chair more suitable for a lawn than the middle of a dusty room at Compton Livestock Company in San Angelo. Wearing a billed cap with the logo of Bentwood, the local country club, and a short-sleeved blue shirt that stretches snugly across his barrel chest, he chews on an unlit San Antonio-made Travis Club cigar. He gave up lighting the smokes years ago, but that doesn't go for chewing. He gnaws through two cigars each day. He rocks and waits for the trucks from the Encino to arrive.

Randee beats the trucks by hours.

A stiff wind chases her into the dingy white house that serves as Compton's offices in San Angelo's livestock district. She slams the door, then turns to face the buyer.

"Well, I hope you've been able to sleep since you stole all those lambs from me," she growls. Her face is a serious scowl, but her hazel eyes smile.

"I been sleeping good. Never better," he says, then chomps down on the cigar.

It is the beginning of a good-natured banter, a contest of sorts that masks the fact that Randee really has won this round in the buying-and-selling game. Since contracting with Bill the week before at seventy-eight cents a pound, the lamb market has taken a dip. She knows it and is glad. He knows it and must shrug it off—but they both know the game isn't over.

Bobby has stayed at the ranch to help load the trucks, Randee driving ahead to meet the driver and to participate in an Internet auction of 100 of their calves. It is the first time they've tried this method of selling livestock, but they both like the idea of leaving the animals in the pasture until after a sale is complete, avoiding the stress of shipping the animals to market and then trucking them back home if the price isn't right. Shipping stress can be costly to both cattle and sheep. Lambs can drop sometimes as much as four pounds from pasture to scales. It's important to unload the trucks quickly. The sheep are then herded onto a large scale in groups, then the weight is recorded and divided by the number of animals in the group for an average weight that will determine the final size of Randee's check.

The longer it takes for the truck to arrive, the longer to unload, the hotter the sun, the less the sheep will weigh. Every ounce means money in someone's pocket. At the end of the day, she is satisfied with the lamb sale, but the calf sale is a disappointment. At Producers Livestock Auction just around the corner from Compton's, Stan Newsom, a lanky cattle buyer in a dusty black Resistol hat and Wranglers stuffed into the tops of custom-made boots, is polishing off a plate of fried eggs and waiting for the Internet auction to start. He's in charge of the sell. He and Randee hunker down in front of the single computer screen in the corner of the room. They are both optimistic.

Randee and Bobby hope the Internet will bring them buyers from out of state, buyers with green pastures. "This way, you get buyers from all over the country, and if you don't get the price you want you don't have to haul them back home," Randee says. There is little give-and-take, then finally an offer worth entertaining. Randee shifts in the chair and thinks. No. It's not enough. She sits tight betting that something will give, but it doesn't. She keeps the calves.

She is disappointed, but it's not the first time. "You have to have faith that everything will work out for the best," she says. It does. A few days later Stan locates an out-of-state buyer who contracts for the calves at a price that makes her smile. "We were relieved to be able to find a home for them at a price we can accept," she says. "So I guess the Internet was good for us."

～

Randee is always looking for that innovative twist. Like most Texas ranchers, she leases land to hunters and depends on that revenue. At least thirty gas wells dot her land, too, but she is always at war with the oil companies. "Those guys come out here and throw their trash all over everyplace. It makes me mad," she says. Never shy about venting her anger, she once left a large bag of garbage on the oil company's doorstep.

"They got the message," she says.

Still, ranchers must be adaptable to survive. A couple of years ago, Randee became one of the first in this southern region of the Edwards Plateau to try the Australian method of baling wool rather than putting it up in bags. "I went to a woolen mill, and after I saw that, I knew baling was the way to go," she says.

This willingness to find another way may be her biological heritage, a legacy passed down from kinsmen determined to build a home in this rocky land. Her great-grandfather, Robert Francis Halbert, came from Alabama to this desolate corner of Texas long before Sonora's boundaries were drawn in 1891. At least by 1900, maybe earlier, he and his wife owned large tracts of land and hauled water in by wagon, paying a dollar a barrel. He lived to be ninety-six and died in a San Angelo hospital as his wife's funeral service was being conducted.

They had two children, Robert Alpha and Suelena Omega. Robert Alpha is Randee's grandfather. He was a respected and adaptable rancher who met his wife, Annie Battie Huggins, at Brownwood's Howard Payne College. Randee's mother, Bobbie Halbert Fawcett, was their daughter. She, too, was a person of uncommon grit.

In 1939, Bobbie's father sent her to Europe hoping to broaden her horizons. She and nineteen friends were on a ship bound for home the day Poland was invaded. One evening as everyone gathered for dinner, the dining salon was plunged into darkness. The ship had been torpedoed and was sinking. Bobbie and her friends were plucked out of the sea by the crew of a Norwegian freighter. Soon after, she wed a handsome West Point graduate, but when he was killed in World War II, she went home to Sonora and began her ranching career in earnest. She married Lee Fawcett, a man whose family also ranched thousands of acres south of Sonora. Randee is their only child.

When Randee was only five or six her father and grandfather bought a ranch in Missouri. It was the 1950s and a withering drought held Texas in an unforgiving grip. Randee's dad and grandfather meant to move their livestock to Missouri until the drought was over. The family lived in a motel while houses and barns were built, but little Randee was itching to come home.

"I did not care for the Missouri lifestyle … so it wasn't long before I griped enough that I got to come back to Texas," she says. She lived with ranch hand Pedro Samaniego, his wife, Margareta, and their children. Her mother came home before Randee started school. Her dad traveled back and forth between the two ranches.

After the drought ended, Randee's grandparents came back to Texas, but her father kept the Missouri ranch until the late 1970s, she says. "He sold it and that was the first time he ever had some money to do with what he wanted, but then he got sick and never got to enjoy it," Randee remembers. Lee Fawcett died in 1979 of congestive heart failure.

∼

Randee and Bobby live in the low-slung house her parents built in the 1950s. Nestled under an ancient oak tree, it is head-quarters for the Encino Ranch, but Randee and her first husband remodeled it when it seemed as if their life together would never end. It is the place she came to after the wreck—alone, the marriage finished, only the divorce left to go. It is here that she willed herself to walk again. First with a walker, then with a cane, and finally on her own, with only a small limp as an outward reminder of that terrible day. Doctors said it would never happen, she would always be a cripple. They were wrong. Here her life had purpose, meaning, direction. "Someone had to take care of this place," she says. "It was going to be me."

She made mistakes, she says. She played too hard, resented too deeply, and finally set about letting go of all the old hurts. She allowed the heart-deep wounds to heal, the gratitude to flood in, she says.

She concentrated on running the ranch and in the end, she says, she found happiness. Now she and Bobby share the house, and their lives, with a cheerful menagerie. Buck is the barking Chihuahua; Rio Grande, a handsome white Labrador; Changa Mae, a flat-faced mongrel; Curly Sue, a sweet-tempered mutt that likes to lie close to a black-and-white cat called Bandit. The two Manx cats, Tuffy and Freddy, loiter in the bedroom. Bobby's dog, Colorado Bull Dog, a black-and-white bull terrier, is pouting because his master left him home on shearing day. He lies in the sun, tears wetting his wrinkled face. Curly Sue licks away the moisture. Chili, a grinning brown Lab with a graying muzzle and a bad case of arthritis, stays outside. When his first owner died, he, too, got a death sentence, but Randee said, "Bring him to me."

She always thought she'd leave this land to her son and that it would remain in the family for generations to come, but she knows that dream will never be fulfilled. Once she thought of adopting a daughter, someone who would care for the ranch as she had—not a child, a grown woman who had become her friend. But in the end, she decided against that plan.

Randee prepares bottles to feed two motherless Spanish goats, two abandoned baby deer, a calf and two lambs she named David and Flop. When she calls, half a dozen registered miniature donkeys press to the fence, hoping to get an affectionate pat.

Life is not easy, but it is interesting. "I have learned something new every day, and the decisions that need to be made affect how much bread we have on the table," she says. "I really try to think things out."

But one riddle won't be solved. Who will inherit this land? Who will love it as she does? Who will bend to the endless responsibility and at last discover the shape and color of their own heart? Who belongs here at the very center of the earth?

The Hardest Ride & July 31, 2005

Rancher Steve Murrin cherishes moments with his independent wife, Dashelle. Courtesy, the Fort Worth Star-Telegram. © *Jill Johnson.*

AS SOON as she finishes the last bite of cabbage and cornbread at Mama Lou's Country Kitchen, a tiny four-table soul-food eatery in the heart of Fort Worth's Como neighborhood, Dashelle Murrin reaches for her lipstick. She's fond of saying, "Keep your wings level and your lipstick on," and she takes her own advice. But like most things in her life, applying lipstick has its own ritual, a time-worn groove that lifts the most ordinary moments to another level, making every deliberate action a celebration of her own singular, determined life. It is the life she was always meant to live, she says, but only a miracle made it possible.

Dashelle is one of Cowtown's most respected horsewomen, a breeder of Holsteiner and Oldenburg horses and a cutting-horse enthusiast known for her sportsmanship—and her independent spirit. She rode in the amateur division of the National Cutting Horse Association's Summer Cutting Spectacular, which ends today, but after months of practice and preparation, she finished with a score of 206, not terrible but not good enough to move to the final rounds.

She is tall and lean with ramrod-straight posture, and it's easy to see why she was once a Neiman Marcus model whose regal bearing made almost everyone think she was from Europe instead of Burleson, fourteen miles south of Cowtown—but that was before the auto accident and the limp that made modeling impossible. The limp is noticeable now only when she's tired, and even then it's as hard to see as the extra quarter-inch that's been added to her boot heel.

At Mama Lou's, Dashelle retrieves a bulging Le Sportsac makeup bag from her purse and pulls out a round mirror with Neiman Marcus engraved on the silver case. She carefully outlines her full lips with a pencil, starting with the very pronounced Cupid's bow. It's the first of a three-step process.

Her friend, Valjeanne Rutledge, Val for short, picks a sliver of fried chicken off Dashelle's plate and pops it in her mouth. Val has already polished off her own hungry-man portion of meatloaf and pinto beans, but she wants a tiny taste of the chicken, too.

"Now that's good," she says in an exaggerated Texas drawl, then wipes her mouth and fishes around for her own lipstick. She slathers the color between her pinched lips in two quick motions and fluffs her red hair. She's done.

Dashelle is just getting started. She paints her lips with Chocolate Impulse, her favorite shade (she doesn't fool with light colors). Gloss goes over that. There's no paint on her short, rounded nails, and her thick fingers are long and strong with swollen knuckles that hint of future arthritis. Her wedding ring is a plain band, but several silver bracelets adorn her brown arm. She tucks the lipstick and mirror back into her bag and pulls out her Armani sunglasses. She's ready to go.

Actually, Dashelle has been on the go since at least five-thirty A.M., when she let the cattle dogs out of the kennel behind the 1930-vintage ranch house she shares with her husband, "Cowboy" Steve Murrin. "Cowboy" Steve is a rancher and former city councilman. He is also a Cowtown character who is sometimes spotted in TV commercials and is known as much for his white hair, handlebar moustache, and western accoutrements as he is for the Texas-style parties he sells at several Stockyards locations and at his West Fork Ranch on the edge of town. After twenty-one years of marriage (her first and his second), he says Dashelle would get along fine without him, but he couldn't make it without her. "In two weeks, I'd run off in the ditch," he declares.

In 1985, only a miracle kept him from testing that sentiment.

The coolness of fall hung in the air that October evening. On a whim, Dashelle climbed into a pickup with a friend, Laura Miller, a dressage teacher, who was taking a sick horse to Texas A&M University for treatment.

The women were on Highway 6 near Marlin as twilight wrapped its dusky wings around the bare fields that stretched along the narrow roadway. They were looking for a place to stop so they could check the horse. A light rain had just begun to fall, and as they rounded a curve, they could see a roadside park only a few yards ahead. It was the perfect place to pull over—but it was much too far to reach in this lifetime.

At that moment, an eighteen-wheeler roared around the curve, its cab already jackknifed against the heavy trailer. It was sliding toward them, its headlights blazing through the gathering gloom.

There was no place to go. No time to think.

In that split second before the impact pitched her headlong through the windshield, Dashelle knew with certainty she was plummeting into a crucible that would brand her as one of its own forever.

"God, help me," she shouted, but her voice was lost in the thunder of breaking metal and glass.

One minute her friend was at the wheel, the next she was gone forever. The truck driver was dead, too, and so was the horse, but Dashelle was alive, pinned inside the big rig's mangled engine, sticky with blood, her left elbow a mushy sack of shattered bone, her right leg splintered. She was drowning in pain.

A man in a dark coat peered down at her through the wreckage. "I'm a minister," he said. "What can I do?"

"Pray," she said—and then, "Don't leave me." She stretched her hand through the coffin of twisted metal. He took her hand and stayed with her while an emergency crew cut her out of the wreckage. He went with her to the Waco hospital, too, and waited until Steve arrived.

When Dashelle's friend, Val, got the news, she gathered up a bag of makeup and struck out for Waco. "Well, I knew immediately Dash would need lipstick," she says. But when she saw her friend, in casts and bandages, her eyes swollen, her face and lips cut and stitched, she knew it would be a long while before Dashelle could use lipstick again. She waited until she was alone and then Val cried.

The mystery man checked on Dashelle a few days later and explained that he'd taken a job with a church in Fort Worth. "When you're well enough, please call me," he'd said, and gave her the church's number.

Later, after several surgeries to repair her crushed leg and arm, torn lips, and lacerated face, Dashelle did call, but no one at the church had ever heard of the man.

"If he wasn't an angel, he was surely sent by God to be with me," she says. "It's a miracle I survived."

~

Recovery was slow. Steve and Dashelle were living in town while Steve served on the city council. One day, Mark Miller, the husband of the friend who died in the wreck, knocked on Dashelle's bedroom window. His life had been broken and changed, too, but he wanted to lift her spirits. He stood outside the window holding the reins of Dashelle's horse. Tears streamed down his face.

She saw him only faintly through a liquid curtain of sorrow.

Dashelle was a long way from well. She spent close to a year in a wheelchair, then there were crutches and, finally, a cane. As soon as she could drive, she visited her friend's grave.

Friends say they saw only Dashelle's usual stubborn resolve as she fought to get well, to ride again, and to carry on with the life she almost lost, but Dashelle suffered more than broken bones and torn tissue—she ached with survivor's guilt.

Slowly, the broken parts mended. Pink skin replaced the scabs. The feeling of culpability lifted.

Christmas came and the Murrins went to Val's house to celebrate. "Cowboy" Steve stuck Christmas ribbons all over Dashelle and made her wheelchair pop a wheelie as he rolled her through the house. Dashelle laughed. It was the sound of life.

"He's loving her," Val remembers thinking.

At last Dashelle was strong enough to ride, but riding wasn't enough. She insisted on saddling her own horse. Even now, her left elbow is a gnarled knot that will not fully extend. Back then, it was weak and stiff, but she ignored the pain and stubbornly tried to lift the heavy saddle onto the horse. Again and again, the saddle crashed to the ground, and with each failure, Dashelle set her jaw and tried again.

"Oh, it broke my heart to watch her throwing that saddle up there over and over," Val says. "But she was going to ride again and saddle the horse herself again. She always believed it would happen, and it did."

~

Dashelle doesn't call the horrific car wreck a turning point. That came in a more private moment only a few years ago, she says.

Dashelle was the only child of rodeo performers Shirle and Johnny Maines. Shirle had been raised in luxury in Chicago, the child of wealthy parents. Her mother was a socialite, her father a respected stock trader at the Chicago Board of Trade. Shirle grew up with nannies and servants and learned to ride dressage at an early age. But in the span of one short year, she lost both her parents and her brother to accident and illness. They weren't around when she fell for a Texas rodeo cowboy and moved to Fort Worth. Johnny Maines was an announcer and bucking horse rider. Shirle was a trick rider. Dashelle became part of the rodeo show by the time she was seven or eight—but it was not an entirely happy family.

"My father wanted a son," Dashelle says. "I paid the price for that."

Dashelle took competition seriously, and by the time she was in high school, she was not only an accomplished horsewoman but also a swimmer with Olympic potential. After graduation, she enrolled at Arlington State College, the forerunner of the University of Texas at Arlington. She was the only woman competitor on the men's swim team.

Her father never attended any of her meets, she says, and she resented it. He died while she was in college, but by then divorce proceedings were in the works.

Johnny Maines was in his fifties when the end came, and Dashelle had no idea that he was proud of her.

She wouldn't know until years later when she found his wallet with a newspaper clipping of one of her swim meets carefully tucked inside.

"Why couldn't he have just said something?" she asks. A prickling animosity needled her for years. Then, only a couple of years ago, when she converted her family films from eight-mm to VHS, she found something surprising. Watching those films was a catharsis, an unexpected moment of forgiveness and understanding. It was, she says, transforming. A deliverance.

Her father stood before the camera, but this time she saw him not as her daddy but as a man with his own set of hurts and disappointments, his heart bound by invisible chains, the weight of unexplained burdens holding him back.

"I came to realize it wasn't his fault," she says.

∼

If Dashelle questioned her father's love, she is secure in her husband's devotion. He cherishes her, say friends, and he proves it in unusual ways such as tucking the laundry tags he pulls off his starched shirts and jeans into her purse and pockets—little reminders that he's thinking of her. She hides cards for him to find. Once, he gave her a case of WD-40 and a little whisk broom for her pickup truck. It's one of her favorite gifts, not far behind the golf cart with the West Fork brand on the side that he presented to her so she could scoot down to the barn and back more easily. He has one, too.

Friends who know them well say they are opposites who were made for each other. At sixty-seven, Steve is still a free spirit who loves company and has never had two days alike in his life. She is happiest when elevating routine to ritual.

She is a neatnik who makes the bed every day and dresses it with a dozen fancy pillows. The bedroom chair might as well be his closet. He piles his clothes there, he says, but she doesn't pick up after him. "She controls her stuff and leaves his alone," Val says.

He never throws anything away. She doesn't stash unnecessary items.

He drinks. She doesn't.

"It's not a moral issue," Val says. "She drank in college, of course, but she lost the taste for it. Now she watches me drink."

Although raised as a Catholic, Steve never attends Mass, but he says Dashelle's "great faith is one of the most important things about her." She "doesn't wear religion on her sleeve," he says, but she is a stalwart of her nondenominational church and a leader in the prayer group there. "We don't go into deep discussions about it, but I totally respect her beliefs," he says.

At fifty-eight, Dashelle knows what she likes, too: people, not parties. When they do attend a party, they go in different cars. She drives her four-year-old Dodge diesel pickup with the dent in the side. He arrives in a small recreational vehicle dubbed "the turtle." She leaves when she's ready, which is almost always before Steve does.

The sun never catches her sleeping. Steve doesn't get up until she calls him to breakfast. By then, she has already tended to the dogs and the horses. "Horses need a routine," she says. Breakfast is at seven-thirty A.M. each day. You can set your watch by it.

She always uses cloth napkins and sets the table with a fork, knife and spoon. Even the way she sings out "Briiick-fast" while standing at one end of the long hall, the syllables resonating with a conspicuous nasal twang, has become part of the morning ritual. Before she clears the table, neighbor Jimbo Calhoun or someone else drops in for coffee.

The routine varies only on the mornings she pulls a horse 115 miles to Wichita Falls to work with a cutting-horse trainer. On those days she leaves at four A.M.

It is, she says, exactly the life she was meant to live—an unrelenting destiny that has been pulling her forward since childhood, but only a miracle made it possible to live it.

PART SEVEN

Family Ties

ૹ ૹ ૹ
ૹ ૹ
ૹ

River of Tears ❧ June 22, 2003

Linda Delaney has become reclusive since learning of her mother's murder. Now, as the killer is brought to justice, she must face the truth. Courtesy, the Fort Worth Star-Telegram.

FAYETTEVILLE, Georgia— Investigator Bruce Jordan tore through the Clayton County evidence room. He ripped off box lids and quickly rummaged through the contents before moving to the next carton. A team of crime-scene technicians came behind him, sorting more carefully through the containers, but Jordan was looking for one damning bit of evidence that he knew would crack a series of Georgia murders that had gone unsolved for more than twenty-five years. It took Jordan, now a lieutenant colonel with the Fayette County Sheriff's Department, just ten minutes to locate a blood-stained cushion that had been listed on the original evidence report.

"This is it," he said, holding up what he knew was the key to the Flint River murders.

Almost a thousand miles away, in Fort Worth, Linda Delaney had no idea her life was about to change.

On New Year's Eve 2002, Jordan and his most trusted teammate, Sergeant Tracey Carroll, also of the Fayette County Sheriff's Department, telephoned Delaney. "We're going to re-open the case against Carl Patton," he told her. "I hope this is good news."

Delaney was stunned.

In October of 1977, her mother, Betty Jo Ephlin, a gregarious, headstrong Fort Worth native, had been murdered and her body dumped in Georgia's Flint River. Ephlin was one of five people who had died in a killing spree fueled by jealousy, revenge, and greed.

Carl Patton Jr., a swaggering tough guy who acted as a collector for his uncle's drug deals, had been the only suspect all those years ago. Delaney had always believed that the man could have been convicted then, but she said the Clayton County district attorney insisted that the blood evidence, semen samples—even the metal pipe with Patton's bloody fingerprints on it—weren't enough to convict.

Now Delaney is fifty-three, a single mother of three who has lived almost half her life with a ferocious anger and a prickling fear that had left precious little room for grief. She never talked about her mother's death, didn't cry, but she did have nightmares. She was suspicious, too, and moved often, hoping she'd be hard to find if Patton should come looking. Then, in February of this year, Jordan led a posse into Patton's house in rural Georgia during the early morning hours and arrested the man. Jordan and his team had everything the district attorney would need to go to trial, he said, but Patton surprised everyone by confessing to the five killings, saving himself from the death penalty, and receiving instead several life sentences.

Suddenly the law said that justice had been served, the crimes had been solved. Ephlin's killer was behind bars, and her daughter was expected to be grateful, relieved, but Delaney couldn't shed years of anger and resentment in the blink of an eye.

Important questions still disturbed her sleep, but now she would have to look to herself, not the law, for the answers. Why had this happened to her mother? Could she ever surrender her anger? Where would the answers take her?

⁓

More than a year ago, Jordan was slogging through cold case files while researching a true crime book, when he came across the

Flint River murders folders. He was surprised to find, after all these years, an evidence list so long and detailed. He was a high school kid when the crimes made sensational headlines, and one of the murders remained the only unsolved homicide in Fayette County during the long tenure of his friend, Sheriff Randall Johnson. (The other four killings fell into other counties' jurisdictions.) Jordan set the case aside, wondering if he could unravel the mystery, as much for his friend's sake as anything else. So in the fall of 2002, he and Sergeant Carroll began focusing on the victim who fell in their jurisdiction, Liddie Evans, who had a rare blood type. Jordan was sure that new DNA technology could help solve Evans' murder. He just didn't know that solving that crime would settle all five murders at once.

∼

Delaney knew she should have breathed easier when she got the news that Patton would spend the rest of his life in jail. But her stomach churned with a roiling anger when she learned that Patton's wife, Norma Patton, who had known about the crimes for years, had turned state's evidence and received no more than a slap on the wrist for her part in the murders.

For "concealing the death of another," Norma Patton received the maximum penalty under a 1977 statute in effect at the time of the murder: a $1,000 fine and a year's probated sentence. Delaney was infuriated, and the old resentment gnawed at her spirit with a new vengeance. She'd waited so long for justice. How could this happen?

Because Carl Patton had confessed and entered a plea bargain, there had been no trial, just a hearing. It was one more way of robbing the family of closure, Delaney thought. She didn't want to hear all the gruesome details of her mother's death, but in some awful way she needed to. She had to have some sign that it was really over.

That sign came last month, when Delaney was invited to an awards luncheon in Fayetteville, Georgia, to honor the team of investigators that solved the Flint River murders. Delaney, a part-time bookkeeper who mows baseball fields for extra cash, wanted to attend, but she couldn't scrap together the price of an airline ticket, and her car wouldn't make the long trip. Realizing how important this was to her, Delaney's oldest son, David Jones, thirty-four, said he'd split the cost of a rental car.

Maybe at least seeing the people who broke the case get a bit of deserved recognition would help revive her crumpled spirit. While she was in Georgia, Delaney meant to see Norma Patton if only from a distance. She wanted the woman to know that she was there. She wanted Norma Patton to understand that she was never going away. That alone would seem like something of a victory.

"For all these years, everything I've done has been for Mother," Delaney said. "Everything I do from here forward, I'm doing for me."

~

Linda Delaney coaches baseball for the Optimist Club today, but she never had much of a childhood herself. Before she turned fourteen, she was the primary caregiver for her little brother and a father stricken with multiple sclerosis, while her mother worked two jobs to pay the family's bills. And then, when she was sixteen, Delaney found her father dead after he shot himself in the head. Delaney was still reeling with grief over her father's death, when, two months after the funeral, her mother married a man ten years her junior. Delaney was at once angry and embarrassed. The marriage didn't last long, and her mother quickly married again—this time to a man named Wayne Ephlin, a long-haul truck driver. Delaney approved of the marriage, and the couple had one happy year together before Wayne Ephlin was killed in a fiery truck crash just outside Fort Worth.

After that, something in Betty Jo Ephlin changed, says Delaney. Betty Jo left Texas for California, and her life became a mystery to her family. Betty Jo had a raunchy sense of humor. She smoked and drank—and still managed to drag sunshine into every dingy room. She had a devil-may-care attitude that was appealing. Her collar-length hair was dyed as black as a crow's wing and was always neatly turned out. She fancied turquoise and silver jewelry and wore an eye-catching necklace that said "Oh Sh—." Always a jokester, she made friends easily and liked to stay out all night, but by 1977, the family realized that her life was taking a dark turn. She was keeping secrets, they knew.

"I've got to go away," Betty Jo confided to her sister one day in the summer of 1977. "I can't tell you where I'm going, because if anyone comes looking for me you can say you don't know where I am and you won't have to lie." She wouldn't say more.

In August she married Fred Wyatt, a Georgia truck driver with a prison record and a rap sheet that included armed robbery, auto theft, and drug dealing. Betty Jo never took his name and didn't tell her family about the marriage until September, when she introduced her daughter to him. Delaney and Betty Jo met at a Denny's in Fort Worth, and the minute Delaney laid eyes on the man, her skin prickled and her stomach turned over. This guy was bad news, and she knew it. Even more disturbing was her mother's appearance. Betty Jo had put on weight. She was bloated and blotchy. Her hair was a mess, and she was edgy and apprehensive. Wyatt was clearly in charge.

"He wouldn't let Mother say anything," Delaney remembered. "I'd ask her a question, he'd answer it. I asked her to go to the ladies room with me really just so we could talk, but he wouldn't let her go."

Delaney begged her mother to stay a few days with her. "We'll all go to Georgia together later," she pleaded, but Betty Jo wouldn't stay. That was the last time Delaney saw her mother alive.

∼

Why her mother would marry a man like Wyatt was one of the questions that always tormented Delaney. But when Betty Jo Ephlin met him in Georgia in the late 1970s, something sparked between them. The ex-con liked what he saw, a sassy, fun-loving woman always ready to push the envelope. Delaney is convinced that her mother did not know about Wyatt's prison record or that he had recently lived with a vindictive and jealous woman who called herself Marie Wyatt.

Surely Betty Jo Ephlin didn't know that Fred Wyatt had hired his nephew, Carl Patton, to kill Marie's husband so the two could be together—and that he'd gotten away with it. When Marie learned that Wyatt and Betty Jo were legally married, she was boiling mad and bent on revenge. She took out an insurance policy on Wyatt and forged his name; then she hired Patton to kill him for half the insurance money, according to police investigators. She wanted Wyatt's new wife to die first, say the authorities.

Wyatt was on a long-haul trip on October 13, 1977, when Patton and his childhood friend, Joe Cleveland, showed up at Betty Jo's home. She knew them, of course, and opened the door. She didn't know that they had already conspired to kill her.

After they killed her, they dumped her body in the Flint River.

In Texas, Betty Jo's family worried when she failed to call on her grandson's birthday. When Thanksgiving came and went without word, Delaney filed a missing persons report.

Wyatt was the next to go. When Wyatt returned from a trip, Patton shot him, put his body in a car and left it on the railroad tracks where it was sure to be hit by a train and look like an accident. That might have been the end of the killing spree except that Cleveland told his secret to his girlfriend, Liddie Matthews Evans, a mother of four. Evans told her mother, and when word got back to Patton, he decided to put an end to all the talking.

He killed his childhood friend first, then turned the gun on Evans. After she was dead, he ripped her jeans open with a knife and raped her corpse. "It was the last indignity I bestowed on her," Patton told the investigators in February. He was angry and blamed her for having to kill his friend. He dumped Cleveland's body in the Ocmulgee River, but threw Evans into the Flint River near where he'd disposed of Betty Jo's body a few months earlier.

In December of 1977, the Flint River flooded, and when the

muddy, swirling water receded, a duck hunter discovered Betty Jo's badly decomposed body on the Clayton County side of the waterway. Evans was found that same day—on the Fayette side of the county line. It was just the break Jordan would need twenty-five years later.

~

Delaney was numb when she learned that her mother's body had been found only a few days before Christmas of 1977. She flew to Georgia to identify the remains and was escorted by law enforcement officials to Patton's house and asked to list her mother's belongings on a steno pad. When she arrived, Patton was sitting in a living room furnished with her mother's things, reading the search warrant. His wife was wearing a vest Delaney had given to her mother.

Patton focused his steely eyes on Delaney. "You look just like her," he said.

Enraged by his cocksure demeanor, Delaney attacked Patton, throwing herself at him in a blind fury. Law enforcement officials pulled her away, and she demanded that Norma Patton remove the vest.

During his confession twenty-five years later, Patton said that he can't remember if money changed hands for Betty Jo's murder, but it is certain that he ended up with many of the dead woman's possessions: living room and bedroom furniture, her clothes—even family photo albums were found at his home. Among other things, Marie Wyatt had taken the dining room table Betty Jo had been sitting at when she was shot. Delaney identified more than 100 items belonging to her mother in Patton's and Marie Wyatt's homes. Marie Wyatt would never be brought to justice in court. She died a few years ago of cancer.

~

Jordan wasn't trying to solve Betty Jo Ephlin's case when he cracked the Flint River murders. Floodwaters had pushed her body across the river, out of his jurisdiction. Evans was in his county. It was Evans' rare type-A blood that had soaked the floral cushion Jordan found in the evidence room—cushions that had been taken from Patton's camper.

"I always told my people that we didn't have to solve all these murders," Jordan said. "I always said we had to solve just this one." He hadn't counted on Patton confessing to all the crimes.

But Delaney knew that without Jordan's work, her mother's murderer would still be free. So on a recent day in May, Delaney packed her own tokens of gratitude: small plaques she had made for Jordan and his partner and a larger one for the entire team. She got in a rental car with her son and drove fifteen grueling hours to present them at an awards luncheon held at a small restaurant.

There were only twelve other guests, including the host, Sheriff Johnson. No wives. No brothers. No other victim's family members. But it didn't matter. For Delaney it was a singularly significant meeting.

For years Delaney had pushed and prodded and nagged Clayton County law enforcement officials to try the case against Patton. She had prayed angry prayers asking God to strike down the man who'd killed her mother. The indignation swelled and festered and demanded all her attention. There was no room for grief, no time for tears. Now unexpected tears were often close to the surface.

When it was Delaney's turn to speak, she held up her plaques. "To Bruce Jordan. My heartfelt thanks for a job well done. Linda Delaney," she read.

She hadn't meant to cry, but as she handed the awards to Carroll and Jordan, the tears came unbidden just as they had the day before when she stood on the Flint River bridge remembering her mother. "You gave me back hope when I didn't have any left," she said, and her voice cracked.

What had been vital two hours earlier had vanished like a river fog burned off by the heat of a Georgia sun. The desire to confront Norma Patton was gone.

"I don't need to do that anymore," she said. "She's just not important." Delaney drove out of town without a backward glance.

∼

As night fell, Delaney admitted that for a long time she had been mad at her mother, angry and frustrated and puzzled that such a spirited, funny woman had chosen to get tangled up with the likes of Fred Wyatt and all the rest. "What could she have been thinking of?" Delaney asked.

It's a question that's come to her a thousand times in the past twenty-five years, and she knows it's easy to find excuses—but impossible to uncover the truth. She and her children and even her grandchildren are forced to live with the consequences of her mother's choices—her mother's secrets. Now she must find a way to keep from drowning in the sorrow of it all.

Adam's Way ❧ June 25, 2006

All Adam Murray wanted for his graduation was a yearbook, even though his picture wasn't in it. Courtesy, the Fort Worth Star-Telegram. *© Jill Johnson.*

IT IS late May, a few days before high school graduation, and Adam Murray is showing me some of the places he and his family have lived. I am behind the wheel, threading our way through heavy traffic on Arlington's busy Collins Street. Adam is eighteen, a big kid with a tender heart who loves the idea of family so much he has become his mother's parent, insisting she find treatment for her drug habit—and loving her when she slips.

They've lived in hovels and homeless shelters and now a subsidized apartment, but he has never considered running away. His mother needs him too much, he says, and he won't leave her. This overwhelming need is Adam's blessing and his misfortune.

Both are molding him into the man he is becoming—one who shatters all the stereotypes. Unlike so many teens with turbulent backgrounds, Adam has a quiet confidence, a comfortable attitude. He is easy to be with, an old soul with an inner compass who instinctively understands the importance of loyalty, honesty, and hard work.

He has lived in a house filled with shouts and threats, dark anger and explosive resentment. He has seen his own family crumble. He knows what it is to be adrift in the wide, inhospitable world. But this is his only family, and on this day he talks of one day building a house large enough for all of them: his mother, his sister, maybe a wife, and some children of his own—with a smaller house out back for his dad. He laughs. It is, he knows, an impossible dream.

Adam leans forward, peering through the windshield, trying to recognize some obscure landmark. "There," he says, pointing, and I take a quick left turn. He motions again to the right, and we drive through a small complex of single-story apartments facing a barren courtyard. The gray paint is nicked and peeling. A dumpster in the middle is overflowing, and a stiff wind blows bits of paper about.

"Shabby, isn't it?" he asks. We circle the courtyard and when we reach the exit, Adam turns and looks back over his shoulder. "Pitiful," he says.

It is a simple, clear-eyed assessment. He is not embarrassed or ashamed. He can't change what has been, and so he focuses on the future.

∾

Adam has no tattoos, no piercings. He doesn't smoke or drink or do drugs, and he doesn't run with those who do. He has watched his parents do all of that. He says he'll be fine if he does exactly the opposite. He considers that irony, and a boyish smile tugs at the corners of his mouth. His round cheeks are smooth and his hands dimpled at the knuckles. His newly trimmed hair is combed straight across his forehead and, like most teens, he wears baggy shorts and a T-shirt, but Adam is far from ordinary.

We drive past his father's two-story house, then circle past Arlington's Martin High School. Over the past four years he has attended at least nine different schools. He liked Martin best, even though his family was teetering on the edge of destruction when he enrolled there.

We turn toward Kennedale and meander down country lanes in a semi-rural area until we find the tiny bungalow where his earliest memories are anchored. He twists in the seat, points up a road, remembers the people who lived there. He's all smiles.

This was a good time in his life. His mother volunteered at the community youth association. His father's carpet-cleaning business was doing well. Adam was a standout on the baseball and football teams and won some trophies. And then some secret memory rises up, and he falls quiet. Like any teenager, Adam answers questions but offers little more. With prodding, he talks about the night a few years ago when he and his mother moved into a shelter for battered women, and about the day last year when a friend took them to the Presbyterian Night Shelter, one of few shelters in North Texas that accepts families with teens. He listened to the radio and looked out the window and tried not to think as they drove, he says. "When we got there, an old man was sitting in a recliner in the yard. I looked at him and thought, 'This is so pitiful,'" he says.

The hum of the engine fills the space between us. "Being homeless is not as scary as people think," he says at last.

Adam has a job and a dream, but if he could have his heart's desire right now, he knows what he'd choose. "I want my mother sober," he says, and for a moment the boy is gone, replaced by a man who knows exactly what he wants—and has no idea how to get it.

~

At Christmas, Adam wanted just two things: a set of sheets and his high school annual. He got both those things—and more—but the yearbook, that record of childhood's end, was a disappointment. Classes had already begun when Adam transferred to Western Hills High School, but according to one of his teachers, Adam had no trouble catching up in his computer class and soon was working on the college level.

Adam fit in and didn't take himself too seriously, the teacher says, but he knows almost nothing about Adam's background. He shows me plans for a two-story house surrounded by a forest of trees that Adam designed in three days. The house has a music room with a grand piano and a game room with pool table. The teacher sees only "someone with great potential." The teacher also sees the boy who fills the holes in his soul with food and includes a vending machine in the atrium of the house he designed.

In years to come, it will be hard for anyone to see that Adam attended Fort Worth's Western Hills High School at all. Because he enrolled late, Adam never had a senior picture taken. His image does not appear in that yearbook that he so wanted to own. Worse, there wasn't even a "photo not available" notice where his picture should have been. He wasn't captured in any candid shot either. There is no record of Adam.

"It's OK. My friends' pictures are there," he says as we navigate Arlington's busy streets. But he has had the yearbook for days and no one has signed it. There's not one sugary sentiment or macho taunt scrawled on the slick pages to memorialize the day.

"When does that happen?" he asks.

~

There are two creaky Chippendale-style chairs at the maple table in Pam Murray's tiny apartment kitchen. She coughs as she eases into one. The sound is deep and raw, her voice a sandpaper sigh. She lights a cigarette.

Pam is Adam's mother. She is forty-two, a big woman with shoulder-length brown hair and the pasty skin of someone who has been ill for a long while. She is also smart, articulate and witty—a cunning storyteller. For almost three hours she weaves a spellbinding tale of a childhood filled with sexual abuse, a dark place rife with anxiety and anger. She talks of getting high on pot with her parents, of a fractured family constantly on the move, of life on the streets at fourteen, of the frightening cruelty heaped by her common-law husband, Adam's father. She says that, until a few years ago when she injured her back, she always had a job, often working as a telemarketer.

She also talks about using every sort of street and prescription drug. She says she has tried to quit and has stayed clean for months on end, but stress always breaks her resolve. "That's how I numb up," she explains.

Eventually she lost sight of herself, abandoned all pride, cast off all belief in a new tomorrow. "I was so beat down I didn't even know who I was anymore," she declares in a hoarse whisper. She weeps and smokes and pulls at her long hair. "I have no faith in the human race anymore," she says.

She leans across the table and looks me in the eye. "When I was little, I had a dream," she says. "It's the only thing that got me through all the abuse. I dreamed I could change all this. I could have a family that was normal and loving."

～

Pam doesn't attend Adam's high school graduation. She's in detox. She uses both prescription and contraband drugs, but she had been clean for more than a year. Then, one day, the stress became too much, she says. She called Adam at work and told him she'd slipped. She wanted to wait until after graduation to start the program, but Adam said waiting wasn't an option. So she went as a sort of graduation present for her son.

On graduation day Adam moves along in the line of seniors dressed in green caps and gowns just as he has all year, calm and quiet, focused on some distant goal. His twenty-year-old sister is somewhere in the stands with her boyfriend, but Adam doesn't seem to care. He says his relationship with his only sibling has always been fractious.

His father is in jail.

Adam walks across the stage to receive that hard-won diploma as the speaker intones, "Adam Michael Murphy."

His name is Murray, not Murphy, but Adam never falters. He strides across the stage and takes the diploma and the proffered flower. The flower is to be a token of admiration and thanks that every graduate has been given to present to someone who had helped them through those high school years.

In the parking lot, after the ceremony is over and the hats have been tossed in the air, Adam says he'll just keep the flower.

"They got my name wrong," he says and doesn't turn around. His shoulders droop. Adam climbs into a van with his sister, but before they get away, Wanda and Harley Butler wave them down. Adam is surprised to see these old friends. He leaps out, all smiles. They have saved his day.

~

The Butlers are still in their thirties, but they were Adam's house parents in 2001 and 2002 when he and his sister lived at All Church Home for Children, a ninety-year-old Fort Worth institution that serves families in crisis. Adam's family was certainly in a state of emergency that year. His mother was serving a prison sentence for welfare fraud.

Pam Murray explains the crime by saying that the family was barely getting by and she was taking food stamps while failing to claim income she made as a telemarketer.

She received four-and-a-half years of probation for the crime—but as soon as she left the courthouse the terms of that probation went up in a puff of smoke as she lit a joint and took a drag—just to relieve the stress.

She says she'd been smoking pot since she was a tot and she wasn't about to stop. She continued to smoke, and naturally the mandatory urine checks kept coming back dirty. The court sent her to one rehab program after another, but it did no good. When Pam landed before the bench for the fourth time, she says the judge had had enough. "I couldn't believe they'd send me to the penitentiary for smoking pot," she says, tears flooding her eyes. "When the judge passed that sentence, I lost it," she says and begins to sob.

Now she says that going to the pen was the best thing that ever happened to her, but on the day she learned her sentence, she could think of only one thing. "I knew I had to find a place for my kids, and I wasn't going to leave them with their father." She sniffles and wipes her face with a tissue. All Church Home was the answer.

Those months were some of Adam's best. "Before I got to All Church Home, I pretty much accepted pretty much everything," says Adam. "When I got there, I learned that there are so many more things than what I had. I was there for two summers. We had passes to everything: Six Flags, Hurricane Harbor. . . . They showed me that I could have more," he says.

The Butlers were part of that influence. Standing with them in the parking lot after the graduation ceremony, Adam looks relaxed and so much younger than his eighteen years. Harley slaps him on the back. Wanda pats his shoulder. They are smiling and teasing. They appear carefree. A passerby might think they are family.

"I'm hungry," declares Harley. "Let's go eat."

They take Adam to Razzoo's and play catch-up. Later, Wanda tells me Adam is unusual. "I see it every now and then—a kid will come my way who is a great kid with a bad background. I don't know if someone along the way makes them want more or if it's just the way they are." She says Adam is trustworthy, truthful and loyal. "When he was at All Church Home, he didn't lie. He didn't steal. He didn't cuss his parents. He followed the rules. He said, 'Everyone loves me,' and he's right, everyone does love him," she says.

Adam was in trouble only once during his stay at the home, she says. He fought with a boy on the school bus and was suspended from class for a couple of days. "He said something about my mom," Adam explains, and it's clear that, after five long years, he still feels justified.

Adam's loyalty is firmly established. He will never abandon his mother. She needs him, and that need has made him resilient and resourceful and determined.

"Being needed is nice," he says. Now she needs him more than ever. He is the breadwinner, and his $6-an-hour job as a telephone troubleshooter for an Internet provider is the only money coming into the house. They are living without a net: no insurance, no credit, no savings, no car.

～

Adam is determined to beat the odds and make a better life for himself. He wants to be a video-game designer and dreams of going to school in Arizona, but he says he can't leave his mother until he is certain she can take care of herself. Pam says she will go with him wherever he goes.

He hasn't taken any of the college entrance exams and says he'd like to start at a small school, maybe a junior college first, but he doesn't know what to do next. He is a puzzling mix of man and boy. He thinks he may have to put school on the back burner for next year while he works, but he's thinking of the future.

"Life has taught me that the world is not an easy place, and that family is the most important thing," he says.

Adam is sure he'll fall in love one day and have a family of his own: a normal, loving family, the fulfillment of his mother's dream.

"I have a destiny," he says. "I'm just not sure what it is yet."

Reweaving History ℘ *November 19, 2006*

Kathleen Hicks and her mother Judge Maryellen Hicks (right) went searching for their white ancestor. Courtesy, the Fort Worth Star-Telegram.

"YOU DON'T choose your family. They are God's gift to you, as you are to them."

—Archbishop Emeritus Desmond Tutu in *God Has a Dream: A Vision of Hope for Our Time*

It has always been the messy stories that interest me most. I'm drawn to those subjects that don't fit easily into any box, the ones that, even when all the reporting is done, leave unanswered questions. Something in that silence speaks to mankind's deepest longings and most ferocious fears. It is a reality that the heart recognizes and from which it sometimes turns away.

It is the history that we've all carried on our backs through the millennia, a story embedded in the tangle of our DNA—the ancient whisper of the blood.

It is the untidy business of race in America.

And so it was that on a Saturday morning in early 2004, I found myself in a spacious townhouse surrounded by a collection of African art and the smells of cinnamon and brewing coffee. Family portraits lined the walls, and a cornucopia of breakfast rolls was artfully spread on the kitchen bar. I had come to learn the story of just one American family—a family with both black and white forebears, but a family that in every way defines itself as African American.

Former State District Judge Maryellen Hicks is known as a fiery champion of civil rights, an adamant supporter of the NAACP, and a woman enormously proud of her African heritage. But like thousands of Americans who identify themselves completely by their African lineage, she has at the very least one white forebear.

What, I wondered, did this family say about that white ancestor? What did they know for sure? Maryellen and her family were hesitant to hold their private history up to the public spotlight, but in the end they agreed.

I had no idea then that this hunt would lead me through decades of America's history and acquaint me with the wonders and the frustrations of DNA testing. I understood only dimly that the family's most cherished stories might take unexpected, even unwelcome, turns. And so *Star-Telegram* news researcher Marcia Melton and I started as all genealogists do, with the family stories.

"His name was Henry Durham," Maryellen said. "He was my grandfather's father, and he was white, but Mary was African." She leaned across the breakfast table and smoothed a golden finger across a framed photograph of her great-grandmother, a dark woman wearing a high-collared dress with a brooch at her throat. There is no photograph of Henry.

Maryellen took a deep breath. "This was a love story," she said, and so began the tale of one family's history and my search for just one man.

Henry had come from Ireland by way of Ellis Island, Maryellen said. One day, while riding through the countryside, perhaps in Indian Territory, he spied Mary and that one glance seared his heart and sealed his fate. He fell hopelessly in love with her.

They married and had many children.

Henry dreamed of owning his own farm, but when at last he was able to buy a place of his own, the family was harassed and tormented by angry neighbors who would not tolerate a white man living with a black woman and raising a family. At last the threats became so violent that one dark night, Henry and Mary loaded their family into a wagon and left the farm and most of what they owned behind.

Maryellen and her sisters did not know Henry or Mary Durham, but they do remember some of their children, particularly their own grandfather, Bruce Durham, and one of his brothers, William J. Durham, an attorney and civil rights defender who was close friends with Thurgood Marshall and later argued cases before the Supreme Court. Bruce moved from Greenville to West Texas and opened a taxi cab company, a barbershop, and a beauty salon in Odessa.

"He would always have someone drive him," remembered Maryellen's sister, Francis Parks, director of Students Offering Services at Syracuse University in New York. "He would get into the passenger side, and, at his invitation, we would often get into the back seat, and we'd be delighted. I don't remember ever seeing him write a check, but he would go into his pocket and pull out a wad of bills."

Maryellen and Francis have rich memories of their grandfather, and they are proud of the man he was, the businessman who wore dress shirts, never short sleeves, had his size-seven boots custom-made, bought his cars in Dallas, planted trees in front of his corner business in West Texas, and sent their mother to a university in the East.

"Here was a man who came out of the soil, and he encouraged his daughters and his granddaughters to go to university. He dreamed with them. He dreamed for them. He was most insistent that they stretch," Francis said. "Grandfather Bruce was a feminist. I always see him as the first feminist I ever met. He wanted his daughters and granddaughters to examine and challenge and explore. He could have marched with the suffragettes," she said.

Even if his philosophy had not set him apart, certainly his light complexion and European features would have. He was a man so fair-skinned that he could have easily passed for white, said his daughter Billie Jo Walton of Sherman. She remembered that at the train station, the conductor would often show him to the white section.

His granddaughter, Francis, remembered that fact, too. "He would say 'No, thank you,' and go into the coach where the colored folks sat. Our grandfather could have been a remarkable trickster. He could have passed, if he had chosen to. None of us can, but my grandfather could have without anyone turning a head," said Francis. "I imagined that he looked much like his father, my great-grandfather, but I don't know that."

It was easy to gather stories about Bruce, who died in 1961. But was he really the son of a white man who loved a black woman in a day when such love was forbidden by law?

We set to work.

〜

It didn't take long to discover that Bruce's father, Henry Durham, did not come from Ireland by way of Ellis Island, which opened in 1892. According to the 1880 U.S. Census, Henry was living in Wood County, Texas, with Mary and their first two children, Ella, six and Zach, three, at least a dozen years before Ellis Island opened. The census also lists Henry's place of birth as Texas and Mary's as Missouri. His occupation was barber.

But there is one other interesting notation in the census record: under the box for race, Henry is listed as a mulatto, a man of mixed race. That detail raises many questions. How was the census information taken? Did the census-taker simply assume that a light-skinned man living with a black woman had to be of mixed lineage, or did Henry declare that he was mulatto?

If Henry himself testified that he was mulatto, the question becomes more complicated, because the *family believes* that Henry was a white man. But in 1880 Texas, it was unlawful for whites and blacks to marry or to live together and raise a family.

It would be another eighty-seven years before the Supreme Court called any ban on interracial marriage unconstitutional.

Clearly, Henry's relationship with Mary was loving and long-standing. They had eleven children; ten survived, and he was there to help raise them all. Would he have claimed to be what he was not for love's sake?

We turned to DNA testing for the answer.

Several labs specialize in testing for African lineage. Howard University has thousands of samples concentrating on areas of West and Central Africa, where most blacks brought to the U.S. as slaves had their beginnings. The DNA taken from an African-American woman will likely point to family origins in places such as Nigeria, Benin, Togo, Ghana, Sierra Leone, Senegal, and Angola, but we were interested in the European side of this family, so for our test we chose Family Tree DNA, a private lab. Then we went looking for the right donor.

Maryellen gave us a sample, but her DNA could trace only the female side of her family, and we were not surprised when the results indicated that her roots were in Africa. The only way to find Henry's lineage is through his male descendants—the male line had to be unbroken. It had to be Henry's son's son's son's son. The line could not have a woman in it. It could not for instance come from Henry's son's daughter's son.

It took almost a year to locate Peter Durham, one of Maryellen's California cousins, who agreed to swab his cheek and send the sample in for testing.

We hoped that the lab could tell us into which generation their white ancestor fell.

We were disappointed. The lab could not pinpoint the gener-ation for us, but we did discover that Peter Durham and his great-grandfather, Henry, came from Viking stock. Peter identifies with the African side of his lineage, but he shares a blood bond with people in Germany, Sweden, Norway, Scotland, England, Ireland, Wales, and France. If Henry Durham was not the white ancestor, then was it his father?

The only other solid clue is in the 1870 Census. In that record, a Henry Durham, a teenager of about eighteen, is working as a farm laborer in Van Zandt County. That Henry Durham is also listed as mulatto.

Is that "our" Henry? Maybe. So if he is, in fact, mulatto, then who is his father? The 1860 slave records pointed to two possibilities and two different families. According to one family's online genealogy, a Tennessee slaveholder presented his fifteen-year-old stepson whose last name is Durham with a thirteen-year-old slave girl as a gift in 1844. By 1860 the stepson had a wife and children of his own and had moved to Texas. The 1860 U.S. Census and slave schedules report that he also owned an eleven-year-old girl and an eight-year-old boy, both listed as "black" on the slave registers. Could the boy be Henry? Because Henry was born about 1853, the age is about right. This man had no other slaves listed, and the mother of these children is not mentioned.

At first, we were certain that this was our Henry. But DNA reports suggest that Henry's kinsmen may have been named Dunham, not Durham. According to the 1860 slave register, an eight-year-old boy listed as mulatto was living with a slaveholder named Dunham in Grimes County.

In either case, the child's name is not mentioned and no matter how we worked, we could not jump this barrier. Our search had ended in disappointment. Without a name on the records we were reduced to speculation.

~

And there lies the sad and sobering truth. Slaves were sometimes listed by a single name: Sally, Ezra, John. Sometimes only as girl, boy, female, or male, followed by ages. The famed African-

American educator Booker T. Washington wrote that after emancipation, former slaves thought "it was far from proper for them to bear the surname of their former owners, and a great many of them took other surnames. This was one of the first signs of freedom," he said.

It was understandable, an eloquent statement of independence, but it adds to the problem of tracing African-American lineage. If Henry was half white, the custom and the law of the day forced him to live as a black man. Even if only one of his eight grandparents had been of African lineage, social custom would have marked him as black. In dozens of states, social custom was also the law, and the "one drop rule" meant that even "one drop" of African blood made an individual black.

During this unsettling time, some Americans who looked European were classified as blacks, too. From about 1900 to 1919, the courts bulged with cases protesting this rule. It would be 1967 before the Supreme Court declared laws based on the "one drop rule" were unconstitutional.

If Henry was indeed the child of mixed race, the law and social custom branded him as black. What is certain is that Henry lived his life with Mary and that together they raised a large family. His descendants are certain that the bond of love between them was unshakable.

For his great-granddaughters, this is what counts. "There is something which loving does," said Francis. It gives strength and courage. It makes every tribulation worthwhile. But Henry's mixed heritage and theirs leaves them sometimes teetering on the edge of a well that has no bottom. "We may have enjoyed some privileges because of our light skin," said Maryellen, but in no way does that bleach her identity as an African American.

Her sister Francis pointed to famed African-American writer W.E.B. Du Bois for an explanation. "He called it a kind of 'schizophrenia,'" she said. In 1903, Du Bois, the first African American to earn a Ph.D. from Harvard University, a pioneer in sociology, and one of the founders of the NAACP, wrote about what it meant to be of mixed lineage.

"One ever feels his twoness ... two souls, two thoughts, two unreconciled strivings; two warring ideals in one dark body. . . ," he wrote.

And that, it seems, is the marrow of this bone.

Every race is in a war of survival, trying ever to preserve itself. Any mixing of races is a threat to that survival, and there is some primal instinct, some dark fear that says one may be swallowed by the other.

Will the day come, I wonder, when a child can choose to celebrate all the ancestors who have come before? Or, with every heartbeat, will we always hear the drumming of only one race, chanting softly to the spirit: You are mine. You are mine. You are mine.

PART EIGHT
Something About Me

Remembered Rain ⅋ *July 2, 2000*

I WAS five—almost six—the first time I saw rain. Surely, it had rained in San Angelo before that afternoon in 1952, but I can't recall it. I don't know why I should remember this brief episode so clearly. I can't remember the first time I saw snow. Maybe the rain lifted Momma's spirits so that I thought all our disappointments were behind us. I didn't know then that I would be ten years old before the savage drought that held West Texas in a suffocating grip was broken.

In a drought there's always some rain—just never enough. A drought is a thief who sneaks into the land to lap up the water and the commerce while occasionally taunting the earth with stingy rains here and there.

It never begins with one great catastrophe as a tornado or a flood might. There is no definite point of time that looking back you can point to and say, "There, that is the moment it began," or, "That is when it ended." Drought is like the sudden realization that life has changed and you with it, but you cannot say how this happened—or when.

∼

All my memories of the Texas drought of the 1950s are like faded watercolors that I see through a lens stained the color of the arroyo sand. I remember the dust, the heat, the swarms of grasshoppers that rippled out before you like waves on the water as you walked across the brittle grass, their wings making a whirring, clicking sound.

The drought was young the afternoon of my remembered rain. My teenage brother said the shower was like a girl in tight, red shorts—only a tease, but now I see it as a promise of things to come.

Momma and I stretched out on the bed on that summer afternoon in 1952 and she read to me, probably from *Aesop's Fables,* tales that always had a moral, or maybe it was *Arabian Nights,* one of my favorites. I loved this story of a clever woman who saved her own life by telling such fascinating tales that her cruel husband, who had already killed many other wives, let her live so she could finish the stories of Sinbad, Ali Baba, and Aladdin and his magic lamp. I'm sure that's where I first got the notion that a storyteller is a good thing.

The abelia bush outside the open window was in bloom, but there was a new smell in the wind, something sweeter than the perfume of the hardy white blossoms. Momma closed the book and turned onto her stomach, propping her chin in her cupped hands. She was sad again I knew. I can see her still in my mind's eye, her dark eyes bewildered and clouded with grief. She seemed tired and somehow lonely. Even as a child, I knew she was just going through the motions of reading to me, finding little joy in the moment.

In November of 1951, my baby sister, Martha, had died. "She's a little angel now," Daddy said. I couldn't imagine that tiny baby, all red and shriveled, with wings, but I didn't argue.

I'd been with them when they picked out the miniature casket. Outside on the sidewalk, Momma had leaned against the buff-colored bricks of the funeral home and cried. There hadn't been much sound, only a small whimpering noise—and tears. Lots of tears.

I held her hand tightly and jumped up and down to get her attention but she seemed not to notice. Daddy put his arms around her, their shadow fell against the funeral home wall, melding into one image. My shadow stood alone. I made it dance and jiggle in the bright sun.

Actually, I was relieved that Martha had not survived. I was glad she was an angel. I'd been terrified that my mother would die instead.

Momma had been cross and sick throughout the pregnancy. One night, as the family listened to the radio in the living room and Momma fried potatoes in the kitchen, a man came to the door. I remember very well that he was selling cemetery plots. My brother, who was then about seventeen, opened the door, and my father got up from the brown armchair as if to talk with the man, but Daddy never even turned down the radio.

"Look here, I'm a young man. I have a young family," Daddy said and his wave encompassed me and my older brother and sister. "I don't have any use for a cemetery plot."

The man turned to go, but he hadn't reached the street before Momma came to the kitchen door. She leaned against the doorjamb, a big spoon in her hand, an apron stretched tight across her pregnant belly.

"Call him back," she said. Her voice was hard, commanding. "You do need a cemetery plot." Then her voice became softer, darker. "One of us isn't going to make it," she said. They stood very still, their eyes locked on each other, and then Daddy moved slowly to the door to call the man back.

A prickly shiver shot down my spine and exploded into my stomach. My mother was going to die? I knew about death. I'd seen our neighbor slaughter goats. My cat, Freckles, had been hit by a car and was buried under the mesquite tree at the corner of the house. We had a dog once that left for a while and then came home, but I knew dead things never came back. I knew I didn't want my mother to die and leave me forever. I wanted to be with her always.

My ears buzzed and my stomach flip-flopped like a fish on a line—a fish that was dying, but not dead yet. The buzzing was like a swarm of flies that had found the goat's bloody and discarded skin. The sound grew louder as Daddy called the man back.

Momma was right, of course. The baby, born with many complications, did not survive, but in a way neither did my mother. For months, maybe years, she was given to ferocious fits of temper and dark hours filled with brooding, followed by crying jags. "Walk on eggs, Mother is nervous today," my older sister would warn as she boarded the city bus headed for the high school across town.

A family in the next block had a new baby, as it did almost every year, and my mother attached herself to it. She cradled it in her arms and sang to it. I'd try to climb into her lap only to be gently pushed away. She loved me, I knew, but I was not enough.

Thanksgiving and Christmas came and went. Spring turned into a hot summer. Oscillating fans stirred the stifling air, but at night, it often grew too hot to sleep inside. Like so many other families, my family sometimes took blankets into the yard and laid them on the brittle grass, hoping for some breath of cooler air. There was usually a radio propped in the window. I always woke in my bed, so someone must have carried me into the house in the small hours of the morning.

Everyone talked of rain, but no rain came. A drought that spread across the Southwest grew worse. West Texas baked under an angry sun. The old-timers who said they'd seen it this bad before didn't sound so sure anymore.

Preachers took up the cause. Every church had multiple prayer meetings to beg God for rain. I remember very well sitting near the front of the sanctuary at First Baptist Church at more than one of these meetings. My mother always carried paper and crayons in hopes I'd amuse myself through the sermon. I, like most children of that day, always chose brown when coloring pasture scenes. Green pastures weren't part of my experience; neither were blue skies. Stirred by the wind, the sand was a constant curtain between the heaven and the earth. The sky of my childhood was always tinged red with dust. I had no idea that clouds cast shadows.

I had little experience with clouds, but even at five or six I was a veteran of the wind. It never stopped. It pushed giant tumble-weeds into town to be caught in hedges and fences. It blew a hot breath on the dry land stirring dust devils that twirled across the withered pastures where ranchers burned the thorns off prickly pear cactus to use as cattle feed.

The dust storms were so fierce the sun was sometimes only a faint orange glow behind the heavy veil of sand. Sometimes it would be snuffed out entirely, dropping the whole town into an eerie and unbelievable darkness. Lake Nasworthy, the city's water reservoir, became little more than a muddy puddle in places, bone dry in others. The lake bed split open in wide, dry cracks. I remember sitting down in one of these fractures, the dust caking my knobby knees. My legs stretched out straight in front of me. I can still see my brown sandals. My whole world was brown.

On that summer afternoon when I lay with my mother on the bed, I remember the loud splat of fat raindrops against the dusty walk. Mother became suddenly alert. She went to the window. I was frightened.

"What is it?" I asked.

She smiled. "It's rain. It's rain," she'd said. Together we went out on the front porch. The rain was coming faster then, not washing the sidewalk clean, but promising to.

It came harder, blowing sideways across the withered grass, turning the dirty sidewalk into a shimmering ribbon. The thunder rumbled above our heads and the wind whipped the rain onto the porch across my bare legs. As it slowed, Mother walked out into the shower, the fat drops spotting her blue dress.

I walked with her, and when we reached the curb, it was almost over. A narrow stream of muddy water filled the gutter. We sat on the curb and let the rivulet run over our toes.

It was as if the rain had for a brief moment washed away some dark presence. Mother went into the house and baked a chocolate cake. For years after that, Mother always baked a chocolate cake when it rained.

That rain was not enough to break the drought. Many dry years followed. It certainly was not the end of my mother's depression, but it was in some small way a start. By the time the drought ended, she would have a new baby to hold, a little girl born in the summer of 1953.

My older sister and brother would move away and start their own lives. I would begin school and learn right from the start that storytelling was indeed a very good thing. When my first-grade teacher ran out of things for the squirming class to do, she'd let me stand near her desk and spin a yarn. I'm embarrassed and amused to remember that I sometimes illustrated these on the chalkboard. I'm pleased to recall that my classmates listened. Storytelling is like having a magic carpet, I remember thinking. It carries you away to the land of make-believe where it might rain every morning, if you choose, and there's always enough love to go around.

The drought broke in 1956 or 1957. The lakes and the stockmen's tanks filled again—and then came the floods. Gushing torrents of muddy water swelled the rivers and careened through the country, destroying property in a flash. The townspeople drove out to see the ruined places and marvel at the flood's power. My family looked, too, but I was never afraid of this abundance of water. I was never troubled by the thunder or the lightning.

I feared the dry times. I still do.

A Walk in the Shadows ℘
Sunday, November 30, 1997

DID IT start with the moccasins? Maybe not. Maybe it began earlier, but it's the moccasins that I remember. A year or so ago, my mother began to wear beaded rubber-soled moccasins everywhere. Pressed for an explanation, she opened her dark brown eyes wide, straightened her back, and declared that the Publishers Clearing House made her do it.

Momma thinks the Publishers Clearing House controls the most mundane aspects of her life. Once I found a tray filled with precisely arranged trinkets on the guest-room bed. There were several tiny ivory gods her brother had sent her from Burma during World War II; a string of beads carefully laid in an oval; a tiny ceramic rose—all placed just so on the tray.

"It's that Publishers Clearing House," she declared. "If they come to your door and you're not doing exactly what they say, they won't give you your millions."

I laughed. She laughed. She put on her moccasins and off we went to lunch at Luby's. Momma and I have laughed often during the past few years, but in secret—when my house is quiet and empty—a choking lump fills my throat and I am overwhelmed by a terrible homesickness.

Mother is traveling alone into a land filled with mists and mysteries. Sometimes it is peopled with fairies and giants and little children who live under her bed. It is a place I cannot find.

"There's a hitchhiker in my brain," Momma tells me over a plate of Chinese food. Suddenly, at seventy-seven, Mother likes Chinese. "He's taking bites of my memory," she complains. Her hands snip like scissors around her head. A look of genuine aggravation crosses her face.

It's true. Her memory is going, going, almost gone. Daddy has been dead for seven years, and a year ago, Mother still lived alone in the house where I was raised. It is a little white frame house where red geraniums still grow in the side yard and violets bloom near the back door. I was married under the trees there. But all the old neighbors have gone now, settling in retirement centers or closer to children in other cities. Mother hung on stubbornly even when the last of those old friends sold their home across the street and moved. Always a solitary woman, Momma became isolated, flying solo in a world with few landmarks. It was a world more and more of her own creation.

One day she tells me that she has had a long visit with Jim Bass, a West Texas Ford dealer. "You know his name isn't really Bass," she says in a conspiratorial whisper. "His name is Fisher, but that's a sacred name. He is a Navajo Indian. He told me, but he can't tell just anyone."

I am stunned. "Momma, I know Mr. Bass, and he's not an Indian. His name isn't Fisher; it's Bass."

Momma folds her arms across her chest in a defiant gesture. She looks smug. "Mary, you don't know everything," she says and walks away.

That is only the beginning of Momma's preoccupation with names. We are eating cherry pie at Luby's when she asks whether I know a man named Goodman. No, he doesn't live in San Angelo or Fort Worth—maybe Houston. She'll have to call my brother Bill, who lives in Houston, she says and see if he knows Mr. Goodman.

"Mr. Goodman owns all the electricity in the country," she explains as she sips coffee. "He's told me I can't turn off my air conditioner, but he says the electric bill won't be but $10 a month."

I am too flabbergasted to protest. "His name isn't really Goodman," she says, bending so close only I can hear. "He's a

Swede, but his name is so hard to pronounce the neighbors just started calling him that good man who lives over there."

I soon learn that Goodman is the label on the new window unit air conditioner my sister has installed in Mother's bedroom—but Momma is riveted on that name. She asks me over and over again if I know Mr. Goodman. The questions stop only when we go to bed. They start again at five-thirty the next morning, with the first cup of coffee. All day long she asks if I know Mr. Goodman, and always she tells me the story of his name, so foreign, so difficult to pronounce that neighbors simply gave him a new, more appropriate moniker.

Finally, late in the afternoon as we stroll through the mall, she seems to forsake her obsession. We have a pleasant dinner. She doesn't mention Mr. Goodman. Luck is with me, I think. We head for home, but just as I turn onto her street Momma touches my arm.

"Mary, I've been meaning to ask you about a man named Goodman," she says. Her tone is serious, worried.

I laugh. Momma laughs. "Have I asked you that before?" she asks.

~

It is clear that Mother cannot continue living by herself. Things are disappearing from her house: the vacuum cleaner, a lamp. She doesn't know where they've gone. I worry for her safety.

My younger sister lives in San Angelo near Momma; she drops in often and calls each day. All the responsibility rests on her shoulders. She fills Momma's fridge with fresh fruits, milk, and ice cream, Momma's favorite treat.

Still, I feel certain that Mother isn't eating well. She can't remember to eat, I argue. She seldom feels hungry, just sick and dizzy. Even so, my younger sister is more reluctant than am I to move Mother out of the house she has had for fifty years. My sister hires a nurse to spend several hours each day with Momma.

That lasts less than a week. Momma pulls the drapes and

refuses to answer the door when the nurse knocks. At last, my younger sister relents. In April, we find an intermediate care facility in San Angelo. There is an opening. I think it is a good omen— a gift from God. All meals are served in a dining room. There's no cooking in the rooms. Not even a coffeepot is allowed, but there is a small dormitory-size refrigerator with a tiny freezer compartment.

My younger sister says she is too close to the situation, too emotional to actually help pack the boxes, load the truck. She says she'll go to Lubbock that day. I think she's right. She can stay a little removed. Once I've gone back home to Fort Worth, and my older sister, Fran, returns to Killeen, she is the one who has to pick up the pieces, withstand Mother's pleas to go home again.

Fran and I say we'll handle the move. My husband says he'll help.

I tell Mother what is coming, but before we hang up the phone, the "hitchhiker" has gobbled up that bit of information. She says she loves me. I say I love her. It is like the light of phosphorous churned up by a ship cutting through a dark sea.

I have T-shirts printed. Momma's name, "Maxine," is stamped in bold, black letters on the front, "Boss" on the back of the one she wears that day. Ours say, "Maxine's Movers."

She is angry when we arrive. Her eyes flash fire. She says she can't move away from her house. Finally, she puts on her T-shirt and smiles an uncertain smile.

We begin throwing things into the Ryder truck. Our goal is to have her bedroom reassembled before dinner. She wanders from room to room. A little boy perhaps six years old shows up, hoping Mother will look at a magazine with him. Mother tells him she's moving away and gives him a book of birds, a going-away gift. Fran takes Mother ahead to the center. I go with my husband in the truck.

Mother is agitated and combative, but we push ahead setting up her bed, asking her to put on the sheets. The bedroom is finished in time for dinner. Fran and I sit with her at her assigned table. She is withdrawn, tentative, shy. She says little, but smiles at others around the table.

After dinner, Momma seems suddenly clearheaded, more rational. She says she knows this is the best thing, but she hates to leave her home. For a moment the angry cloud that has covered us all day lifts—and then it is bedtime and the water in the shower won't get hot fast enough. Momma begins to cry. She doesn't stop until almost morning.

Exhausted, Fran and I try to get comfortable on the sofa bed in the living room. Mother sobs and prays. Louder and louder grow her lamentations. She begs God to let her die before morning.

My sister and I lie in the dark praying, too, and I am certain all of Heaven can hear my heart breaking.

The next day, we take Momma to the grocery market. We buy pineapple juice, a tray of assorted cookies, and teal-colored paper napkins. We're giving a come-meet-Momma party. Never mind that she pouts when she hears the news.

"No. No. No," she says. "No one will come."

At supper, my sister and I visit each table, inviting everyone to Momma's room in an hour. They arrive in half that time. Momma stands by the door greeting these strangers as if she's known them her entire life. My sister and I pass cookies, pour juice, and find seats for everyone.

When it's over, we're exhausted, but Momma is smiling. "All these people are my friends," she says. We are dumbfounded. Mother has always been a loner, someone who seldom had a cup of coffee with a neighbor.

It is as if she has forgotten who she is. Once painfully shy, Mother adopts a more gregarious disposition. "I never could think of a thing to say before. Now I say any ol' thing that comes into my head," she observes with a giggle.

There's no question about it. Momma is changing. She does

still look at the newspaper headlines through a magnifying glass, but she is no longer the avid reader she once was consuming everything written about American Indians, Eskimos, holistic remedies, and gardening. Her ferocious temper has cooled, too. She may now fume or huff, but she doesn't explode. Maybe the hitchhiker has gobbled up that bit of self-knowledge, too.

The one thing she doesn't forget is her little house.

The next days are rocky. She begs to go home but looks forward to going to dinner early so she'll have plenty of time to talk.

After two weeks, I visit again, and when she asks to go out to her house, I take her. She walks through the musty rooms still messy from the hurried move. She picks up her Bibles, opens a few drawers, and sighs.

"You can't go home again," she says. Her eyes are clear, her voice firm. I am filled with a savage yearning for the yesterdays we spent together in these rooms. I remember sitting beside her in that chair there as she read to me from *Aesop's Fables, Black Beauty,* or the *Arabian Nights.* I knew early the Bible stories of the creation, Daniel in the lion's den, Gideon, Moses on the mountain, baby Jesus and the star of Bethlehem.

For a moment, I can hear her voice soft and full as she reads poetry to me. I see the highwayman from the poem riding over the purple moor; Paul Revere astride a stallion as he warns his countrymen that the British are coming; fields of daffodils bending in the wind. I am transfixed by the melody of the memory and the pictures dance again in my head. It is like the spark struck by flint, a bright flash that is gone in an instant.

"Just boards and a roof," I say. "You still have all the memories." I lie to ease the moment. Mother doesn't own the memories now. I do.

Over the phone each week, Momma complains about her failing memory. On one visit I give her a reporter's notebook. I tell her that I must write down everything or I forget, too. She smiles and seems pleased. A few days later I call and when I ask what she's done that day, she consults the notebook.

"We had a birthday party at supper," she says. "There were three people celebrating. I didn't get their names. Let's see, we sang *The Tennessee Waltz* and the *Yellow Rose of Texas*. We had a cake all decorated, too."

In a few days she forgets where she's left the notebook. She also loses her purse and telephones me.

"Mary do you have my purse?"

"No, Momma. I'm in Fort Worth; you're in San Angelo."

"Well, I thought maybe you had my purse," she says. "I've looked under my pillows on the bed and under the sink, and even in that tiny little refrigerator."

She says that if she can only find that purse she'll call the Ford dealer and have a new car delivered. She needs a few items from the store and can't get them without a car.

"What do you want?" I ask.

There is a brief silence on the other end of the line. I can feel her resolutely straightening her back. I am certain she is wearing the moccasins.

"Ice cream," she says.

I laugh. She hesitates and then I hear the little chuckle, but I feel the tears hot and stinging and a choking wave of memory and fear rises in my throat.

A Valentine for My Friend, Doris ℘
February 14, 2004

Doris Dinkins knew the secret of staying young-at-heart. Courtesy, the Fort Worth Star-Telegram.

IT WAS early summer, and twilight was settling softly between the houses; the streetlights were beginning to glow. I was still in my twenties, and my friend Doris Dinkins was close to sixty—a good five years older than my mother. We'd been neighbors for about a year, and we were becoming unlikely friends. We'd taken a short walk and had just made the turn toward home when she told me the secret.

"Mary, would you like to know how to stay young at heart?" she asked.

"Of course," I said.

"You pick the age you're most comfortable with yourself," she said, her words slow and distinct, as if each carried wisdom's heavy weight. "Then you stay there in your mind, forever." Her eyes sparkled behind the big lenses of her glasses. "See, I'm thirty-five," she declared and giggled.

In that moment I understood that Doris really had given me a treasure, but I could not guess that over the next three decades I would go again and again to the well of our friendship, each time drawing up some unexpected bounty. I wouldn't say Doris is a mentor, a teacher, or even a venerable "wise woman." She's not salty or sassy, lettered or religious. But she is a woman who is flexible, responsive, cheerful—and growing older with a bit of pluck. She turned eighty-eight in August but says she still feels younger than her years.

"Oh, you might have to add six months on some days," she told me recently. "Today I feel about thirty-five and a half," she said. "Some days I'm pushing forty—but not today."

Not today. The words crackled in my head.

What a powerful idea, I thought.

I might feel old someday—but not today. I might feel sick or tired of life always nipping at my heels someday—but not today. I might feel nervous or unsure or stupid or fat or unloved or any of a thousand dark passions, but today I choose something different.

"Why not today?" I asked.

"Oh, I found a new floor exercise on TV, and it's really helped my aches and pains," Doris said.

Yoga enthusiasts call it the cobra position, but Doris calls it "the seal." "You know, it looks like a seal in a circus act," she told me.

Doris is a vegetarian who has been doing floor exercises for more than fifty years. It began when her oldest son contracted polio in 1951. She joined him in an exercise routine as he recuperated. Even when that son became a man and moved away, Doris continued stretching and bending. Conditioning her brain was just as important to her.

Lucky for me, Doris embraced the computer age with enthusiasm. E-mail has made it easier to keep our friendship vital. Doris had a home computer before I did, and the first one she owned was hardly "user friendly," so she took courses to tame the monster. When she discovered the World Wide Web, it was as if she'd found a worldwide playground.

Doris sends me a couple of e-mails each week, sometimes more, and I can count on her to forward the most amazing photos and funniest jokes—the ones worth opening. Once she sent me a CD she had burned with her favorite love songs and, more recently, the Web address for an Indian newspaper. She thought I should read what others in the world were saying about America's involvement in Iraq. It's always been hard to think of Doris as my "older" friend—not so surprising, I guess, since she's a perpetual thirty-five and I'm "forever forty-three."

When we were next-door neighbors in the 1970s, it was easy and comfortable to stop by her house, and I dropped in often. Her husband, Ross, who was then retired and who died in 1983, was usually in the kitchen. Doris hardly ever cooked.

She worked at a mortgage company then, only one in a long list of jobs she'd held, including a stint as an advertising copy-writer and a stay-at-home mom who typed doctoral dissertations for college students. By the time we knew the Dinkinses, their nest was empty. One son was married, and the other was away at college, but Doris and Ross seemed to enjoy our company, and we enjoyed theirs.

My husband and I were often invited for supper, usually on the spur of the moment. One cold winter evening, we were having a potluck dinner in their den and they began to laugh about their life together. They'd dated for nine long years when Ross received his draft notice. World War II was in full swing, and Doris gave up any hope they'd marry—so she rushed out and joined the U.S. Marine Corps—only to learn that Ross had failed his physical. He proposed in a telegram. She said "yes," and Ross spent the war years following her around the country as she worked as a marine recruiter.

I remember that night was filled with laughter as they recalled those lean years: the dumps they lived in, the scarcity of gasoline and sugar, the abundance of friends.

It was a wonderful reminder that one year is not like the next, that the world keeps spinning and those who are on bottom today may be on top tomorrow—that friends and family are like gravity, anchoring our hearts to humankind.

After the war, Doris and Ross came back to Fort Worth with every intention of starting a family, but that beginning was not as sure-fire as they had hoped. One year melted into another, and no baby came. It was a story I could relate to.

Doris was in her thirties when the first boy was born—old by the standards of the day. By the time my husband and I celebrated our sixth wedding anniversary, I wondered if there would never be a child in our home.

"When are you going to start a family?" Doris asked me one night as we started off on a walk.

I confessed my fears, and the next time I stopped at her house, Doris was crocheting a baby's receiving blanket. "This is a magic blanket," she said. "By the time I finish this, that baby will be on the way."

She was right.

Doris and Ross enjoyed their own sons' company and, naturally, the "boys" became our friends, too. One day about two years ago, when Doris was in her mid-eighties, she experienced a searing pain in her abdomen. She didn't call her sons or me for help but drove herself to the emergency room. Physicians quickly found a large tumor on her ovary and rushed her to surgery.

The next day, she summoned me to the hospital. In the dimly lit room, I could see the IV bottle above the bed. Monitors bleeped. Doris was alone, her eyes closed, her breathing shallow. I stepped closer.

"Doris?" I whispered, and her eyes fluttered open.

"Mary," she said weakly. "You'll have to talk to the boys. They're very upset."

My own heartbeat quickened. She seemed so fragile, so small. I took her hand.

Doris swallowed hard and seemed to be searching for the right words. "They know this means they'll never have a brother or a sister," she wheezed as she tried to squelch a laugh.

Doris has a habit of laughing at life—even when life is no laughing matter.

Always interested in nutrition and exercise, she'd never considered that she might have to face any serious illness. A diagnosis of cancer in the 1980s left her stunned. She survived, but her life and the picture she had of herself had changed.

"That was the first time it leaked into my brain that I wasn't going to live forever," she told me recently. That simple declaration made me flinch.

I certainly understand that everyone's days are numbered, but I can't imagine losing Doris. She has been one of my most supportive fans, reading my work, encouraging me to tackle a book, lifting my spirits with her offbeat brand of humor.

I'm ashamed to admit that I've not been as good a friend to her. I've been satisfied to communicate with her through e-mail and the occasional phone call. I'm embarrassed to say I hadn't actually seen Doris in well over a year, but a few weeks ago I picked her up to run an errand. She opened the door, and when I bent to hug her, I wondered if she had always been so short.

She still wears her trademark pinky ring of pavé diamonds, but I was surprised to see that her hands tremble a bit now and her step is no longer confident. She's seldom hungry anymore, and her vision is fading, too.

She asked me if I knew the quickest way to clean the house.

"No," I said.

"Take off your glasses," she advised.

She held my hand as we made our way down the steep steps from her second-story condo and made a joke about needing a steadying influence in her life.

I might have worried—except that on that day Doris said she felt a solid thirty-five.

Graduation ℘ Tuesday, May 16, 1995

THE WHOLE family is coming—even my baby sister. All my husband's people will be here. They're bringing my mother. We're celebrating. Our son, Ben, is graduating from high school. None of us want to miss this commencement, this rite of passage, this beginning, this time of promise, this moment of hope. It's a happy time.

So why does my heart squeeze shut when he slips into a sports jacket and rushes off to work?

We like the young man Ben has become. We like his friends. We think he makes good choices—not the decisions we'd make, you understand—but good choices all the same. We think he's interesting and funny. We're proud of his strong work ethic, his determination, and his tender heart.

So why do I feel the tears, hot and stinging at the corners of my eyes, when he gives me a quick hug and I catch the smell of his cologne?

It seems like only yesterday he and his buddy Cameron were digging in the sand pile behind the house, riding Big Wheels, catching tadpoles in the creek.

If I close my eyes I can see them playing with G.I. Joes at the head of the stairs or jumping in shimmering puddles of water as they cross the street. I recall the Easter egg hunts, the fireworks on the Fourth of July, the Christmas trees. I remember his first hunt, the first time he drove a car, his first date. I'll never ever forget a day a year or more ago when Ben insisted I ride his horse. He was saddling Duffer when I got to the barns.

"Let me work him out a little and then we'll get in the arena," he said.

I hadn't seen him ride in at least six months, but when he swung into the saddle I sensed something was different. He adjusted his hat as they cantered to the gate. I stood leaning against the fence as they loped across the pasture. A light breeze caught his shirt, puffing it out across his shoulders and back. He put the horse though the paces, turning, backing up, stopping. He was confident, assured, in control. It was a magic moment. In those seconds he was transformed before my eyes from a boy to a young man. I would never see him the same way again. Now he's ready to start a new phase of life.

I'm glad—but lately I've found I worry more. At night I sometimes lie awake examining the little anxieties that wiggle from beneath the covers. I remember the times I was cross, unreasonable, unbending. I wonder if I've said all I should have said.

I told him to be happy, but did I tell him what that will cost? The price of happiness is your whole self. Dedicate yourself completely to a task, forget the clock, forget the compensation, forget the outside voices. Wring every good and bad experience from it and in the end you may have the opportunity to be your best. That's happiness.

I told him to be strong, but did I tell him strong people have charity written on their hearts? Be generous with your goods, your time, and your judgments. Remember that most people are doing the best they can.

I told him to go to church, but does he know it doesn't count unless he worships, unless he holds within himself a sense of the sacred? My spiritual experiences or his dad's or his grandparents' can't be borrowed. That's a personal pilgrimage.

I told him to be a man of action, but did I say that sometimes it's best to make things temporary? Relationships can be destroyed by quick decisions based on emotion. Don't be pushed to make a move before you're ready.

Did I tell him enough fairy tales?
Did I read him enough Scripture?
Did I tell him to work every day to be a human being?
Did I say "I love you" often enough? Is it too late?
Oh, what's the matter with me?
We're celebrating.

Remembering Guy &ᵃ
Thursday, November 28, 1991

MAYBE IF I tell you, I will understand.

Maybe if I write it down and go to sleep, pleasant dreams will come back to me.

Maybe I'll stop crying on the freeway.

Maybe I'll put it away.

It's been a whole year since my brother died. We buried him the day before Thanksgiving in a Houston cemetery. Sick for years, first with lung cancer, then with a brain malignancy, Guy fought and suffered and finally died.

We had plenty of time to prepare for that day, but we mourners weren't ready. We were numb. I remember a gray day of low clouds and the flag-draped casket. The commands to the honor guard were muffled by a jet screaming overhead.

"Ready. Aim. Fire."

Mother jumped at the first volley of the twenty-one-gun salute.

My brother, Bill, was stoic. He seemed not to watch the honor guard's mechanical, expert folding of the flag, or the slow final salute.

The haunting notes of "Taps" drifted into the soggy air. My sister, Fran, sobbed.

Hold on. Hold on, I told myself.

Dad had died the February before, and after that funeral we had laughed and cried and remembered our times together—but this was different. He was our brother and he was only fifty-four.

The specter of our own mortality stalked among the gravestones eyeing each of us. "Don't waste it; life may be over before you're ready," it whispered.

It would be days before the memories crept back.

Guy was more than a decade my senior. Even now, I think of him as a handsome, happy-go-lucky high school boy with thick auburn hair and a ready smile. Or I see him lean and trim in Air Force blues home for Christmas. I remember all the times he would scratch on my window screen late at night. I'd unlock the back door and we'd talk until dawn.

I can't think of him as he was when I saw him last: bloated from chemotherapy; his beautiful red hair gone, replaced by a fine fringe of gray; his face and neck red with shingles.

No, I see him spinning tops on the driveway or strapping on a scuba tank. I remember being lifted onto his shoulders and touching the ceiling.

When I was a very little girl, before my younger sister was born, I slept in the dining room and Guy slept on an iron bed on a screened back porch. I remember waving at him through the window. I can still see his smile as he snuggled under layers of heavy blankets.

Guy and Fran were only a year apart in age and looked like twins. I thought they were beautiful—especially when they danced. They would roll the living room rug back and put on some records and suddenly the tiny room was filled with magic as they danced into the night.

But all the memories are not happy ones. Guy was often argumentative and hot-tempered. There were years when he and Dad didn't speak.

He married four times. He fathered four children he didn't help raise.

He was a rambler and a rebel and a rascal. When I was an adult, I often found him too difficult to enjoy, but he was my brother and to lose him was to slash a gaping hole in the part of my heart I keep for family.

With all his bad points, with all his good points, I want him back . . . if only for one more Thanksgiving dinner. I need to stay up and argue with him until dawn. I want to hug him . . . just once more. But his death has made a strange change in me. I don't want to spend time on the social "ought tos." I've stopped having dinner with people I don't like. I don't do things I don't think are important. I've become even more frank. I'm more likely to fight than compromise.

I hear the specter whisper: "Life's short. Don't waste it."

Old Man in Winter ⊱
Sunday, January 27, 2002

ONCE UPON a time I had a cat.

Actually, I've owned many cats in my life. I should say my former life. Now I have dogs, but I've always had animals. Once I had a little Spanish goat. Then there was the hawk, a beautiful creature that had not yet learned to fly and ate from my hand, but that was long before the cat called Cis was born, long before I learned what it really means to decide.

I think of him now because it's January, the season of deciding. December is the month for dreaming, but January demands more.

Cis was a big tabby the color of fresh-cut pine. He was one of a litter of three kittens born to a stray tortoise-shell mama cat we called BC for Big Cat. BC was a traveling cat when she found us in the early spring of 1972, and if she only meant to rest in our kitchen for a day or two, she soon decided we would be her people. In late March, she gave birth to three kittens: Cicero, called Cis; his brother, Fat Boy, who was my favorite; and a female we dubbed Fluffy because she alone had a long and luxurious coat. We kept the little family in a box in the bathroom, safe, we thought, from predators, but we hadn't counted on the most deadly threat of all.

One night before the kittens had even opened their eyes, BC, and half a dozen other neighborhood pets, got some poisoned bait tossed over backyard fences. BC came back from her late-night constitutional, had a seizure and died in the living room. The elderly neighbor's little lap dog died the same night. A German shepherd pup collapsed the next morning in front of a gathering of neighborhood children.

My husband and I were furious, bewildered, and sad. We couldn't understand why anyone would do such a horrible thing. We kept the kittens alive by feeding them every two hours night and day with an eyedropper. By the time they were grown, these cats owned our hearts. They returned our love with unqualified devotion—and then our son was born.

The cats were two years old when Benjamin arrived. The cats were not happy. They stalked away in a huff. They made friends with people down the alley and even stayed away overnight. One morning I found them all lined up on a desk adjacent to the crib, their backs turned to our baby, their tails twitching in irritation, and I knew without a doubt that this was a cat's most powerful display of contempt.

It took time, but eventually Fat Boy and Cis came home to stay, baby or no baby. Fluffy was never really our cat again. The neighbor kept a heating pad on the sofa for her, and Fluff thought it the perfect place to spend a cold winter day. When we moved in 1976, Fluffy stayed with that neighbor. The boys—and the baby—came with us.

Fat Boy was more affectionate than Cis and decidedly easier to have around. He ate and slept and hunted birds a bit, but Fat Boy caused no problems. Cis was a walking disaster. He howled and fought and controlled a wide territory. He prowled the creek behind the house and sometimes dragged dead water rats up to the door as if they were trophies. He refused to stay inside at night, but demanded to be let into the house at first light. If we ignored his call to unlock the door, he stationed himself on the bedroom windowsill and began an obnoxiously loud lament that always woke the neighbors. He was too full of vim and vigor for his own good, but by 1990, Cis had mellowed. He was eighteen then, inveterate for a tomcat. Fat Boy had died a decade earlier, and Cis was no longer the handsome ruler of a large domain. He had become a shrunken stay-at-home with a matted coat.

He no longer moved with the liquid grace characteristic of cats. Instead, he hobbled along on arthritic feet, unable to retract his claws. Sometimes he actually grunted as he walked. We began to call him the Old Man.

Most of his teeth were gone. His eyesight was fading and his hearing wasn't what it had been; still, he never failed to limp out of harm's way when a car started—until that fateful afternoon.

Ben was frantic as he tore through the house, shouting for me to follow. "He's not dead, Mom. He ran," he cried. I knew immediately that Ben had run over the Old Man. I raced after our son, certain that when we did find Cis, it would be over. I was wrong.

Ben pulled the Old Man from behind the air-conditioning units. One hind leg dangled crazily, but there was no blood. We wrapped him in a towel and made a wild dash to the vet. Cis sat quietly in Ben's lap, and I tried to prepare us both for the inevitable.

"Ben, the Old Man is really hurt," I said. "He probably just didn't hear the truck start." I looked at our sixteen-year-old son. He'd known Cis his whole life. He stroked the cat's head and blinked away tears. "It's not your fault, but Cis is old and frail. He might not have made it through the winter anyway."

Ben was stoic. I saw the muscle working in his jaw as he clenched his teeth. "Son, the doctor may have to put him down."

Ben shook his head. "No," he said.

The Old Man was quiet. He seemed almost curious about the neighborhoods that flashed past the car window. He didn't howl or scratch. He rubbed his whiskers against Ben's fingers. I held my tongue.

As we waited in the tiny examination room for the vet, some of the staff came in to smooth Cis' worn coat and croon encouragement to him. He began to purr.

The doctor scrutinized the fracture. He peered over his half glasses. I held my breath.

"I don't know how you feel about this cat," he said. "You all need to talk this over. It will be expensive, but we can set the leg."

I couldn't believe my ears.

"We'll stabilize him for now. You think about it overnight. He's tough. He can make it, but it will mean a long, confined recuperation. Let us know tomorrow what you decide."

~

You decide?

You decide.

The words were hammer blows.

You decide if this old friend you raised by hand will live or die. You decide what to do with this one of nature's best examples of independent living, this member of the family who carved out his own space in your life. You decide what happens to this companion who talked to you, sang to you, and always reminded you that no matter what happens, you can land on your feet.

Deciding means that you take responsibility. You don't settle. You become resolved. You choose. There is no turning back. Will you take the blessing or the cursing? Will you choose happiness or dissatisfaction? Will you love or simply wait to be loved? Will you invest your mind, your time, your heart or will you hold back? Will you honor the sacred? Will you trust? Will you change? Will you grow, forgive, let go? Will you be your brother's keeper? Will you be accountable? You decide.

Deciding is a profound act, but for years when I told the Old Man's story I made it funny. I could make a joke out of my drive to the grocery store after hearing the vet's words. People always chuckle when I say I sobbed all the way.

They smile when I tell them that my husband went to tell the doctor to put the Old Man down and then changed his mind. They laugh when I tell them that the vet let the Old Man have whatever he liked for dinner—fried chicken or spaghetti, one of the Old Man's favorites.

I made the old cat's two surgeries and months of recuperation sound like a comedy, but when I think of him now, I can't laugh.

I can't even smile. I remember how we had to let him go on a cold winter day, his eyes matted and his breathing labored. We couldn't bear to see him suffer any longer. We decided it was best to ask the doctor to help him step out of this world.

He was there through so many of our early years together. Even now I feel a knot in the chamber of my heart where I've stored all the stages of our family's life. Once it was a jagged stone of memory. Now its sharp edges have been ground down, worn smooth and polished by a river of Januarys.

The Forgotten Photo 🐝
Wednesday, August 7, 2002

LAST YEAR, I inherited a large box of miscellaneous photographs from my mother. I recognized hardly anyone in this dubious treasure chest, but after carefully looking at each picture, I tucked the box away in a closet, strangely unable to part with any of the contents. There were snapshots of young men in uniform, dogs, fishermen, and naked babies on blankets. It was one family's history thoughtfully captured on film—with seldom a word scribbled on the back for identification. It was easy to forget most of these pictures, but one small photograph stuck in my mind, and later I dug through the box to find it again.

The people are strangers to me, the house unfamiliar, but when I study the picture, a hungry yearning comes over me, and I am at once homesick for a place I have never been. In this tiny black-and-white photograph, five boys dressed in their Sunday best pose on a lawn before a comfortable home. The photographer likely stood in a dirt driveway across the street so that the entire house, with its broad steps and wide front and side porches, would be centered in the frame. With a magnifying glass, you can see a porch swing in the shadows.

If there were a "scratch and sniff" strip on this photo, it would smell like Sunday's fried chicken and fresh-cut grass. You know without being told that around twilight, the family will gather on this porch and a cool south breeze will blow away their cares. There will be laughter and maybe music. The children will play night games and catch fireflies.

As darkness falls, the oldest boy will shake off the younger children and join the adults on the porch. He'll hunker down on the steps, petting the old dog that lounges there, listening to the gentle ebb and flow of the conversation. He won't say much, but he'll remember it for years to come; the creak of the rocker on the board porch, the sigh of the porch swing, the smell of honeysuckle on the trellis.

Uncle Jim will turn the crank on an ice cream freezer. The men will smoke cigars or pipes. Neighbors will amble along the sidewalk, shouting greetings and maybe even coming onto the porch to sit a spell. They'll remark on the preacher's sermon, the latest political race, the state of the economy, and the weather— always the weather.

Before World War II, most houses had porches. In the South and Southwest, porches were a practical matter, offering shelter from the broiling sun and a cool retreat on hot evenings. More important, these outdoor living rooms were gathering places as pivotal to the community psyche as is the kitchen table. It was a day when neighbors knew more than each other's names. They knew one another's stories.

I have sat on porches such as these and rocked in the swings there, but the porches from my own childhood are not so grand. My parents' modest porches were of the post-World War II variety: little rectangles of concrete tacked onto the front and rear of a two-bedroom bungalow. The front porch was too small to accommodate a rocking chair or a swing, but it held a checkerboard just fine and was a shady place to play jacks on hot afternoons. The rear porch was screened, and the door always closed with a satisfying thwack.

The house in the photo was clearly built before World War II, but I wonder when the picture was taken. The back of the photo looks like a postcard, not an unusual characteristic of antique photos. The passing years have left it the color of tea-stained linen. How many years? I ask. I search the Internet for postcard information, hoping to narrow the window of time when the photo might have been taken, but after an hour I am no closer to solving the puzzle. I call a local history buff, who refers me to Dalton Hoffman at the Cattle Raisers Museum. "If anyone can help you, he can," she says. I thought he'd need to see the photo, but he doesn't. He just asks questions.

"Does it say 'post card'?" he says.

"Yes."

"Is the card divided: correspondence on one side, address on the other?"

"Yes."

"Look at the stamp area. Does it have AZO on each side?"

"Yes."

"Are there arrows at the corners?"

"Yes."

"Are the arrows pointing up or down?"

"Up," I say.

He doesn't hesitate. "It was taken before 1916," he declares.

I am amazed at his expertise. In less time than it takes to toast a piece of bread, he has answered my question—and changed the way I see this picture. I look at the photograph again. It is older than I had imagined.

These people have never heard of Babe Ruth, the Jazz Age, or Prohibition. Women can't vote. There is no Miss America. Maybe they know that the unsinkable Titanic sank; that New Mexico and Arizona are states. Maybe they know about the Panama Canal. Maybe they've heard about a war far away in Europe.

I take out the magnifying glass and focus on the boys on the lawn. I wonder if the oldest marched off to that war, the First World War—and if he came home. I wonder if one of these boys contracted polio, if one came down with tuberculosis. Which one married happily and which did not? Did one drink too much? Did one gamble? Did one of them become a captain of industry? Did one of them break away from the family? Did one become bitter? Which ones learned to forgive? I wondered how this family fared through the dark days of the Great Depression and, after that, World War II.

The possibilities for suffering and sanctity are everywhere. The picture seems such a blissful interlude, an almost magical setting where it only takes a south breeze to carry away all worry. I study the photo, hoping to remember this house with its wide porches and feel once more the terrible longing, the deep need to return to a place I have never been before, a magic place of all possibilities.

Silencing a Killer ❧ Sunday, June 19, 2005

Donna Henry Goodwin was one of the milllions of children stricken with polio during the frightening epidemic of the 1950s. Courtesy, the Fort Worth Star-Telegram.

SAN ANGELO—It stalked the children in the summer months, slipping silently through shadows on sunlit afternoons crippling and killing the little ones, holding entire towns hostage with no hope of ransom. After fifty years, one generation has all but forgotten—and the next generation has never known—the fear of polio or the exhilaration America felt when at last there was a way to combat that enemy. In the spring of 1955, the nation's children lined up for injections of Jonas Salk's vaccine. From that day forward, polio in America was officially on the run, but not before the seven-year plague that began in 1949 had exacted a terrible toll. For decades, this crippling virus that attacks the spinal cord had terrorized American cities. In 1907, it hit New York City. In 1916, it was Brooklyn. By 1921, even the toney enclave of Hyde Park on the Hudson River wasn't safe.

No one could guess then that the worst was yet to come—and in the most unlikely of places: San Angelo, Texas, a burgeoning town of fewer than 50,000, 250 miles west of Fort Worth and 150 miles north of the Mexican border.

For seven summers, polio hammered the town. The infection

rate soared to thirty times that of the national average, but for me, polio had only one face, and it was freckled.

~

No one knows why San Angelo was hit so hard. There had always been small, intermittent outbreaks of polio; Fort Worth had one in 1944. There was another in San Angelo in 1946. Still, it seemed a golden time. The national economy was booming. In cities, the suburbs were sprouting. Soldiers just home from World War II were marrying, buying houses, starting families. San Angelo almost doubled in size. The sky was blue and there wasn't a cloud in sight.

Three years later, in 1949, polio became epidemic, and it was hard for anyone to be optimistic. More than two dozen San Angelo children were hospitalized in less than a month—and at least seven died. Overnight, San Angelo's friendly people grew anxious about shaking hands, and travelers either drove past the town or sped through the dusty streets, afraid to stop to air up their tires or to drink a sip of water. Swimming pools and movie houses closed. Even the Baptist Sunday school was shuttered for a weekend.

Every day, trucks rumbled through the streets, spraying great toxic clouds of DDT. Children on bicycles peddled behind the trucks or danced along in the mist. The toxin killed mosquitoes and flies believed to carry the disease. But birds died, too, and still polio would not retreat.

The local newspaper printed each new case, listing the patient by name and address. The town prayed for those stricken families—and avoided them. The epidemic reached a furious climax in 1952, claiming more victims nationwide than ever before. Headlines in the San Angelo *Standard-Times* screamed, "Polio Strikes Once Each Hour in Texas" and "1952 Polio Siege Worst on Record." That's the year my memories of this time begin. That's the year polio found Mickey.

Her real name was Donna Gene Henry. At six, she was tall and thin with red hair and a generous sprinkling of auburn freckles dotting her face from forehead to chin and covering her arms and legs. Even her bony knees were freckled. She and Jan Sternard and Gail Stone were my playmates, kids who lived just around the corner in the baby-boom era that followed World War II. They weren't the only kids on the block, of course. They had brothers and sisters, and other houses were just as full of children. But they were like family—always in my life.

Summer's heat still hugged the dusty earth as school bells rang. We were off to first grade. Mickey remembers that her left arm ached, and that she had trouble holding the lunch box her mother had packed. By evening, she burned with fever. The doctor hurried to the Henrys' house. Doctors always came to homes in those years. He shook his head. It didn't look good. Mickey was moved to a polio ward in the basement of Shannon Hospital. The ward served all of Tom Green County's polio patients, black, white, brown—something unusual in a day when segregated wards were the rule. From there, she went to Gonzales Warm Springs, a medical center in South Texas reserved for the most severe cases.

I learned the seriousness of my friend's condition over supper one evening. Daddy said the same blessing at every meal. It had been his father's prayer, too, and it never varied.

"Heavenly Father, smile upon us. Give us thankful hearts for these and all Thy many blessings. Amen." But one night he added, "Watch over little Mickey and her family."

I looked up. Mother and Dad held hands. Their heads were bowed; their eyes squeezed tightly shut. There was a platter of fried potatoes on the table and the smell of fried onions hung in the hot room. A tingle crawled up my spine. I knew it was bad.

∽

Gonzales was 300 long miles southeast, and parents were not allowed to stay. Visitation there—and in almost all polio treatment centers—was very strict. Families were allowed only two hours each week on Sunday afternoons. So six-year-old Mickey was left in the care of strangers, white-uniformed nurses in an antiseptic place. The Henrys never missed a visiting hour and were never late, Mickey says. Some families couldn't afford weekly trips, and she remembers that her mother always made time to sit with those children, too. The routine at the center seldom varied: school, occupational therapy, physical therapy, naptime, lunch, water therapy, and movies on Saturday night. Before physical therapy, patients were wrapped in hot cloths to relax the muscles and relieve the pain.

But even after all the treatment, the muscles in Mickey's left shoulder were devastated. Her arm hung like a limp rag, and the disease's attack on her right hip and leg were evident. She was fitted with a leg brace, a crutch, and a hand brace, but that was only the beginning.

The town was on edge, but as frightened as people were, they wanted to help. The National Foundation for Infantile Paralysis launched a media blitz that put polio research square in the spotlight's glare. The foundation was the first to use a poster child to drive home the message that research could conquer polio—all it took was money and the women set out to raise it. In San Angelo, waitresses pinned little banks to their shirts and patrons dropped in their change. My mother, like so many of America's women, volunteered to collect dimes—and quarters and dollars—from neighbors who left their porch lights burning. Hardly any house was dark.

Nationwide, the Mother's March of Dimes raised $250 million between 1951 and 1955 for the National Foundation for Infantile Paralysis. That was big money in those years. Those dollars funded the work of Jonas Salk's search for a polio vaccine. His research rival, Albert Sabin, followed in 1962 with a vaccine that was given orally on a sugar cube. Those vaccines eradicated polio in this country.

They just didn't come soon enough for Mickey or millions like her.

~

When Mickey returned that summer from Gonzales, her mother wouldn't let the neighborhood gang into the house, but one afternoon, we went around to Mickey's open bedroom window and talked to her through the screen. She lay flat on her back with her feet jammed into a contraption at the end of the bed. We played quietly under her window in the sand, building little ranches in the shade. Pebble fences surrounded pastures of pebble sheep and pebble cattle. Pebble people walked the corrals.

Mickey's mother found us there and shooed us away, but she was so gentle we came back on at least one other afternoon.

Mickey says she doesn't remember those visits—but she doesn't remember the iron lung that frightened Jan so completely, either, or the leg brace that is so vivid in my memory. Her older brother confirms those bits of information. Yes, she was in an iron lung. Yes, of course, there was a leg brace and high-top shoes and a crutch.

Maybe she was too young or too scared. Maybe there were too many other things to remember. She went back and forth to Gonzales for five years, from 1952 to 1957, and suffered through a number of surgeries to repair the damaged shoulder.

Mickey does remember the children who were forbidden to walk past her house.

~

The family on the corner had a big garden always in need of weeding, a barking black dog—and a new baby almost every year. After Mickey got sick, those children walked blocks out of the way to reach the schoolhouse. They gave the rest of us a wide berth, too, but I recognize that now only in hindsight.

"Well, everyone was frightened to death," says Dr. Ralph Chase as he settles into a chair in his home office. Now eighty-two, he has retired from a pediatric practice that began in 1953, the year after polio hit its all-time high across the nation.

The first day in the office he treated fifty-eight patients. "Can you believe it?" he asks, gray eyes blinking behind glasses. He is a man with a perpetual smile and an easy laugh. To everyone in town he is "Uncle Ralphie." His wife is called "Sweet Virginia."

"Why, the new doctor is supposed to sit around for two months and wait to see someone, but these doctors were sending me patients," he says. It didn't matter. Uncle Ralphie threw himself into the work. "Every time a child got a fever, the parents were certain they had polio, so they'd call the doctor," he remembers. The only sure way to diagnose the disease was with a spinal tap, but once the diagnosis was made, doctors could do very little, says Chase. And then one bright day, he found something that was almost as good as a magical elixir.

Chase ends every conversation, e-mail, or correspondence with, "You are a wonderful person, and I love you." He says that endearment was more potent than anything he had in his medical bag.

"I'm just an average doctor, but I'm a first-class cheerleader," he declares. "I learned that what my patients really needed was someone to cheer them up. So I began encouraging them. Then I began encouraging their parents, too. I've been doing it ever since."

∼

The man who really could do something, the man Chase and many others calls the real hero of the San Angelo epidemic, was the late Lanier Bell, a physical therapist who'd been at Pearl Harbor when the Japanese attacked. Wounded three times before the war ended, his lumbar spine was surgically fused. He knew all about pain and suffering. Yet, Chase remembers that Bell sometimes put in twenty-two-hour days and showed the greatest kindness to those stricken with polio. When he learned that one family could not afford the gas to drive their little girl to Gonzales, he took her himself.

One day a family smuggled a dog into the ward to see a very sick little girl. Of course, animals were strictly forbidden in the hospital, but this bear of a man quietly looked the other way, knowing the child would not survive. At every turn he seemed to find ways to show kindness, but others did not always return that compassion.

Bell had one daughter, Lorna, who lives in Arizona. She remembers a lonely childhood with few playmates. "People were afraid to let their children play with me because Dad worked with polio patients," she says in a recent phone conversation. It was a fact that wounded Bell, who gave so much to other people's children.

Bobby Eckert was Bell's first patient in 1946. Eckert was nineteen, a blue-eyed blond with a year of university life under his belt. He liked fried chicken, strawberry shortcake, Tommy Dorsey, and Betty Grable—but he didn't care for raisins or girls who wore high heels with socks. Like the rest of the country, even drought-bitten West Texas was giddy with possibilities. Eckert was part of that happy-go-lucky, make-it-happen world. The sky was the limit. And then, just as suddenly as a flash flood can turn a dry creek into a rampaging torrent, Eckert was pulled down, twisted, and turned—and marked as one of polio's own. The disease attacked Eckert's shoulders and arms. One day he had flulike symptoms, the next he could not lift his hands.

Eckert remained confident. "I always knew I'd recover," he says sitting in his comfortable home on a recent afternoon. "I just wanted to hurry up and get back to school." While Bell put Eckert through the paces, the young man's grandfather fashioned two tiny ladder-like contraptions for him. The idea was to walk his fingers up and down the rungs, building muscle and endurance, but when an oilman offered young Eckert a job that required using a microscope, Eckert wasn't strong enough to lift his arms.

The oil man, who wouldn't take no for an answer to his job offer, built an apparatus with springs that would give Eckert's hands the needed lift and installed it over his desk. It worked, and Eckert spent many productive months there.

Eckert pauses remembering that man's generosity and tears flood his eyes.

∾

In truth, polio was not as threatening a disease as the media made it seem, says Chase. More children died of cancer or accidents than polio, he explains, but the fear of that specter was enormous. The National Foundation for Infantile Paralysis used that apparition to find new ways to raise money and awareness. In 1955, the Salk vaccine clobbered polio, and the Sabin vaccine in 1962 finished it.

While thousands were permanently crippled, many more survived with few scars.

Eckert regained use of his arms, but the muscles in his back are shrunken and his spine a bit twisted. Those who don't know of his battle with polio would never guess. He became a CPA in San Angelo, married, and raised a family.

Mickey gave up the leg brace and crutches years ago, but she has a slight limp and has never regained full use of her left arm. She married, moved to Minnesota, and has two grown children. Jan became a professional Girl Scout director in Brownwood.

I lost contact with Gail.

San Angelo has grown to almost 100,000, and most of those citizens probably can't remember the polio epidemic that began in 1949, but if I close my eyes, I can still see Mickey smiling through the window screen and hear my father's suppertime prayer.

ACKNOWLEDGMENTS

I WANT to acknowledge so many people, beginning first with all those brave souls who let me tell their stories. I also want to thank Judy Alter and TCU Press for preserving these stories in book form. These pieces are little snapshots of people's lives, but they are also a small look into our shared history, a time already gone. Since these stories were written, the lives of all these people have changed. Some have had new successes; some have known disappointment. There have been births, deaths, divorces. These people live in these pages as they were then, not now.

Many thanks to the *Star-Telegram* for giving permission to reprint these stories and most especially to former publisher Wes Turner and executive managing editor Jim Witt for their support. As I compiled these selections, I could not help but remember former *Star-Telegram* editor Mike Blackman who took a chance and gave me a job after I'd been out of the business of journalism for twenty years. I want to thank Mike for sticking with me while I found my voice.

Others gave me a hand up along the way too. I recall the kind encouragement of the late Karen Potter, one of my first *Star-Telegram* editors and of the stubborn prodding of former *Star-Telegram* editor Julie Heaberlin. Almost all the essays in this collection are a result of her constant insistence.

I also want to thank research librarian Marcia Melton who worked on a number of these stories with me. However, none would have been worth the ink without the attention of the *Star-Telegram's* hard-working copy editors including Sandy Guerra-

Cline, former copy chief Ruthanne Brokeway, Cathy Harris, Cathy Frisinger, Carol Nuckols, Felicia Smith, and others.

The list of friends who have encouraged me through the years is long and includes such supporters as author Jeff Guinn who has always cheered me on—and even nagged a bit. Others who have made a difference in my life include Charles Caple, Mary Alice Smith, Becky Brumley, Linda and David Moore, Christi Moore, Lynda Hill, Stephanie Owen, and so many others. I am grateful for my second son, Cameron Moore, who helped me navigate the sometimes mysterious world of computers and to attorney Bob Bodoin for without his patient work this collection would never have become a reality.

My own family has generously made room for my writing schedule, and I am especially thankful for my son, Ben Rogers, who always told me I was a good storyteller. But most of all I am indebted to Charles Rogers, my husband and my friend whose story is forever a part of my own.

ISBN 978-0-87565-374-7

Dancing Naked
ISBN 978-0-87565-374-7
Paper. $18.95

ISBN 978-0-87565-383-9

Dancing Naked
ISBN 978-0-87565-383-9
Cloth. $27.50